GMO Food

Books in the **Contemporary World Issues** series address vital issues in today's society such as genetic engineering, pollution, and biodiversity. Written by professional writers, scholars, and nonacademic experts, these books are authoritative, clearly written, up-to-date, and objective. They provide a good starting point for research by high school and college students, scholars, and general readers as well as by legislators, businesspeople, activists, and others.

Each book, carefully organized and easy to use, contains an overview of the subject, a detailed chronology, biographical sketches, facts and data and/or documents and other primary source material, a forum of authoritative perspective essays, annotated lists of print and nonprint resources, and an index.

Readers of books in the Contemporary World Issues series will find the information they need to have a better understanding of the social, political, environmental, and economic issues facing the world today.

GMO Food

A REFERENCE HANDBOOK

David E. Newton

ABC-CLIO

Santa Barbara, California • Denver, Colorado • Oxford, England

Library of Congress Cataloging-in-Publication Data

Newton, David E.

GMO food : a reference handbook / David E. Newton.

pages cm. — (Contemporary world issues)

Includes bibliographical references and index.

ISBN 978–1–61069–685–2 (hard copy : alk. paper) — ISBN 978–1–61069–686–9 (ebook) 1. Genetically modified foods. 2. Genetically modified foods—Social aspects. 3. Genetically modified foods—Risk assessment. 4. Transgenic plants. I. Title. II. Title: Genetically modified organisms food. III. Title: Genetically modified food.

TP248.65.F66N49   2014

664—dc23   2014021910

ISBN: 978–1–61069–685–2

EISBN: 978–1–61069–686–9

18 17 16 15 14   1 2 3 4 5

This book is also available on the World Wide Web as an eBook. Visit www.abc-clio.com for details.

ABC-CLIO, LLC

130 Cremona Drive, P.O. Box 1911

Santa Barbara, California 93116-1911

This book is printed on acid-free paper ∞

Manufactured in the United States of America

Humans have been altering the genomes (genetic composition) of plants and animals for millennia. At first, these modifications were largely trial-and-error events in which organisms with desirable traits were crossbred with each other to produce new plants or animals better suited for food, for transportation, for working in the field, to be resistant to pests, or for other purposes. The first major breakthrough in the process of genetic modification occurred in the late nineteenth century with the discovery of the genetic units (*genes*) through which characteristics are transmitted from generation to generation. Breeders and biological researchers had no way of using this new knowledge, however, to improve the traditional methods of producing new organisms by crossbreeding.

The next major breakthrough, however, did cross that hurdle. In 1953, American biologist James Watson and English chemist Francis Crick showed that genes were not more nor less than chemical molecules of a substance called deoxyribonucleic acid (DNA). That discovery opened new vistas for the modification of plants and animals because DNA, like any other chemical, can be modified, at least in principle, in the same way any other chemical can be modified. For the first time in history, researchers were able to change the chemical structure of DNA from a cat, alligator, or tobacco plant, thereby producing a new type of cat, alligator, or tobacco plant. And thus was born the science of genetically modified organisms (GMOs).

Among the most obvious targets of the new technology were food organisms, plants and animals that are bred primarily as foodstuffs for humans, domestic animals, and other organisms. The technology made it possible, for example, to create new types of plants that are resistant to pesticides, making it possible to use those pesticides on crops without affecting the crops themselves. It also made possible to development of animals used for meat that are fatter or leaner, that mature more quickly, that are less susceptible to disease, or that have any one of a number of other desirable traits.

The success of this new technology is reflected in the fact that, as of 2013, 90 percent of all the cotton and corn and 93 percent of all the soybeans grown in the United States is genetically modified. Worldwide, the amount of land under cultivation for genetically modified (GM) crops has risen from essentially zero in 1996 to more than 70 million hectares (170 million acres) in developed nations and just slightly less than that amount in developing nations. Today, crops are modified for a host of purposes, including pest resistance, disease resistance, cold tolerance, drought tolerance, resistance to salinity, improved nutritional value, and the synthetic production of drugs and other useful chemical products.

Despite the undeniable success of GM crops at this point in history, critics have raised a number of concerns about the development, production, and use of such foods. Those critics often argue that, even after years of research, scientists and the general public simply do not know enough about potential health risks of GM foods. They are concerned that such foods may cause cancer in humans and other animals to whom they are fed or that they may produce allergic reactions in people who have a predisposition to such conditions. Critics also worry about the potential harm that GM foods could cause to the natural environment. They suggest that genetically engineered traits might be transferred in nature to unintended target organisms, producing frightening "super-organisms," which might be resistant to human control because of their modified genomes. Critics also point out that once GM plants and animals are released to the natural environment, there may be no way to control or recover those organisms, should they turn out to be more dangerous than first thought. Finally, individuals and organizations who object to the use of GM technology fear that this technology will only make developing nations even more dependent on developed nations and multinational corporations than they already are.

This book is designed to provide young adults with the factual background they need to better understand the controversy over GM foods and with the tools to continue their own research on the topic. Chapter 1 provides background and history about the development of genetic engineering technology over the centuries, with special emphasis on the period since the 1950s. Chapter 2 reviews some of the most important problems and issues associated with GM foods, including the advantages and disadvantages of the development and use of such products. Chapter 3 provides an opportunity for stakeholders in the debate to express their personal views on some specific aspect of the overall issue of GM foods. Chapter 4 includes profiles of a number of individuals and organizations that have been or are involved in the controversy over the development and use of GM foods. Chapter 5 includes a number of important documents—court cases, laws, position statements, and the like—associated with the topic of GM foods, as well as some statistical data about the production and use of such foods. Chapter 6 is an annotated bibliography of print and electronic sources that contain additional information about GM foods. Chapter 7 is a chronology of important events from prehistory to the modern day on the topic of GM food. Glossary lists important terms used in the discussion of the topic.

GMO Food

Be fruitful and multiply; fill the earth and subdue it; have
dominion over the fish of the sea, over the birds of the air,
and over every living thing that moves on the earth.
(Genesis 1: 28, New King James Version)

One of the first commands issued by God, according to the holy book of the Christian religion, is for humans to "subdue the Earth," taking command over all the plants and animals that God had placed on Earth. At the dawn of human civilization, no matter what religious beliefs one holds, such was largely the situation in which early humans found themselves; they stood alone against the rest of the natural world. They had no cows to supply them with milk, no mules to carry their burdens, no horses to ride to distant places, and no corn or wheat with which to make their meals. Everything they needed they had to find in the natural world and kill or collect it for their own needs.

Slowly that situation began to change. Humans realized, first of all, that they could domesticate some of the wild animals around them as sources of milk and meat, as beasts of burden, and to supply hides and other body parts for tools and

---

Marshall Nirenberg shared the 1968 Nobel Prize in Physiology or Medicine with Har Gobind Khorana and Robert W. Holley for solving the genetic code and showing how it functions in the synthesis of proteins. (National Library of Medicine)

ornaments. No one knows precisely when the first animals were domesticated, although some authorities suggest a date of about 8000 BCE as the period during which first goats, and then sheep, were domesticated for human use. Residents of Mesopotamia were learning about the domestication of not only animals but also plants at about the same time. They found ways of taking plants that grew naturally in the environment around them and growing them under controlled conditions not only as sources of food but also as raw materials for clothing, housing, and other basic needs.

Hybridization

Many millennia after humans began the domestication of wild plants and animals, they took a significantly more advanced step: They began to create entirely new plants or animals, not found in nature, by cross-breeding two different species of natural plants or animals, a process known as *hybridization*. Probably the first animal hybrid was produced by crossing a horse and a donkey. When the cross involves a male donkey (jackass) and a female horse (mare), the product is called a *mule*. A cross between a female donkey (jenny) and a male horse (stallion) results in the birth of a *hinny*. Hinnies are depicted in Egyptian tomb paintings as early as 1400 BCE, and mules can be identified in Mesopotamian art dating to the first millennium BCE (Sherman 2002, 42).

The origins of plant hybridization are also somewhat difficult to trace, although there is some evidence that the first rice hybrids may have been produced by about 2000 BCE when rice native to Japan (*Oryza sativa japonica*) was hybridized on the Indian subcontinent to form a new strain, *O. sativa indica* ("Indian Archaeobotany Watch: Lahuradewa 2008"). *O. sativa japonica* also made its way to the African continent by about 1500 BCE, where it was domesticated and hybridized with a native form of rice, *O. barthii*, to form a new species, *O. glaberrima* (Hirst, "History of Rice, Part One"; Linares 2002, 16360).

For more than 3,000 years, agricultural workers have continued to use hybridization techniques to improve the quality of domestic plants and animals. To a large extent, these techniques have relied on trial-and-error methods of crossing different organisms with each other to produce certain desirable traits. The fact that experimentalists did not know the scientific basis for the production of hybrids did not mean that such methods were often not elegant, sophisticated, and productive. Over time, in fact, they produced hybrid animals such as ligers (a cross between lions and tigers), beefalo (cow and buffalo), cama (camel and llama), savannah (domestic cat and serval), donkra (donkey and zebra), and dzo (domestic cow and yak), as well as hybrid plants such as the *Amarcrinum* (a cross between the *Amaryllis* and *Crinum* genera), peppermint (spearmint and watermint), *Chitalpa* (desert willow [*Chilopsis linearis*] and southern catalpa [*Catalpa bignonioides*]), Leyland cypress (Monterey cypress [*Cupressus macrocarpa*] and Alaska cedar [*Chamaecyparis nootkatensis*]), and limequat (Key lime and kumquat).

Hybrid technologies can be subdivided into two major categories: intraspecific and interspecific. In the former case, individuals from two different species are interbred to produce a new species (e.g., the liger or buffalo), sometimes to produce a plant or animal with some new and useful physical characteristics, and sometimes just to prove that the breed can be produced. In the latter case, two individuals from the same species are interbred to improve the overall quality of the species. The inbreeding of the maize plant over the centuries, as an example, has resulted in a modern plant that looks and tastes entirely different from the parent plant from which it originated, a small plant with cobs only a few inches in length and eight rows of kernels ("Corn in the United States"). The very significant accomplishments of hybridization can be appreciated today simply by looking at the 161 different breeds of dogs recognized by the American Kennel Club, the 40 different breeds of cats recognized by the Cat Fanciers Association, or the more than 2,000 varieties of roses recognized by the American Rose Society ("AKC Breeds—Complete Breed List"; "CFA Breeds"; Quest-Ritson and Quest-Ritson 2011).

The Birth of Genetics

The first real attempt to obtain a scientific explanation for the process by which hybridization occurs dates to the work of the Austrian monk Gregor Mendel between 1856 and 1863. In one of the most famous set of experiments in the history of science, Mendel patiently crossbred differing strains of peas (*Pisum sativum*), carefully recording the properties of the progeny of each cross for two or more generations of the plants. As a one-time teacher of mathematics and physics, Mendel understood the importance of collecting precise quantitative data about the changes that occurred as a result of his crossbreeding efforts. The laws of hybridization that now carry his name illustrate this commitment to quantitative thinking. One such law, for example, predicts that the ratio between two forms of a trait (e.g., color) in a crossbreeding will always be 3:1, whereas the ratio between two forms of two traits (e.g., color and size) will always be 9:3:3:1 (O'Neil 1997).

Perhaps the most important conclusion Mendel was able to draw from his research was actually a very simple one: The physical traits of pea plants that are transmitted from parent to offspring are apparently encoded in some type of unitary particle, to which Mendel gave the name *Elemente*. He was fully able to describe how physical traits (which he called *Merkmal*), such as color and size, were passed down from generation to generation by imagining various ways in which these *Elemente* combined with each other during the mating of female and male plants.

In one of the great oddities of the history of science, Mendel's momentous discoveries were essentially lost for more than three decades after he reported them to a small local group of scientists, the Natural History Society of Brno (Naturforschenden Vereins Brünn), on February 8 and March 8, 1865. Then, in 1900, those results were almost simultaneously rediscovered by three researchers independently, the Dutch botanist Hugo de Vries, the Austrian agronomist Erich von Tschermak, and the German botanist Carl Correns, all of whom immediately recognized that Mendel's discoveries made possible for the first time a new field of science that could be used to understand and direct the hybridization of plants and animals. The dispute that arose as to which of these three men should receive credit for this rediscovery inspired many more biologists to seek out Mendel's original papers, and his work at last began to receive the recognition that it had long deserved (Moore 2001). And thus was born the new science of genetics.

The renaissance of Mendel's work raised the question as to what the unitary particle, Mendel's *Elemente*, should be called. De Vries had already adopted the notion of a unitary hereditary factor, which he called the *pangen*, which he thought of as being invisibly small but still larger than a chemical molecule (Wayne 2010, 270). Finally in 1909, the Danish botanist Wilhelm Johannsen suggested a name for the unitary particle by which it is still known today, the *gen* (in Danish and German), or *gene* (in English).

The Gene

By the first decade of the twentieth century, genetics had begun to expand and grow. Some early discoveries about the transmission of hereditary traits were being reported. However, one of the most basic questions in the new science remained unanswered: What is a "gene"? Most practitioners understood the notion that hereditary traits were carried from one generation to the next on or within some type of unitary particles, but what precisely and exactly was that particle? True, many geneticists did not worry too much as to what a "gene" was as long as they could design experiments that played out successfully— even if they didn't know exactly what a gene looked like. Whereas other researchers recognized that discovering the physical and chemical nature of the gene was ultimately essential to developing a true and productive science of genetics, and they embarked on a campaign to discover what that unit really consisted of.

For most researchers, the primary candidate for the gene was some kind of protein molecule. Proteins are complex chemical substances that consist of various combinations of about two dozen simpler molecules known as *amino acids*, joined to each other in a variety of ways. Proteins are very large molecules, consisting of hundreds or thousands of amino acids in virtually every imaginable combination. And that fact explains why proteins were thought to be good candidates for genes: The many different sizes, shapes, and compositions proteins could have meant that they could code for an endless variety of physical and biological traits, which is just what we see in the natural world.

A relatively small number of researchers, however, focused on a different candidate molecule known as *deoxyribonucleic acid* (DNA). Nucleic acids had been discovered in 1868 by German chemist Friedrich Miescher, who originally called the material *nuclein*, because he found it in the nuclei of cells. (Miescher's student, Richard Altmann, later suggested the term *nucleic acid* for the material, the name by which it is known today.) Miescher knew nothing about the chemical composition of nuclein or its biological function. He considered the possibility that it might be involved in the hereditary transmission of genetic traits but later rejected that notion (Dahm 2008; Wolf 2003). In fact, research on the chemical structure and function of nucleic acids moved forward very slowly and with few practical results for many years. For example, it was not even until 1935 that the Russian chemist Andrei Nikolaevitch Belozersky was able to isolate a pure sample of the material, making it possible for researchers to proceed with an analysis of its structure and function.

Much of the early research on DNA produced findings that appeared to be trivial and of questionable value at the time. For example, in 1950, Austro-Hungarian–born American biochemist Erwin Chargaff discovered that two of the nitrogen bases found in DNA, adenine (A) and thymine (T), always occur in the same ratio to each other, and the other two nitrogen bases present in DNA, guanine (G) and cytosine (C), also occur in the same ratio, although the two ratios are different from each other. So according to this so-called Chargaff's rule, if there were 5.2 g of A in a sample of DNA, there would also be 5.2 g of T, and the presence of 3.5 g of C necessarily implied the presence of 3.9 g of G. So what possible significance could that information have in thinking about genes? The answer to that question would come in only three years, and when it did, it turned out to be an essential part of the description of what a gene is.

In fact, by the early 1950s, enough information about DNA had accumulated that a few research teams were close to answering that fundamental question: What is a gene? The winners of the contest (and a contest is very much what it was) was a somewhat unusual research team working at Oxford University in Great Britain. The team consisted of a somewhat brash young biologist from the United States, James Watson; a more reserved physicist-turned-chemist from Great Britain, Francis Crick; a New Zealand-born physicist-turned-molecular biologist, Maurice Wilkins; and a brilliant, but somewhat ignored, English x-ray crystallographer, Rosalind Franklin. In a series of events too long and complex to be told here, the team—often not working together happily as a team—finally discovered the chemical structure of DNA. Crick and Watson announced the result of their work in a now-classic paper published in the journal *Nature* on April 25, 1953. (Crick and Watson received the Nobel Prize in physiology or medicine, along with Wilkins, but without Franklin, in 1962.)

The Watson–Crick model of DNA consists of two very long strands of atoms (the *backbone* of the molecule), where *long* means tens or hundreds of thousands of atoms. The atoms are grouped into two characteristic groups, a sugar called *deoxyribose* and a phosphate group, which is a collection of one phosphorus atom and four oxygen atoms. So each of the two strands of the DNA molecules looks like this:

S - P - S - P - S - P - S - P - S - P - S - P - S - P - S - P - S - P - S - P - S - P - S -.

Figure 1.1   Backbone of DNA Molecule

where S represents a sugar grouping and P a phosphate grouping.

Attached to every sugar group is one of the four (and there are only four) nitrogen bases found in DNA. Each of the four nitrogen bases—adenine, thymine, guanine, and cytosine— consists of about two dozen atoms, some of which are nitrogen atoms (and hence their name). So a complete DNA strand looks like this:

```
S - P - S - P - S - P - S - P - S - P - S - P - S - P - S - P - S - P - S - P - S - P - S -
I     I     I     I     I     I     I     I     I     I     I     I
C     A     C     T     G     G     G     C     A     T     G     C
```

(The placement of nitrogen bases is random in the molecule.)

Figure 1.2   Nitrogen Bases in DNA

where A, T, G, and C stand for the four nitrogen bases, and with the possibility of placing *any* nitrogen base anywhere on the strand. To get an idea of the size of a DNA molecule, imagine that the formula shown in here runs across the width of this page, the next page, and all the pages of this book, without showing even a small part of the molecule.

As soon as they drew this model, Watson and Crick knew that DNA would be an ideal candidate for a gene. Moving all those A, T, C, and G nitrogen bases around on the DNA backbone made possible an almost infinite variety of structures,

certainly enough to account for every known genetic characteristic. At first, they did not know *how* that all took place, but
they certainly had their suspicions. Indeed, in the last sentence
of their 1953 paper they noted that "[i]t has not escaped our
notice that the specific pairing we have postulated immediately
suggests a possible copying mechanism for the genetic material"
(Watson and Crick 1953, 738).

Only one step remains to provide a complete description of
the DNA molecule. The two strands of the type shown in earlier are lined up opposite each other so that the nitrogen bases
on one strand are lined up opposite the only nitrogen bases
on the other strand to which they are attracted: every A with a
T, and vice versa, and every C with a G, and vice versa (i.e.,
Chargaff's rule), and the two strands are twisted around each
other to form a *double helix*, almost like a spiral staircase.

At this point, all that remained was to solve the final part of
the puzzle: Given the chemical structure of a DNA molecule,
how do the four nitrogen bases code for a physical trait, such
as blue eyes, red hair, or left handedness? (Note that it has to
be the bases that hold the key because the background strand of
sugar and phosphate groups is always the same in every DNA
molecule.) A number of researchers contributed to answering
this question, but credit for cracking the code usually goes to
American biochemist Marshall Nirenberg, working with colleague Johann H. Matthaei at the National Institutes of Health
(NIH). In some ways, the answer was easy. Researchers knew that
the basic process had to be something like this:

nitrogen bases — direct production of —> amino acids —
which make —> proteins.

Each different protein made by this process is responsible by itself
or in combination with other proteins for a specific genetic trait:
blue eyes, red hair, left handedness, and so on. The question really
was *how many* nitrogen bases and *in what arrangement* were
needed to account for the production of the approximately two
dozen amino acids used in the synthesis of proteins?

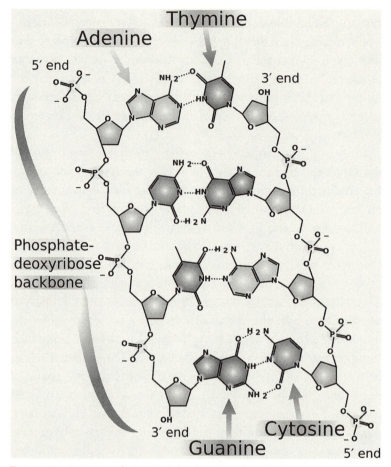

Figure 1.3   Structure of a DNA Molecule (Madeleine Price Ball)

It is obvious that a single nitrogen base cannot code for two dozen amino acids because the four nitrogen bases in DNA could then code for only four different amino acids. How about a genetic code consisting of two nitrogen bases? In that case, one DNA molecule could make 16 amino acids. Go ahead and try it. See how many different ways you can put together two nitrogen bases, such as:

AA   AT   AC   AG   GC   GT   ...

You should be able to come up with 16 different combinations, not enough to make two dozen amino acids.

However, what about sets of three nitrogen bases? Again, try it yourself and see:

AAA   AAT   ATA   ATT   CGT   CGG   CGA   ...

This system will work. With a set of three nitrogen bases—called a *triad* or *codon*—a single DNA molecule can code for 64 different amino acids. That is well beyond the number of amino acids used in proteins, but, as it turns out, it provides redundancy for the DNA molecule. A single amino acid, such as arginine, can be made by any one of six different triads: CGU, CGC, CGA, CGG, AGA, or AGG.

The final step is to determine which arrangement of nitrogen bases codes for which amino acid. Nirenberg got the process working to answer this question with an elegantly simple experiment. He prepared a DNA molecule that contained only one nitrogen base, adenine (AAA), and found that this molecule codes for the amino acid lysine. Another DNA molecule consisting only of cytosine (CCC) coded for the amino acid proline. By using somewhat more complicated DNA molecules consisting of other combinations of nitrogen bases, Nirenberg and other researches were eventually able to produce a complete genetic code that tells which amino acid is coded for by every possible combination of nitrogen bases. Table 1.1 shows what that code looks like. In the table, the first nitrogen base in the code is shown on the left side of the box, the second nitrogen base on the top of the box, and the third nitrogen base on the right side of the box.

All very interesting, perhaps, what does this discussion have to do with the genetic modification of foods? The important point of this story is that the Watson–Crick discovery turned the question of the biological properties of an organism—the colors of its flowers, the amount of meat on its carcass, its ability to resist attack by insects, and the like—into a chemical problem. A plant that is able to live in a very salt environment,

Table 1.1   The Genetic Code

		2nd base				3rd base
		T	C	A	G	
	T	TTT = Phe	TCT = Ser	TAT = Tyr	TGT = Cys	T
		TTC = Phe	TCC = Ser	TAC = Tyr	TGC = Cys	C
		TTA = Leu	TCA = Ser	TAA = STOP	TGA = STOP	A
		TTG = Leu	TCG = Ser	TAG = STOP	TGG = Trp	G
	C	CTT = Leu	CCT = Pro	CAT = His	CGT = Arg	T
		CTC = Leu	CCC = Pro	CAC = His	CGC = Arg	C
		CTA = Leu	CCA = Pro	CAA = Gln	CGA = Arg	A
		CTG = Leu	CCG = Pro	CAG = Gln	CGG = Arg	G
1st base	A	ATT = Ile	ACT = Thr	AAT = Asn	AGT = Ser	T
		ATC = Ile	ACC = Thr	AAC = Asn	AGC = Ser	C
		ATA = Ile	ACA = Thr	AAA = Lys	AGA = Arg	A
		ATG = Met/ START	ACG = Thr	AAG = Lys	AGG = Arg	G
	G	GTT = Val	GCT = Ala	GAT = Asp	GGT = Gly	T
		GTC = Val	GCC = Ala	GAC = Asp	GGC = Gly	C
		GTA = Val	GCA = Ala	GAA = Glu	GGA = Gly	A
		GTG = Val	GCG = Ala	GAG = Glu	GGG = Gly	G

for example, can do so—taking the simplest possible view—because its DNA consists of a sequence of nitrogen bases that codes for the amino acids from which proteins are made that are responsible for salt tolerance. If the plant did not have this specific set of nitrogen bases, it could not make those amino acids or the protein that makes it salt tolerant.

So if you have a plant that is *not* salt tolerant to begin with, all you really need to do is to carry out a chemical experiment in which the incorrect nitrogen bases are removed from the DNA molecule and/or the correct nitrogen bases are inserted into the molecule in such a way that the "salt-tolerant" configuration is achieved. As you might guess, this process is a lot easier to describe than it is to carry out in the laboratory. Let us see how it is actually done in practice.

The Process of Genetic Engineering

The modification of a plant or animal's genetic composition (its *genome*) can be accomplished in the following steps.

First, researchers have to decide what physical or biological property of an organism they want to change. Do they want to make a plant that is resistant to rust disease or one that produces fruit that does not ripen as quickly as the natural plant? Or do they want an animal with reduced body fat or one that lays more eggs in a shorter time?

Second, they have to find out what region of the organism's genome codes for that particular physical or biological property. In practice, that means that all or some portion of the organism's genome has to be sequenced. *Sequencing* means finding out what genes are present in the genome, what their chemical (DNA) structures are, and where they are located in the genome.

Scientists have been working on the sequencing of plant, animal, and other genomes for more than 40 years. The first genome of any kind sequenced was that of a virus, bacteriophage MS2, a project completed by Belgian molecular biologist Walter Fiers in 1976. It took nearly two decades to produce the genomes of more complex organisms, such as the first bacterium, *Haemophilus influenzae*, completed by researchers at the Institute for Genomic Research (IGR) in 1995; the first archaeon, *Methanococcus jannaschii*, also produced by IGR researchers in 1996; and the first eukaryote, a yeast, *Saccharomyces cerevisiae*, determined by researchers at 74 European laboratories and announced after a decade-long project in 1997.

The complete sequencing of the first plant genome, that of a weed in the mustard family, *Arabidopsis thaliana*, was completed in 2000 by an international consortium, and a new project has been initiated to determine the function of the more than 25,000 genes present in that genome. The first complete animal genome announced was that of the nematode *Caenorhabditis elegans*, produced by a team at the Sanger Institute and Washington University in 1998, followed two years later by the announcement of the complete genome of the fruit fly *Drosophila melanogaster* by a team from the Celera company, the Baylor College of Medicine, the University of California at Berkeley, and the European Drosophila Genome

Project (DGP). The first draft of the complete genome of humans (*Homo sapiens*) was announced in 2001 by the Human Genome Project and researchers at Celera Genomics, and the final and complete genome was reported in 2006. Efforts to determine the function of each of the 20,251 known human genes constitute a major activity in the world of genetics research today (Hutchison 2007; "Memorandum by the UK Intellectual Property Office (UK-IPO)," Table 2.1).

Third, researchers have to find a way to alter the organism's genome so that it stops producing the wrong (to the researchers) kind of protein(s) and/or to start producing the right (again, to the researchers) kind of proteins(s). Either of these options changes the properties of the organism in the direction that researchers want. How can they make such changes in the genome?

It turns out that changing the structure of a DNA molecule requires only two kinds of tools: a "pair of scissors" to cut open a DNA molecule and a "paste pot" to glue the molecule back together. In a stroke of good luck, researchers learned that DNA molecules already have these devices available to them; in fact, they use them regularly to deal with everyday occurrences with which a DNA molecule has to deal.

The "scissors" first: In the late 1960s, Swiss microbiologist Werner Arber hypothesized that bacterial cells possess a natural ability to protect themselves against infection by virus-type materials (*bacteriophages*, or simply *phages*) by using specialized enzymes that cut viral DNA, incapacitating the bacteriophage. He called these enzymes *restriction endonucleases* or *restriction enzymes*. By 1968, he had been able to identify one such restriction enzyme in the common bacterium *Escherichia coli*, an enzyme that he called EcoB. Within a matter of months, Harvard researchers Matthew Meselson and Robert Yuan had discovered a second restriction enzyme in the *E. coli* bacterium, which they named EcoK.

Two years later, Hamilton O. Smith and Kent W. Wilcox at the University of California at Berkeley discovered another restriction enzyme from the bacterium *Haemophilus influenzae*, which they called HindII. HindII turned out, however, to be a significantly different kind of restriction enzyme from either EcoB or EcoK. The latter two enzymes cut DNA molecules at random points in the molecular chain. Adding either enzyme to a DNA molecule produced different sets of products each time the experiment was done. Whereas HindII targeted very specific parts of a DNA molecule, which became known as *restriction sites*. When added to DNA, the enzyme "searched for" the sequence and cut the molecule precisely at that part. (Today, the two types of restriction enzymes are known as Type I and Type II enzymes.) For the HindII restriction enzyme, for example, the restriction site is in the region:

$$GTPy{\uparrow}PuAC$$

where G is a guanine group, T a thymine group, A an adenine group, C a cytosine group, Py any pyrmidine nitrogen base (usually cytosine or thymine), and Pu any purine base (usually adenine or guanine). The arrow indicates the point at which the enzyme cleaves the DNA strand. Other restriction enzymes cut a DNA molecule at other characteristic points. The PstI enzyme, for example, cuts the molecule at the point CTGCA↑G. (For a history of the development of restriction enzymes, see Pray 2008 and Roberts 2005).

Using a pair of restriction enzyme scissors on a DNA molecule produces the following effect, in which a complete molecule is cut at some distinctive region:

```
- C - G - G - G - T - A - A - G - T - C - C - C - A - G - C - G -
- G - C - C - C - A - T - T - C - A - G - G - G - T - C - G - C -
                              ↓
- C - G - G - G - T - A - A - G - T - C - C - C - A - G - C - G -
- G - C - C - C - A - T - T - C - A - G - G - G - T - C - G - C -
```

Second, the "paste pot" also occurs naturally in cells and is used to repair strands of DNA that become broken as a result of exposure to heat, light, other forms of radiation, some chemicals, and other factors. As this process occurs thousands of time every day in the average human body, some mechanism is needed to repair damage to DNA. That mechanism involves the use of yet another type of enzyme, known as a *DNA ligase*. Ligases have the ability to join together the two ends of a broken DNA molecule, making it once more "as good as new." In the example just above, a ligase is able to restore the chemical bond between adenine and guanine groups in the upper chain and between thymine and cytosine in the lower chain ("DNA Ligase, T4"; "DNA Repair" 2002).

The availability of naturally occurring "scissors" and "paste pot" makes it possible to carry out the process of genetic engineering of any cell. The first instance in which this process was actually carried out in the laboratory was an experiment designed by American biochemist Paul Berg in 1972. He worked with two very simple organisms, a virus that infects monkeys, SV40 (for simian virus 40), and another virus that most commonly infects the bacterium *E. coli*, called the λ (lambda) bacteriophage. Both organisms exist in the form of *plasmids*, circular loops consisting of DNA only.

In the first step of his experiment, Berg cut open the SV40 plasmid using the restriction enzyme EcoRI. He then used the same restriction enzyme to cut out a small segment of DNA from the λ bacteriophage. Each time the restriction enzyme made a cut in one of the viruses, it produced a modified particle (the SV40 modified plasmid) or a DNA fragment (from the λ bacteriophage) with so-called sticky ends. The term *sticky ends* refers to the fact that the open segment of the SV40 virus and the ends of the λ particle contain a short segment of DNA consisting of a distinctive set of nitrogen bases

GCTA

CGAT

that was capable of joining to a comparable set of nitrogen bases from some other source, such as

GCTA
CGAT

Next, Berg inserted the DNA segment taken from the λ bacteriophage into the gap he had created in the SV40 plasmid. Finally, he sealed up this new plasmid using a DNA ligase. The product thus formed is known in general as a *chimera*, a term taken from Greek mythology that refers to mythical animals consisting of body parts of a variety of animals, such as a human body with the head of a lion or some other animal and a tail. The final product is also known as *recombinant DNA* (rDNA), a term that is also used to describe the procedure by which the chimera is produced. Berg was awarded the Nobel Prize in chemistry in 1980 for this research. (He offered a technical description of his work in his Nobel lecture on December 8, 1980.)

At about the same time that Berg was carrying out his pioneering experiments, two other American researchers, Herbert W. Boyer and Stanley N. Cohen, were embarking on a somewhat more ambitious but similar project in their separate laboratories at Stanford University and the University of California at San Francisco. Boyer and Cohen were exploring methods for inserting a variety of DNA segments that coded for specialized properties into plasmids like the one used by Berg. In one experiment, for example, Boyer and Cohen worked with *E. coli* bacteria, one strain of which was resistant to the antibiotic tetracycline (call them the t^+ bacteria), and one of which was resistant to the antibiotic kanamycin (call them k^+).

For their experiments, Boyer and Cohen used a synthetic plasmid called pSC101 ("p" for "plasmid," "SC" for "Stanley Cohen," and "101" because it was the 101st plasmid Cohen had invented). pSC101 was about as simple as plasmids can get, consisting of only two genes, one of which coded for replication of the plasmid and one for resistance to kanamycin. Using the cut-and-paste method described earlier, Boyer and Cohen inserted a third gene into the pSC101 plasmid, a gene coding for resistance to tetracycline. They then inserted the modified pSC101 plasmid into a *E. coli* culture and allowed the bacteria to reproduce. After a period of time, they found some bacteria that were resistant to tetracycline (as some *E. coli* naturally are), some that were resistant to kanamycin (as other *E. coli* naturally are), and some that were resistant to both antibiotics (as none of their bacteria naturally were). They had produced a recombinant form of the bacterium with new properties different from those found in naturally occurring *E. coli*.

Boyer and Cohen went on to conduct a number of similar experiments transferring one or another physical or biological property from one organism to another. In what was probably their most impressive work of all, they eventually found a way to transfer genes taken from an amphibian, the African clawed toad *Xenopus laevis*, into bacteria, where they were expressed over a number of generations ("The First Recombinant DNA").

Concerns about rDNA Research

The work of Boyer and Cohen is sometimes thought to constitute the beginning of the age of modern biotechnology. Certainly, the techniques they developed were soon being put into use by researchers around the world to produce a host of new transformed organisms. For example, German-born American researcher Rudolf Jaenisch and his colleague, Beatrice Mintz, reported in 1974 that they had produced transgenetic mice by transferring a portion of the SV40 genome into pregnant mice, which then exhibited traits carried by the SV40 DNA when they reached adulthood (Hopkin 2011).

Virtually everyone with the least knowledge about molecular biology began to realize the staggering implications of this line of research. For the first time in human history, scientists had discovered a way of potentially remaking life in essentially any form they desired. It is difficult to imagine a more exciting, promising, and also terrifying line of research.

Even as the first new discoveries in biotechnology were being announced, a number of researchers—including many who were themselves active in the field—began to express concerns about the possible risks to humans and the natural environment of such research. Of course, there was almost no precedent for the research being conducted, and no one really knew what might happen if an engineered organism managed to escape from a laboratory. What effects might it have on human health or on the environment. These concerns were partially based on the fact that one of the most common organisms used in the research was *E. coli*, a bacterium found commonly in the environment and, more importantly, in the digestive tract of humans and other animals.

As early as 1973, the potential risks posed by rDNA research were discussed at a meeting, the Conference on Biohazards in Biological Research, also known as Asilomar I, held in January 1973 at the Asilomar Conference Center, Asilomar State Beach, California. That meeting was sponsored by the National Science Foundation and the National Cancer Institute and attended by about 100 researchers. The risks associated with the use of viruses in research were the major theme, and only modest attention paid to rDNA research in particular (Peterson and White 2010).

At another series of meetings held in June of the same year, a major annual session known as the Gordon Conferences, Boyer reported in an off-the-record session about his research, and attendees at his meeting immediately recognized potential problems that this research was likely to involve. They agreed to write a letter to the National Academy of Sciences (NAS) and National Academy of Medicine (NAM), recommending that these federal agencies initiate a more formal analysis of the risks that might be associated with rDNA research projects (Peterson and White 2010).

The NAS responded to that letter by recommending the formation of an informal study group of rDNA researchers to consider this question. In July 1974, that group of researchers wrote a letter to the journal *Proceedings of the National Academy of Sciences of the United States* (now *PNAS*) reporting on their deliberations. The group included Berg (who was chair of the group), Boyer, Cohen, Daniel Nathans, Watson, and David Baltimore, who was a year later to win the Nobel Prize in physiology or medicine for his work in molecular biology. The signatories of the *PNAS* letter made four specific recommendations for dealing with the potential dangers posed by rDNA research:

1. A voluntary moratorium on certain types of rDNA research that might possibly increase the risk to human health of such research.
2. Careful consideration to experiments in which animal DNA is introduced into bacterial DNA.
3. The creation of an advisory committee within the NIH with the responsibilities of overseeing an experimental program to obtain better information about the safety of rDNA research, developing new procedures for minimizing the risks posed by such research, and devising guidelines under which future rDNA research should be conducted.
4. Convening an international meeting of scientists to discuss the safety issues created by this new field of research (Berg et al. 1974).

In October 1974, the NIH followed recommendation 3 in this letter by appointing a Recombinant DNA Advisory Committee (RAC), which remains in service to the present day. In addition, less than a year after the *PNAS* letter was published, the proposed meeting was held, once more at the Asilomar Conference Center. It is sometimes known as Asilomar II, to distinguish it from the earlier meeting by the same name. The conference included a total of 153 participants, of whom 83 were molecular biologists from the United States, 50 molecular biologists from other countries, 16 journalists, and four lawyers (Peterson and White 2010). The meeting continued over a period of four days, from February 24 to

February 27, at the conclusion of which participants adopted a general statement summarizing their work. That statement was later published as an article in *PNAS* in June 1975 that consisted of three major elements, based on two general principles. Those principles were the following:

(i) that [physical] containment be made an essential consideration in the experimental design and, (ii) that the effectiveness of the containment should match, as closely as possible, the estimated risk. (Berg et al. 1975, 1981)

The major elements enunciated for reducing risk, according to one historian, could be classified as "physical containment, biological containment, and human behaviour" (Krimsky 2005). In the first category, participants at the conference defined four levels of risk, minimal, low, moderate, and high, and outlined the types of physical containment necessary for each level. The second category involved a review of the types of organisms that should and should not be produced, emphasizing the avoidance of organisms that had a moderate to high probability of being able to survive outside the laboratory. The third category dealt with the types of behaviors that should not be allowed, including some that are now part of even a beginning chemistry student's list of prohibitions, including eating and drinking in the laboratory and carrying materials produced in the laboratory out of the work space (Berg et al. 1975).

The recommendations made by the Asilomar participants were sent to the NAS, which, in turn, forwarded them to the NIH, which responded by reconvening the RAC, with instructions to convert the Asilomar recommendations into guidelines for researchers who wanted to work with rDNA experiments. This decision initiated what was to become a long and contentious debate over the elements that should be included within the guidelines, including debates over the role the general public should have in developing those guidelines, the proper agencies from whom those guidelines should come, how restrictive the final guidelines should be, how important it was to conduct rDNA research at all, and the extent to which the safety of such research could be guaranteed. The first draft of the rDNA guidelines was issued in June 1976, representing a noble effort on the part of the RAC and NIH to satisfy all interested parties. That hope was too optimistic, however, and the committee and the agency continued to work for a number of years on revisions to the guidelines that would become increasingly more acceptable to all stakeholders in the debate. The most recent version of the NIH guidelines is a 142-page document that covers virtually every imaginable issue involved in the conduct of rDNA research as of March 2013 ("NIH Guidelines for Research Involving Recombinant or Synthetic Nucleic Acid Molecules [NIH Guidelines], March 2013"; for an excellent review of the post-Asilomar activities on the guidelines, see Fredrickson 2001).

History of rDNA Regulation

The NIH guidelines on rDNA research issued in 1976 had, according to many critics, one major flaw: they applied only to research funded by the federal government. This flaw prompted a number of members of Congress to consider legislation that would extend and perhaps strengthen those guidelines to include all research of any kind by any entity within the United States. In 1977 alone, for example, 16 discrete bills were introduced into the U.S. Congress on the regulation of rDNA research (see, for example, "Planned Releases of Genetically-Altered Organisms" 1986). That effort did not succeed, however, for a variety of reasons. For one thing, the RAC decided to expand its membership, including more individuals from outside the scientific community and giving critics a greater opportunity to express their views on regulatory issues. Perhaps more important, however, was the growing realization among researchers that rDNA experiments might actually not be as dangerous as they had feared only a few years earlier. Indeed, the late 1970s and early 1980s saw a number of important breakthroughs by researchers who followed the NIH guidelines and voluntarily used the greatest precautions in conducting their work. As researchers lobbied legislators not to proceed with formal legislation, that avenue of regulation gradually disappeared as an option (McClean 1997).

This is not to say that regulatory agencies in the government abandoned their responsibilities to oversee rDNA research under the NIH guidelines. Instead of looking to new legislation for the oversight responsibilities they had, however, they turned to existing laws and regulations and found ways to apply them to the new technology. For example, the U.S. Department of Agriculture (USDA) was among the first agencies faced with ruling on the use of genetically engineered organisms in agricultural projects. To determine whether such projects should be approved or not, they turned to one very old law, the Plant Quarantine Act of 1912, which gave the USDA the authority to regulate plants that might carry pests or diseases that could harm agricultural crops, and the Plant Pest Act of 1957, which had similar provisions for plants imported to the United States (McHughen 2006). The Food and Drug Administration (FDA) followed a similar line, referring applications for the testing of genetically engineered organisms to its Center for Drug Evaluation and Research (Junod 2009).

As progress in rDNA research rapidly moved forward in the 1980s, the federal government finally recognized that a more comprehensive and orderly system was needed to regulate research on and release and commercial production of genetically modified organisms (GMOs). Thus, in April 1984, President Ronald Reagan appointed a Cabinet Council Working Group (the Working Group) to consist of representatives from all executive departments and the Environmental Protection Agency, Council on Environmental Quality, Council of Economic Advisers, Office of Management and Budget, Office of Science and Technology Policy, White House Office of Policy

Development, and National Science Foundation. By December, the Working Group had produced a draft document for publication in the Federal Register, to which public comments were invited. As a result of these comments, the Working Group created yet another committee, the Biotechnology Science Coordinating Committee (BSCC), consisting of a smaller group of members more directly concerned with the regulation of GMOs, the commissioner of the FDA, the director of NIH, the assistant secretary of agriculture for marketing and inspection services, the assistant secretary of agriculture for science and education, the assistant administrator of EPA for pesticides and toxic substances, the assistant administrator of EPA for research and development, and the assistant director of the National Science Foundation for biological, behavioral, and social sciences. This committee reassessed the work of its predecessors and produced yet another version of the Coordinated Framework, which was published in the Federal Register on June 26, 1986 ("Coordinated Framework for Regulation of Biotechnology Products" 1986; Kingsbury 1990).

That document dealt with two large issues: research on GMOs and commercial products made from such organisms. The committee divided up the responsibilities for all the conceivably possible regulatory needs in these areas among the USDA, Animal and Plant Health Inspection Service (APHIS), FDA, NIH, EPA, Food and Safety Inspection Service (FSIS), and Science and Education Administration of USDA (S&E). (The appropriate portion of the document is reprinted in Chapter 5.) For example, research on GMOs that could be contained with a laboratory were regulated by the agency providing funding for the research if it were a federal agency and by NIH, S&E, and APHIS (or voluntarily by researchers) in the case of funding from nonfederal sources. Just who was responsible for what research in the latter case was the point of an extended discussion in the Coordinated Framework. Similarly, the regulation of commercial GMO foods and food additives was the responsibility of the FDA in some cases and the FSIS in other cases, whereas the production of pesticides was usually the responsibility of the EPA and, sometimes, APHIS. (For the final document, see "Coordinated Framework" 1986 or, in a more accessible and essentially similar form, Office of Science and Technology Policy 1986.)

Interestingly, some local and state governments were moving forward on the regulation of rDNA research, whereas the federal government was working its tortuous way through the issue. As early as 1977, for example, the city of Cambridge, Massachusetts, became the first municipality in the world to regulate rDNA research by adopting a version of the NIH Guidelines for Research Involving DNA Molecules. The provisions of the Cambridge Recombinant DNA Technology Ordinance remain in force today and are administered by the city's Biosafety Committee ("Recombinant DNA"). The Cambridge ordinance was especially significant because the city is home to one of the largest and most prestigious research institutions in the world, Harvard University, whose activities in the field of rDNA research therefore became subject to city regulation.

Shortly after the Cambridge action, a number of cities and states across the nation adopted similar ordinance, also often modeled on the NIH Guidelines. These municipalities included the cities of Emeryville and Berkeley, California (both in 1977); Princeton, New Jersey (1978); Amherst and Waltham, Massachusetts (1978); Boston and Somerville, Massachusetts (1981); and Newton, Massachusetts (1982), and the states of Maryland (1977) and New York (1978). (For details of these ordinances, see Krimsky, Baeck, and Bolduc 1982.) A number of these cities are, like Cambridge, home to major research institutions, including Princeton University, the University of Massachusetts (Amherst), Brandeis University (Waltham), and Boston (the home of many important institutions of higher learning and research companies).

Breakthroughs in rDNA Research

Even as governmental entities at all levels were debating the regulation of rDNA research, scientists interested in the topic were moving forward at a significant rate, making a number of critical breakthroughs in the development of GMOs. In 1977, for example, the genetic engineering firm of Genentech, Inc., announced the creation of the first transgenic organism capable of expressing a human gene. The term *transgenic* refers to an organism whose genome has been altered by the insertion of DNA from a different species. In this case, a human gene for the production of the compound somatostatin had been inserted into the genome of the bacterium of *E. coli*, producing a new strain of bacterium that was capable of producing the human hormone somatostatin. Somatostatin is a hormone that regulates the endocrine system and affects neurotransmission and cell reproduction in the human body. The next year, Genetech announced the production of a second transgenic organism, a bacterium carrying a human gene for the production of the hormone insulin, and in 1978, it reported a third such product, a bacterium engineered to synthesize the human growth hormone (HGH). These breakthroughs were significant because they made available for the first time a relatively inexpensive, efficient method for manufacturing a group of extremely important natural products used for the treatment of a variety of human diseases and disorders.

Work was progressing apace among researchers who were attempting to produce transgenic plants and animals with other purposes. For example, the first transgenic animal was produced by researchers at Ohio University in 1981 when they injected a gene for the β-globin protein from a rabbit into a mouse. The host mouse and its descendants then produced blood that carried that protein for a number of generations (Wagner et al. 1981). Almost simultaneously, transgenic mice with other characteristics were reported by four other research teams ("Transgenic Mice Formed by Nuclear Injection").

Over the next three decades, researchers produced a number of transgenic animals for a variety of purposes. Among the most popular lines of research has been the production of genetically engineered mice and rats with introduced genetic traits that can be studied for medical purposes. Other transgenic animals have been developed for other types of research or for purely entertainment value. For example, a common line of research has involved the introduction of the gene for the production a protein known as green fluorescent protein (GFP) into a variety of animals. GFP has the specialized property of producing a bright green fluorescence when exposed to light in the blue to ultraviolet range. Researchers sometimes add the gene for GFP to other genes they want to study that are introduced into a host animal. A more mundane application of the technology has been the creation of so-called GloFish that carry the GFP gene and glow in different colors when exposed to light of different wavelengths (Zimmer, "Fluoro Fish").

Other than their use in research and for the production of medical products such as insulin and HGH, transgenic animals have not yet experienced wide use in agricultural or other types of commercial businesses. Such has not been the case at all with transgenic plants. The first such plants were invented almost simultaneously in 1983 by four different research groups. Three of those groups presented papers about their discoveries at a conference in Miami, Florida, in January 1983, whereas the fourth group announced its own discovery at a conference in Los Angeles in April of the same year. The three groups that reported in January had all used similar approaches for the insertion of a gene providing resistance to the antibiotic kanamycin in tobacco plants, in two cases, and petunia plants, in the third case (Fraley, Rogers, and Horsch 1983, 211–221; Framond et al. 1983, 159–170; Schell et al. 1983, 191–209). The fourth group took a somewhat difference approach and introduced a gene removed from the common bean plant and inserted it into a sunflower plant (Murai et al. 1983, 476–482; also see "History of Plant Breeding"). (The matter of priority in discoveries is often a matter of dispute. For example, some historians credit invention of the first transgenic plant to a European research team because they published their results in a peer-reviewed journal first in May 1983; see Herrera-Estrella et al. 1983.)

Again, much of the earliest work on transgenic plants was designed to test a variety of technologies for producing such plants and demonstrating the efficacy of such technologies. The 1983 experiments, for example, were not designed primarily for the purpose of producing new strains of tobacco plants or sunflower plants with commercial value to farmers. That step was soon to come, however, when in 1985 a research team at the Belgian company Plant Genetic Systems (now Bayer CropScience) reported that they had developed a genetically engineered tobacco plant that was resistant to attack by insects that normally caused disease in the plant. The key to this discovery was the use of a bacterium commonly found in the soil called *Bacillus thuringiensis* (Bt). Bt also occurs naturally in the gut of caterpillars of various types of moths and butterflies, on leaf surfaces, in aquatic environments and animal feces, and in human-made environments, such as flour mills and grain storage facilities. Some strains of Bt produce proteins during the process of spore production called δ-endotoxins that are toxic to a large range of insect species. By introducing the gene for the production of Bt into a tobacco plant, the Belgian researchers had created a new form of the plant that was resistant to predators that normally cause disease in the plant (Vaeck et al. 1987).

The significance of this technology, of course, is profound. By adding the Bt gene to any type of plant, that plant then becomes resistant to many of the diseases to which it would otherwise be subject. Farmers do not have to spray a field with insecticide to protect a corn, cotton, soybean, or other type of crop carrying the Bt gene, because those crops are now naturally resistant to many types of insect-caused diseases. Almost simultaneously and also within a short period of time, other research teams announced the development of Bt tomatoes (Fischhoff et al. 1987) and Bt cotton plants (Perlak et al. 1990). Bt technology very quickly became widely popular among farmers throughout the world, and plants modified with the gene were soon available for a number of crops (Betz, Hammond, and Fuchs 2000).

There are at least two major arguments for the use of agricultural plants that have been engineered to contain the Bt gene (beyond the obvious financial benefit to the companies that manufacture and sell the plant seeds). First, the natural environment will benefit because farmers will have to spray less plant-killing herbicide on their fields. Second, farmers will benefit because they will have to buy less herbicide and, therefore, save money. As it turns out, the latter prediction has not turned out to be very accurate. Studies have showed that farmers who plant Bt-engineered crops often use *more* herbicide than they did using traditional, nonengineered plants. (More about this topic is in Chapter 2. For data on this issue, see Benbrook 2012; Superweeds: How Biotech Crops Bolster the Pesticide Industry 2013.)

Bt crops are still being planted around the world today, although they tend to be less popular than other forms of GM crops. In the United States, for example, 5 percent of all the corn planted in 2013 was a Bt varietal, down from a high of 26 percent in 2005, and 8 percent of all cotton was a Bt varietal, down from a high of 18 percent in 2005 and 2006 ("Adoption of Genetically Engineered Crops in the U.S."). Comparable numbers in other parts of the world were much smaller in most cases, largely because of bans on many aspects of GM crops and foods in the European Union and nations economically depended on trade with the Union. In its latest report on the production of GM crops worldwide, the International Service for the Acquisition of Agri-Biotech Applications (ISAAA) reported that two countries, Sudan and Cuba, began using Bt crops for the first time in 2012, whereas the use of such crops increased moderately in some parts of the

European Union. The Czech Republic, Portugal, Romania, Slovakia, and Spain together planted 129,071 hectares of Bt maize in 2012, a 13 percent increase over the previous year and a significant increase, given the continent's general opposition to the use of GM crops and foods ("Global Status of Commercialized Biotech/GM Crops: 2012").

Two exceptions to these trends appear in India and China. In the former case, farmers cultivated a total of 10.8 million hectares of Bt cotton, with an adoption rate of 93 percent, whereas the data for China showed 4.0 million hectares of Bt cotton, with an adoption rate of 80 percent. Adoption rate is defined as the percentage of land planted to a crop that is used for the Bt varietal ("Global Status of Commercialized Biotech/GM Crops: 2012"). A good general overview of the ongoing status of Bt crops can be found at Mannion and Morse (2013).

Types of Genetically Modified Plants

The introduction of pest resistance by the insertion of a Bt gene is by no means the only mechanism by which plants have been genetically modified for use in agriculture. A historically famous example involves efforts to produce plants that survive low atmospheric temperatures at which they would normally be killed by frost. The economic benefits of such a product are obvious because many crops that are routinely destroyed by low temperatures would survive to the marketplace.

The scientific basis for such a product was discovered accidentally in the early 1960s when researchers at the USDA observed that some of the plants being used in an experimental test at the department froze to death during an unexpected frost, whereas others survived the frost. It took more than a decade to unravel this mystery, but researchers eventually discovered that bacteria living on the surface of plants routinely produce a protein on the plant surface that serves as a center on which ice crystals can form, resulting in the eventual freezing of the plant. Some mutant bacteria lack the gene for this protein, however, and are unable to produce the so-called *ice nucleation* protein.

A number of biotech companies began to explore the possibility of producing a genetically modified form of bacteria that lack the ice nucleation gene. In 1983, one of those companies, Advanced Genetics Sciences (AGS), applied for a permit from the USDA to field test a spray, called Frostban, containing so-called *ice-minus* bacteria, which lacked the gene to produce the ice nucleation protein. USDA issued the permit, the first permit for the testing of a GM crop in history. However, the field testing did not occur immediately because outraged activists interrupted the field test by burning the test fields. In fact, it was not until four years later that the test was actually carried out. For a variety of reasons, the strong objection of activists among them, AGS never pursued the commercial development of the Frostban spray (Maugh 1987; Skirvin et al. 2000).

Another early—and failed—GM crop was the Flavr Savr tomato, developed by the biotech company, Calgene, in the late 1980s and early 1990s. The objective behind this research was to develop a tomato that does not ripen as quickly as occurs in nature. A tomato that ripens more slowly might retain the correct color, odor, and taste but would not soften during harvesting, storage, transport to the market, and display time on market shelves. It would save untold amounts of money lost by having to throw away tomatoes that go bad between harvesting and sale.

Researchers learned that the process of ripening in a tomato is controlled by the enzyme polygalacturonase, which attacks and breaks down the pectin in the cell walls of tomato skin, producing the softening of the fruit. They hypothesized that introducing a compound that inactivates that enzyme, a so-called *antisense enzyme*, would interrupt that natural process and slow down the ripening process. Experiments eventually supported this line of genetic engineering, and in 1992, Calgene submitted a petition to the FDA asking for permission to sell the product to the general public. After a two-year analysis of the petition, the FDA concluded that the Flavr Savr tomato was "as safe as tomatoes bred by conventional means" and that there was, therefore, no reason to withhold approval of its sale to human consumers ("Agency Summary Memorandum").

At first blush, Flavr Savr tomatoes and the paste made from them appeared to be very popular, often outselling their traditional rivals at supermarkets. The GM fruit was also popular with food manufacturers, who realized about a 20 percent profit in the distribution and production of tomato products from it. For a variety of reasons, however, initial sales numbers soon began to drop off, and by early 1999, the product had been withdrawn from the market, never to reappear again (Bruening and Lyons 2000; Martineau 2002).

Another approach to the genetic modification of crops is based on a chemical known as glyphosate. The name is a shortened version that describes the substance's chemical composition; it is a phosphate derivative of the amino acid glycine. Glyphosate was first synthesized in Switzerland in 1950 by the organic chemist Henri Martin, who was working at the time for the small pharmaceutical company Cilag. Martin apparently never published his research and did not explore possible biological properties of the substance. It essentially sat on the virtual shelves of the drug industry until 1970, when a chemist working for the Monsanto company, John E. Franz, repeated Martin's synthesis and tested it for herbicidal action. Franz found that glyphosate was extraordinarily effective in killing large-leaved plants of the type that most commonly compete with agricultural crops. Monsanto went on to patent glyphosate under the trade name of Roundup (Duke and Powles 2008; Magin 2003).

Roundup soon became a very popular herbicide among farmers. The product had one serious drawback. As it was most effective against large-leaf plants, it also had a tendency to attack and kill crop plants. Monsanto's solution to this problem was to develop a new generation of GM plants that were resistant to their new herbicide. The challenge of developing such plants was simple in concept, although not so easy in practice. Glyphosate kills plants because it inhibits an enzyme known as 5-enolpyruvylshikimate-3-phosphate (EPSP) synthase, which is essential for the synthesis of three aromatic amino acids: tyrosine, tryptophan, and phenylalanine. Without these amino acids, a plant stops growing and dies. Monsanto's method for developing Roundup Ready–resistant plants was to insert a gene into those plants that inhibits the action of glyphosate. Engineered plants with this gene are, therefore, resistant to the harmful effects of glyphosate on the plant's normal growth patterns. (For a technical description of this process, see Funke et al. 2006.) As with Bt-engineered plants, the expectation is that the use of Roundup herbicide on fields where Roundup Ready plants are being grown results in less harm to the environment and financial benefit to farmers (and the Monsanto company). The extent to which this has actually occurred will be discussed in Chapter 2.

Glyphosate herbicides experienced by far the greatest increase in popularity among American farmers in the period between 1990, when they first became commercially available, and the first decade of the twenty-first century. In one series of ongoing studies, for example, the USDA found that the use of glyphosate herbicides in nine Midwestern states rose from essentially zero in 1990, to about 10 million pounds in 1996, to 30 million pounds in 1999, to 50 million pounds in 2002. During this period, no other herbicide in use experienced such an increase in popularity (Battaglin et al. 2005, Table 1). In another series of studies conducted by the EPA, the use of glyphosate nationwide continued to grow from more than 85 million pounds in 2001 to more than 180 million pounds in 2007, the last year for which the EPA has data ("Pesticide News Story" 2011). Still, in 2013, herbicide-resistant plants accounted for only 14 percent of all corn and 15 percent of all cotton planted in the United States (but 93 percent of all soybean crops) ("Adoption of Genetically Engineered Crops in the

U.S."). How does one account for the remaining parts of corn and cotton acreage planted in the United States in 2013 (71 percent for corn and 67 percent for cotton)?

The answer is that researchers have developed yet another technique for the modification of plants, which involves a process known as *stacking*. An obvious improvement in the development of GM plants might involve the invention of a plant that contains genes for two or more characteristics, such as resistance to an herbicide and delayed development of fruit. The problem is that inserting one gene at a time into a plant is difficult enough, and adding two or more genes to a plant is an extraordinarily difficult technical procedure. However, there is a way around that problem, one that involves mating two GM members of the same species. In such a case, at least some of the progeny of that mating will carry both inserted genes, one from each parent. By continuing this process through additional generations, more and more modified genes can be added to the plant. A group of genes that have been added by this procedure is said to constitute a set of *stacked genes*. The process is also known as *gene pyramiding* and *multigene transfer* ("Stacked Traits in Biotech Crops"). Currently (early 2014), the most complex of these products is a seed called SmartStax, produced in a collaborative effort between Monsanto and the Dow Chemical Company. SmartStax seeds contain eight GM genes for a resistance to a variety of above-ground and below-ground insects and to two kinds of herbicides ("Monsanto's SmartStax Maize").

Plants with stacked genes obviously hold a number of advantages for farmers, and they have become very popular since first introduced in 1995. The most recent data available suggest that stacked plants accounted for about 43.7 million hectares of crops worldwide in 2012, making up more than 26 percent of all GM crops planted. The rate of adoption of stacked varietals by farmers in that year was 31 percent greater than it had been for the previous year. In the United States, the rates of stacked gene varietals were even greater than the worldwide total, reaching (as noted earlier) 71 percent for corn and 67 percent for cotton (but essentially zero for soybeans). Stacked gene plants appear to be growing in popularity fastest in developing nations, with Argentina, Brazil, China, India, and South Africa collectively accounting for about 78.2 million hectares of such crops, nearly half of all biotech crops grown in those countries. These numbers are important because it is in just those countries that population is growing fastest, food shortages tend to be the most severe, and new technologies, such as stacking, more hold the greatest promise for dealing with those issues ("Global Status of Commercialized Biotech/GM Crops: 2012").

Genetically Modified Animals

Research on GM animals dates back at least three decades, a period during which GM animals have been produced for a variety of purposes, such as

- Producing pharmaceuticals for use by humans and other animals
- Decreasing the environmental effects of impact of large-scale, "industrial" agriculture by decreasing the amount of harmful chemicals such as phosphate in manure, thereby reducing water pollution
- Serving as a source of cells, tissue, and organs for use in human transplantation procedures
- Producing certain types of materials with specialized uses, such as surgical sutures and personal protection devices, including body armor for military and law enforcement use
- Producing very specific antibiotics for use against disease-causing bacteria such *E. coli 0157:H7* and salmonella ("Fact Sheet: Genetically Engineered Animals")

Notice that one use not mentioned in this list is the development of GM animals for human consumption. Until late 2013, research had not yet yielded a single animal developed through rDNA research that was approved for human consumption in the United States. That situation changed in 2014 when the FDA granted approval for the sale of a genetically modified form of salmon in the United States. The salmon, sold under the trade name of AquAdvantage salmon, was developed by AquaBounty Technologies and includes a growth-regulating hormone that forces the fish to grow year around, rather than only in spring and summer, as is the case with the natural form of the fish. The hormone makes it possible for the salmon to reach market size in about half the time of its natural cousins, 16 to 18 months, rather than three years. The advantage the fish offers to producers (although not necessarily consumers) is obvious ("Genetically Engineered Salmon").

Conclusion

The Biblical admonition quoted at the beginning of this chapter to take dominion over every living organism on Earth appears to be coming true. Over the last half century, humans have made impressive progress in learning how to change and shape plants, animals, bacteria, viruses, and other organisms for dozens of different purposes, from the production of drugs to the creation of new food varietals. It is hardly a wonder, then, that many scientists see the new age of biotechnology as a period in human history filled with promise and hope, an opportunity perhaps for the first time to feed the billions of hungry men, women, and children around the world.

However, that view would be ignoring some very strong objections and concerns posed by individuals worldwide about the potential risks that GM foods pose to human health and to the natural environment. Ever since the earliest breakthroughs in rDNA research were announced, critics have been asking scientists to slow down and take a closer look at the potential risks posed by their research, or perhaps to abandon that research entirely.

These concerns have thus far not been expressed universally in all parts of the world. As this chapter indicates, for example, there are virtually no laws that limit or prohibit research on GM foods, or even to require labeling of foods that contain GM components, although there are many very complex regulations that companies must follow before their products are approved for public consumption. Such is not the case in the European Union, for example, where concerns about GM foods have resulted in the adoption of very tight controls on research, development, distribution, sale, and consumption of foods that contain GM elements.

Thus, the debate over the use of GM foods continues in most parts of the world, even in the United States, where battles are still being fought about the sale and labeling of such products. Chapter 2 offers a historical review of the anti-GMO movement around the world and a discussion of the arguments currently being offered both for and against the development and marketing of such products, for and against the labeling of GM foods, and other issues that remain before the public today.

References

"Adoption of Genetically Engineered Crops in the U.S." USDA Economic Research Service. http://www.ers.usda.gov/data-products/adoption-of-genetically-engineered-crops-in-the-us.aspx. Accessed on September 8, 2013.

"Agency Summary Memorandum Re: Consultation with Calgene, Inc., Concerning FLAVR SAVR™ Tomatoes." U.S. Food and Drug Administration. http://www.fda.gov/Food/FoodScienceResearch/Biotechnology/Submissions/ucm225043.htm. Accessed on September 8, 2013.

"AKC Breeds—Complete Breed List." American Kennel Club. http://www.akc.org/breeds/complete_breed_list.cfm. Accessed on September 3, 2013.

Battaglin, William A., et al. 2005. "Glyphosate, Other Herbicides, and Transformation Products in Midwestern Streams, 2002." *Journal of the American Water Resources Association* 41(2): 323–332.

Benbrook, Charles M. 2012. "Impacts of Genetically Engineered Crops on Pesticide Use in the U.S.—the First Sixteen Years." Environmental Sciences Europe 24: 24. http://www.enveurope.com/content/pdf/2190-4715-24-24 .pdf. Accessed on September 9, 2013.

Berg, Paul. 1980. "Dissections and Reconstructions of Genes and Chromosomes." Nobel lecture, December 8. http:// www.nobelprize.org/nobel_prizes/chemistry/laureates/ 1980/berg-lecture.pdf. Accessed on September 5, 2013.

Berg, Paul, et al. 1974. "Potential Biohazards of Recombinant DNA Molecules." *Proceedings of the National Academy of Sciences of the United States of America* 71(7): 2593–2594.

Berg, Paul, et al. 1975. "Summary Statement of the Asilomar Conference on Recombinant DNA Molecules." *Proceedings of the National Academy of Science of the United States of America* 72(6): 1981–1984.

Betz, Fred S., Bruce G. Hammond, and Roy L. Fuchs. 2000. "Safety and Advantages of *Bacillus thuringiensis*-Protected Plants to Control Insect Pests." *Regulatory Toxicology and Pharmacology* 32(2): 156–173.

Bruening, G., and J. M. Lyons. 2000. "The Case of the FLAVR SAVR Tomato." *California Agriculture* 54(4): 6–7.

"CFA Breeds." Cat Fanciers' Association. http://www.cfa.org/ breeds.aspx. Accessed on September 3, 2013.

"Coordinated Framework for Regulation of Biotechnology Products." 1986. *Federal Register* 51: 23303–23350.

"Corn in the United States." http://www2.econ.iastate.edu/
classes/econ496/lence/spring2004/corn.pdf. Accessed on
September 3, 2013.

Dahm, Ralf. 2008. "Discovering DNA: Friedrich Miescher and
the Early Years of Nucleic Acid Research." *Human Genetics*
122(6): 565–581.

"DNA Ligase, T4." Worthington Enzyme Manual. http://
www.worthington-biochem.com/dnat4l/. Accessed on
September 4, 2013.

"DNA Repair." 2002. In Molecular Biology of the Cell, 4th
edition. http://www.ncbi.nlm.nih.gov/books/NBK26879/.
Accessed on September 4, 2013.

Duke, Stephen O., and Stephen B. Powles. 2008. "Glyphosate:
A Once-in-a-Century Herbicide." *Pest Management Science*
64(4): 319–325.

"Fact Sheet: Genetically Engineered Animals." U.S. Food and
Drug Administration. http://www.fda.gov/AnimalVeterinary/
DevelopmentApprovalProcess/GeneticEngineering/
GeneticallyEngineeredAnimals/ucm113597.htm.
Accessed on September 9, 2013.

"The First Recombinant DNA." DNA Learning Center.
http://www.dnalc.org/view/15915-The-first-recombinant
-DNA.html. Accessed on September 5, 2013.

Fischhoff, David A., et al. 1987. "Insect Tolerant
Transgenic Tomato Plants." *Nature Biotechnology* 5(8):
807–813.

Fraley, R. T., S. B. Rogers, and R. B. Horsch. 1983. "Use of a
Chimeric Gene to Confer Antibiotic Resistance to Plant
Cells." In *Advances in Gene Technology: Molecular
Genetics of Plants and Animals. Miami Winter Symposia*
20: 211–221.

Framond, A. J., et al. 1983. "Mini-ti Plasmid and a Chimeric
Gene Construct: New Approaches to Plant Gene Vector
Construction." In *Advances in Gene Technology: Molecular*

Genetics of Plants and Animals. Miami Winter Symposia 20: 159–170.

Fredrickson, Donald S. 2001. "The First Twenty-Five Years after Asilomar." *Perspectives in Biology and Medicine* 44(2): 170–182.

Funke, Todd, et al. 2006. "Molecular Basis for the Herbicide Resistance of Roundup Ready Crops." *Proceedings of the National Academy of Sciences of the United States of America* 103(35): 13010–13015.

"Genetically Engineered Salmon." U.S. Food and Drug Administration. http://www.fda.gov/AnimalVeterinary/ DevelopmentApprovalProcess/GeneticEngineering/ GeneticallyEngineeredAnimals/ucm280853.htm. Accessed on September 9, 2013.

"Global Status of Commercialized Biotech/GM Crops: 2012." International Service for the Acquisition of Agri-Biotech Applications. http://www.isaaa.org/resources/publications/ briefs/44/executivesummary/default.asp. Accessed on September 8, 2013.

Herrera-Estrella, Luis, et al. 1983. "Expression of Chimaeric Genes Transferred into Plant Cells Using a Ti-Plasmid-Derived Vector." *Nature* 303(5914): 209–213.

Hirst, K. Kris. "History of Rice, Part One." About.com Archaeology. http://archaeology.about.com/od/ domestications/a/rice.htm. Accessed on August 29, 2013.

"History of Plant Breeding." Colorado State University. http:// cls.casa.colostate.edu/transgeniccrops/history.html. Accessed on September 8, 2013.

Hopkin, Karen. 2011. "Ready, Rest, Go." The Scientist. http:// www.the-scientist.com/?articles.view/articleNo/30726/title/ Ready–Reset–Go/. Accessed on September 5, 2013.

Hutchison, Clyde A., III. 2007. "DNA Sequencing: Bench to Bedside and Beyond." *Nucleic Acids Research* 35(18): 6227–6237.

"Indian Archaeobotany Watch: Lahuradewa 2008." The
Archaeobotanist. http://archaeobotanist.blogspot.com/
2009/06/indian-archaeobotany-watch-lahuradewa.html.
Accessed on August 29, 2013.

Junod, Suzanne White. 2009. "Celebrating a Milestone: FDA's
Approval of the First Genetically-Engineered Product."
About FDA. http://www.fda.gov/AboutFDA/WhatWeDo/
History/ProductRegulation/SelectionsFromFDLIUpdate
SeriesonFDAHistory/ucm081964.htm. Accessed on
September 7, 2013.

Kingsbury, David T. 1990. "Regulation of Biotechnology:
A. Perspective on the US 'Coordinated Framework'." http://
www.scopenvironment.org/downloadpubs/scope44/
chapter14.html. Accessed on September 7, 2013.

Krimsky, Sheldon. 2005. "From Asilomar to Industrial
Biotechnology: Risks, Reductionism, and Regulation."
Science as Culture 14(4): 309–323. http://www.tufts.edu/
~skrimsky/PDF/From%20Asilomar.PDF. Accessed on
September 5, 2013.

Krimsky, Sheldon, Anne Baeck, and John Bolduc. 1982.
*Municipal and State Recombinant DNA Laws: History and
Assessment.* Medford, MA: Department of Urban and
Environmental Policy, Tufts University.

Linares, Olga F. 2002. "African Rice (*Oryza glaberrima*): History
and Future Potential." *Proceedings of the National Academy of
Sciences of the United States of America* 99(25): 16360–16365.

Magin, Ralph W. 2003. "Glyphosphate: Twenty-Eight Years
and Still Growing—the Discovery, Development, and
Impact of the Herbicide on the Agrichemical Industry."
In G. C. Volgas, Roger A. Downer, and H. B. Lopez, eds.
Pesticide Formulations and Application Systems, vol. 23,
149–158. West Conshohocken, PA: ASTM.

Mannion, A. M., and Stephen Morse. 2013. *Gm Crops
1996–2012: A Review of Agronomic, Environmental and*

Socio-economic Impacts. University of Surrey Centre for Environmental Strategy Working Paper 04/13. http://biotechbenefits.croplife.org/paper/gm-crops-1996-2012-a-review-of-agronomic-environmental-and-socio-economic-impacts-2/. Accessed on September 8, 2013.

Martineau, Belinda. 2002. *First Fruit: The Creation of the Flavr Savr Tomato and the Birth of Biotech Food.* New York; London: McGraw-Hill.

Maugh, Thomas H., II. 1987. "Altered Bacterium Does Its Job: Frost Failed to Damage Sprayed Test Crop, Company Says." Los Angeles Times. http://articles.latimes.com/1987-06-09/news/mn-6024_1_frost-damage. Accessed on September 8, 2013.

McClean, Phillip. 1997. "Historical Events in the rDNA Debate." http://www.ndsu.edu/pubweb/~mcclean/plsc431/debate/debate3.htm. Accessed on September 7, 2013.

McHughen, Alan. 2006. "Plant Genetic Engineering and Regulation in the United States." Agricultural Biotechnology in California Series. http://anrcatalog.ucdavis.edu/pdf/8179.pdf. Accessed on September 7, 2013.

"Memorandum by the UK Intellectual Property Office (UK-IPO)." http://www.publications.parliament.uk/pa/ld200809/ldselect/ldsctech/107/107we39.htm. Accessed on September 4, 2013.

"Monsanto's SmartStax Maize 'to be Approved for Growth in October' in EU." RT. http://rt.com/news/smartstax-maize-germany-approval-428/. Accessed on September 9, 2013.

Moore, Randy. 2001. "The 'Rediscovery' of Mendel's Work." *Bioscene* 27(2): 13–24. http://www.cs.uml.edu/~grinstei/91.510/Rediscovery%20of%20Mendel.pdf. Accessed on May 2, 2014.

Murai, Norimoto, et al. 1983. "Phaseolin Gene from Bean Is Expressed after Transfer to Sunflower via Tumor-Inducing Plasmid Vectors." *Science* 222(4623): 476–482.

"NIH Guidelines for Research Involving Recombinant or Synthetic Nucleic Acid Molecules (NIH Guidelines), March 2013." Department of Health and Human Services, National Institutes of Health. http://osp.od.nih.gov/office -biotechnology-activities/rdna/nih_guidelines_oba.html. Accessed on May 16, 2014.

O'Neil, Dennis. 1997. "Mendel's Genetics." http://anthro .palomar.edu/mendel/mendel_1.htm. Accessed on September 3, 2013.

Office of Science and Technology Policy. 1986. *Coordinated Framework for Regulation of Biotechnology.* http://www.aphis .usda.gov/brs/fedregister/coordinated_framework.pdf. Accessed on August 19, 2013.

Perlak, Frederick J., et al. 1990. "Insect Resistant Cotton Plants." *Bio/Technology* 8(10): 939–943.

"Pesticide News Story: EPA Releases Report Containing Latest Estimates of Pesticide Use in the United States." 2011. Environmental Protection Agency. http://www .epa.gov/oppfead1/cb/csb_page/updates/2011/ sales-usage06-07.html. Accessed on September 9, 2013.

Peterson, M. J., and Paul White. 2010. "Asilomar Conference on Laboratory Precautions When Conducting DNA Research—Case Summary." http://scholarworks.umass .edu/cgi/viewcontent.cgi?article=1023&context=ed ethicsinscience&seiredir=1&referer=http%3A%2F %2Fwww.google.com%2Furl%3Fsa%3Dt%26rct%3Dj %26q%3Dasilomar%2520conference%2520was %2520convened%2520by%2520%26source%3Dweb %26cd%3D2%26ved%3D0CC8QFjAB%26url%3Dhttp %253A%252F%252Fscholarworks.umass.edu%252Fcgi %252Fviewcontent.cgi%253Farticle%253D1023% 2526context%253Dedethicsinscience%26ei%3DQfwo UtiUAcPiiwKXroHQDA%26usg%3DAFQjCNFIR 1KKv4q0jLHttdmMVryF5vZqA%26bvm%3Dbv.5177

3540%2Cd.cGE#search=%22asilomar%20conference%
20convened%20by%22. Accessed on September 5, 2013.

"Planned Releases of Genetically-Altered Organisms: The Status of Government Research and Regulation." 1986. Hearing before the Subcommittee on Investigations and Oversight of the Committee of Science and Technology, House of Representatives, Ninety Ninth Congress, First Session, December 4, 1985. Washington, DC: Government Printing Office.

Pray, Leslie A. 2008. "Restriction Enzymes." Nature Education. http://www.nature.com/scitable/topicpage/restriction-enzymes-545. Accessed on September 4, 2013.

Quest-Ritson, Charles, and Brigid Quest-Ritson. 2011. *Encyclopedia of Roses*. New York: DK.

"Recombinant DNA." Cambridge Public Health Department. http://cambridgepublichealth.org/services/regulatory -activities/biosafety/overview.php. Accessed on September 8, 2013.

Roberts, Richard J. 2005. "How Restriction Enzymes Became the Workhorses of Molecular Biology." *PNAS* 102(17): 5905–5908.

Schell, J. M., et al. 1983. "Ti Plasmids as Experimental Gene Vectors for Plants." In *Advances in Gene Technology: Molecular Genetics of Plants and Animals. Miami Winter Symposia*. 20: 191–209.

Sherman, David M. 2002. *Tending Animals in the Global Village: A Guide to International Veterinary Medicine*. New York: Wiley-Blackwell.

Skirvin, R. M., et al. 2000. "The Use of Genetically Engineered Bacteria to Control Frost on Strawberries and Potatoes. Whatever Happened to All of That Research?" *Scientia Horticulturae* 84(1): 179–189.

"Stacked Traits in Biotech Crops." International Service for the Acquisition of Agri-Biotech Applications. http://www.isaaa

.org/resources/publications/pocketk/42/. Accessed on September 9, 2013.

Superweeds: How Biotech Crops Bolster the Pesticide Industry. 2013. Food & Water Watch. http://documents.foodand waterwatch.org/doc/Superweeds.pdf. Accessed on September 9, 2013.

"Transgenic Mice Formed by Nuclear Injection." http://www .informatics.jax.org/silver/chapters/6-3.shtml. Accessed on September 8, 2013.

Vaeck, Mark, et al. 1987. "Transgenic Plants Protected from Insect Attack." *Nature* 328(6125): 33–37.

Wagner, Thomas E., et al. 1981. "Microinjection of a Rabbit β-Globin Gene into Zygotes and Its Subsequent Expression in Adult Mice and Their Offspring." *Proceedings of the National Academy of Sciences of the United States of America* 78(10): 6376–6380.

Watson, J. D., and F. H. C. Crick. 1953. "A Structure for Deoxyribose Nucleic Acid." *Nature* 171(4356): 737–738.

Wayne, Randy. 2010. *Plant Cell Biology: From Astronomy to Zoology.* Amsterdam; Boston: Academic Press.

Wolf, George. 2003. "Friedrich Miescher: The Man Who Discovered DNA." http://www.bizgraphic.ch/miescheriana/ html/the_man_who_dicovered_dna.html. Accessed on September 3, 2013.

Zimmer, Mark. "Fluoro Fish." http://www.conncoll.edu/ ccacad/zimmer/GFP-ww/cooluses16.html. Accessed on September 8, 2013.

Opposition to Genetically Modified Foods

In 1985, the U.S. Environmental Protection Agency (EPA) granted approval to Advanced Genetic Sciences, Inc. (AGS) to conduct a field test on a genetically engineered product called Frostban, consisting of ice-minus bacteria. Ice-minus bacteria are genetically modified organisms (GMOs) capable of preventing plants from freezing at temperatures below which they normally freeze and die (see page 33, Chapter 1). The test was originally scheduled to take place in Monterey County, California, on a small patch of strawberries on December 12, 1985. News of the planned test aroused an immediate and vociferous outcry from the general public. Monterey County officials received so many complaints and expressions of concern from local residents and other critics from as far away as Europe that the tests were cancelled, and the county adopted an ordinance prohibiting the release of GMOs in the county, a ban that continues today (Naimon 1991; "Report on Genetically Modified Organisms in Monterey County, California").

Barry Aleshnick, of Guilford, Vermont, holds a sign at the Statehouse in Montpelier on February 26, 2004, during a protest to call for a time out on genetically engineered crops. Demonstrators went inside to listen to Monsanto lobbyists as they testified before the House Agriculture Committee. (AP Photo/Toby Talbot)

Understandably concerned by public reaction to its planned test, AGS decided to reschedule its experiment in another location, this time working to better inform the public about the nature of the ice-minus bacterium and its potential risk (or lack of risk). The new test site was a 0.2-acre plot of strawberries in Brentwood, Contra Costa, California, on April 24, 1987. Any hopes the company had that the test would go forward smoothly were dashed, however, when protestors mounted another campaign against those plans. They made a number of accusations against the planned test, some supposedly scientific, others political, and still others moral and ethical. Noted iconoclast Jeremy Rifkin, for example, predicted that the release of ice-minus bacteria might "reduce rainfall," and other protesters opined that scientists, bureaucrats, and industrialists were "playing God" in their experiments (Jukes 1987).

During the early morning hours of April 24, protestors gained access to the Brentwood test plot and pulled up 2,200 of the 2,400 strawberry plants scheduled to be sprayed. AGS officials replanted those plants, however, and the spraying went forward without further incident. The experiment was eventually completed, and the test plants were destroyed two months later (Baskin 1987; Crawford 1987).

This type of early reaction against the development and testing of GM crops did not bode well for the industry. Supporters of GM technology had every reason to believe that they might face an uphill battle in convincing farmers and consumers of the value of their new products. This concern was confirmed when a second test of Frostban was disrupted less than a month after the Brentwood incident. About three-quarters of 4,000 potatoes sprayed with the product at a test site in Tule Lake, California, were pulled up by protestors in the early morning hours of May 26, 1987. Again, the potatoes were replanted, and the experiment was carried to its conclusion ("Vandals Uproot Plants Used in Bacteria Test" 1987).

In 2000, a reporter for *The Oregonian*, Portland's daily newspaper, reported on a survey of the types of protests carried out by anti-GM activists, primarily in the West. Some of the incidents he described were the following:

- In 1996, members of the Greenpeace organization spray-painted a giant letter "X" on a field of soybeans in Iowa consisting of GM plants ("Greenpeace Protestors Paint Field").
- In protest against a contract between the biotechnology firm of Novartis and the University of California at Berkeley in 1998, two teams of protesting students played a football game on a test field of GM corn, destroying 14 rows of the corn ("Round-Up Ready Corn under Attack in California").
- Members of the Earth Liberation Front (ELF) set fire in December 1999 to a research facility at Michigan State University where genetic engineering experiments with plants were being conducted, claiming that such research was "one of the many threats to the natural world as we know it" ("Four Arrested in 1999 New Year's Eve Agricultural Hall Arson").
- A group calling itself Seeds of Resistance took credit in August 1999 for cutting down a half-acre crop of experimental GM corn at the University of Maine, hoping to convince workers there to "look into other lines of work" (Tuttle 1999).
- In November 1999, members of an activist group calling themselves the Washington Tree Improvement Association broke into a research facility at the Washington State University Puyallup Research and Extension Center, intending to destroy genetically engineered poplar and cottonwood trees. By mistake, they uprooted 180 nonengineered raspberry plants (Mccomber 1999).

At the time of the *Oregonian* article quoted here, the reporter noted that his own state was fortunate in not having been the target of any serious eco-action in opposition to GM crops and foods, although he quoted a representative of ELF that it "is just a matter of time before Oregon is hit." That prediction was surely correct, because members of ELF attacked the Jefferson Poplar Farm in Catskanie, Oregon, on May 21, 2001, to protest the growing of GM trees at the location (Bartley 2006). This action was hardly the last such event in the history of protests against GM crops and foods in the United States. As recently as June 2013, unknown individuals plowed under a total of about 6,500 genetically engineered sugar beet plants in southern Oregon (Wilson 2013).

Thus, although the GM food and crop industry has moved forward in the United States with considerable success in the past half century, protests by those opposed to such research continue. Those protests reached a zenith in 2013 when two worldwide March against Monsanto events were held on May 26 and October 12. Organizers claimed that more than 2 million people from 436 cities in 52 countries attended the first of these marches and 3 million people from 400 cities in 57 countries attended the second. Organizer Tami Canal explained her group's objective. "If we don't act," she said, "who's going to?" After all, she continued, "They [presumably, Monsanto] are poisoning our children, poisoning our planet" ("Protestors around the World March against Monsanto").

Public Opinion on Genetically Modified Foods in the United States

To what extent, if at all, does the action of protesters, such as these, reflect general public opinion about GM crops and foods? Public opinion polling companies have been taking the pulse of the American public, as well as citizens of other nations around the world, for more than 30 years. No brief summary is adequate to describe the results of those polls, although the general trend over those years appears to be that the general public is (1) generally uninformed about the nature of GM foods and the scientific evidence about their safety, (2) generally opposed to the sale of GM foods and less likely to by such foods if provided the opportunity, and (3) generally in favor of labeling GM foods so that consumers can know when they are purchasing such foods.

One of the earliest surveys of public opinion about GMOs was conducted in 1987 by the U.S. Office of Technology Assessment (OTA). The agency asked a sample of Americans about a number of aspects of biotechnology, including genetically engineered crops and foods. The results of this study must be read in view of the fact that the field of biotechnology was still relatively young. In any case, some of the OTA findings included the following:

- About two-thirds of the people surveyed for the study thought that they had a general understanding of the process of genetic engineering.

- Only about one in five respondents (19 percent) had heard of any possible negative consequences of research in genetic engineering.

- Respondents' concerns about the development of GM crops and foods depended on the perceived risk posed by such items. More than half (55 percent) said that they would approve the use of GM crops if the risk of losing one or more natural plants or animals were 1 in 1,000 or less. That number decreased as the risk of losing organisms increased.

- Members of the general public appeared to be aware of the potential risks posed by the development of GM crops and foods. Sixty-one percent acknowledged the possibility that antibiotic-resistant diseases might develop, that such products might produce birth defects in humans (57 percent), or that they might create herbicide-resistant weeds (56 percent) or endanger the food supply (52 percent). Nonetheless, fewer than one in five respondents expressed any real concerns about such outcomes, regarding them all as highly unlikely.

The OTA concluded that its overall impression was that the general public had some concerns about genetic engineering in the abstract but approved of every specific example of such research when offered the choice. The general summary of the report concluded with the observation that

> obstruction of technological development is not a popular cause in the United States in the mid-1980s. This survey indicates that a majority of the public believes the expected benefits of science, biotechnology, and genetic engineering are sufficient to outweigh the risks. (U.S. Congress, Office of Technology Assessment 1987, 3–5)

A fairly significant number of public opinion polls about the attitudes of Americans toward GM foods have been conducted over the past three decades. Some of these polls have a relatively short-term focus, conducting surveys that last over a year or so. Other polling agencies have conducted a series of polls on the topic that extend over many years, in at least one case more than a decade. The International Food Information Council (IFIC) has been conducting such polls on a regular basis since 2001, with its most recent survey dating to 2012. Surveys were conducted in 1997, 1999, 2000, 2001, 2006, 2007, 2008, 2010, and 2012 ("Consumer Insights Regarding Food Biotechnology").

An example of the type of short-term polling that has been conducted was an especially interesting survey by researchers at the University of Florida, reported in 2004. In this survey, the researchers asked some fairly standards, such as how much respondents actually knew about GM foods in general and in the food industry and what their attitudes about various aspects of GM foods were. They repeated their survey on four occasions, ranging from February 1999 to September 2001. Although responses varied somewhat over this period, they tended to range within a central limit. For example, researchers found that somewhere between 10 and 15 percent of respondents said that they knew "a lot" about GM foods, about 30 percent said that they knew "some," another 30 percent said that they knew "little," and about 20 to 25 percent said that they knew "nothing" (Medina et al. 2004).

When asked whether they knew if GM foods were available in local markets, about 40 percent said yes, and an equal number said no. The remaining number of respondents just did not know. Respondents were then asked how willing they might be to purchase foods that had been genetically modified (1) for the purpose of resisting the action of pesticides (e.g., Roundup Ready plants) and (2) to improve the shelf life or taste of a product. Nearly three quarters of respondents had no problem with the first option (30 percent being "very willing" to buy such products and 40 percent, "somewhat willing"), whereas just over half were agreeable to the second option (20 percent being "very willing" to buy such products and 40 percent, "somewhat willing"). About 40 percent said that they were not likely to buy such products (20 percent) or definitely would not do so (20 percent).

Of somewhat greater interest is long-term trends detected by surveys that have extended over many years. For example, the Pew Initiative on Food and Biotechnology conducted a series of annual surveys beginning in 2001 and ending in 2006, measuring some basic information about public attitudes with regard to GM foods (Pew Initiative on Food and Biotechnology; "The Pew Initiative on Food and Biotechnology" 2006) Some of the findings reported from that series of studies include the following:

- Self-reported knowledge about GM foods ranged from 54 percent at the beginning of the period to a high of 65 percent in 2003 and 2004, back down to 58 percent in 2005 and 2006.
- Support for the introduction of GM foods into the U.S. marketplace remained stable throughout the period at about 27 percent, although opposition declined over that period

from a high of 58 percent in 2001 to a low of 46 percent in 2006.

- The willingness of an individual to knowingly eat GM foods was very much a function of gender, with men about equally equal to knowingly eat or not eat such foods, whereas women were about twice as likely not to eat GM foods as they were to eat them.

- A somewhat common finding supported by the Pew data has to do with how consumers respond after being told that more than half of all processed foods in the marketplace contain GM elements. When consumers receive that information, they tend to feel much more safe about GM foods than without that information. In the Pew surveys, nearly half of all respondents said that they felt GM foods were safe to eat after being provided with this information, whereas less than a third felt GM foods were unsafe. The former number fell only slightly over the five-year period of the surveys, whereas the latter number increased by almost 10 percent.

- One of the quite remarkable findings of the Pew surveys was to whom an individual would turn for trusted information about GM foods. The least reliable source mentioned was the news media, with only 9 percent of respondents selecting this source, followed by biotechnology companies themselves, regarded as trustworthy by only 11 percent, and food manufacturers and government regulators, by 14 percent each. The most reliable source of information mentioned by respondents was friends and family, followed by farmers, with support from 37 percent and 33 percent of respondents, respectively.

Perhaps the best overall view of public opinion in the United States about GM foods is the series of IFIC polls mentioned earlier. Some of the findings produced over the decade and a half of this polling are as follows (all data from individual poll results summarized at Consumer Insights Regarding Food Biotechnology, 2013):

- The number of people surveyed for the IFIC polls who said they knew "a lot" about GM foods remained fairly constant at around 10 percent from 1997 to 2012, with the number claiming to know "some" stayed just under 30 percent until it rose to 32 percent in 2012. Throughout the period, the number who said they knew "little" or "nothing" remained consistently in the low-60-percent range.

- Generally speaking, the number of respondents who knew whether or not GM foods were available in stores was just under 30 percent during the period, with about twice that number (ranging from 59 to 68 percent) saying they just did not know. Around 10 percent believed that no GM foods were available in stores.

- IFIC pollsters began asking respondents in 2006 about their general attitudes toward GM foods and found that about 10 percent were very favorable, about 22 percent somewhat favorable, about 30 percent neutral, about 12 percent somewhat unfavorable, and about 5 percent strongly unfavorable. These numbers have remained relatively constant in the 2008, 2010, and 2012 polls.

- A question that IFIC researchers have consistently asked over the years has to do with the willingness of consumers to purchase and eat foods that have been genetically modified, similar to the query by Florida researchers noted earlier. Their results were generally similar to those of the Florida study, with about two-thirds of responding saying that they would be very or somewhat likely to buy foods that were genetically modified to improve taste or shelf life and about one-third saying that they would not do so. In the case of pest-resistant plants, the IFIC results were somewhat different from the Florida results, with about two-thirds of respondents again saying that they had no problem buying and eating such products and about one-third saying that they were unlikely to do so.

Overall, the IFIC surveys seem to show a somewhat modest increase in public acceptability of GM foods, although it is probably too early to know if this is really a long-term trend or a single-year movement in the data. (For a good overall review of trends in public opinion about GM foods in the United States up to 2008, see Bonny 2008.)

Public Opinion about Genetically Modified Foods in Europe

Observers have long commented on the disparity in views about GM foods in the United States versus the European Union and other developing nations. As one reporter has noted,

the United States and Europe could hardly be farther apart. U.S. grocery stores are well stocked with genetically modified cereals and other products, while Europeans have found ways to keep them off the shelves. (Galbraith 2013)

In polls from the 1990s and early 2000s, European respondents tended to show a disapproval of GM crops and foods by as much as a dozen percentage points or more.

Over the last decade, however, differences between European and American attitudes have begun to disappear. For example, a German website devoted to providing information about GM products, GMO Compass, reported in 2009 that support for GM crops and foods among the general populace in Europe appeared to be inching upward and that fewer and fewer poll respondents were expressing concern about the potential health and environmental effects of such products

("Opposition Decreasing or Acceptance Increasing?"). A similar trend was observed in the United Kingdom, where a 2012 poll commissioned by the British Science Association (BSA) showed that the percentage of respondents who expressed concerns about GM foods had dropped from 46 percent in 2003 to 41 percent in 2012 and the percentage who were not concerned rose from 17 percent to 25 percent over the same period (Vaughan 2012). Perhaps more to the point, pollsters have found that consumers in Europe and the United Kingdom appear to have little hesitation in actual practice to the purchase of GM foods, even when they express concerns or doubts about such products. In one EU survey, for example, more than 80 percent of consumers interviewed in a recent EU poll said that they make no conscious effort to avoid the purchase of GM foods in their daily marketing ("Opposition Decreasing or Acceptance Increasing?").

Probably the best statistical information currently available about European attitudes toward GM crops and foods comes from a 2010 Eurobarometer poll on the topic. Eurobarometer is the Public Opinion Analysis division of the European Commission (EC) that has been conducting surveys about a variety of topics in the European Union since 1973. The major results of the 2010 survey on GM foods are shown in Table 2.1.

As one might expect, general data for the European Union do not necessarily reflect attitudes in individual member states, which tend to vary over a relatively wide range. For example, on the question as to whether or not GM foods make a person uneasy, the response rate ranged from a "yes" response of 88 percent in Greece, 85 percent in Cyprus, and 80 percent in Lithuania to 40 percent in Malta, 47 percent in Hungary, and 48 percent in Ireland. A similar spread was found in the fundamental question as to whether or not GM foods are good for a person and her or his family. Eighty percent of Latvians said "no" to that question, along with 78 percent of Greeks and 73 percent of Cypriots, compared with 37 percent of the Maltese, 39 percent of the Irish, and 40 percent of residents

Table 2.1   European Attitudes on Genetically Modified Foods (percentages)

Issue	Agree	Disagree	No Opinion
Genetically modified food			
Is fundamentally unnatural	70	20	10
Makes you uneasy	61	29	10
Benefits some people but puts others at risk	57	25	18
Is not good for you and your family	54	30	16
Helps people in developing countries	43	37	20
Is good for the economy of your nation	31	50	19
Should be more fully developed	23	61	16
Does no harm to the environment	23	53	24
Is safe for your health and that of your family	22	59	19
Is safe for future generations	21	58	21

Source: "Biotechnology." Eurobarometer 73.1. Brussels: TNS Opinion & Social. http://ec.europa.eu/public_opinion/archives/ebs/ebs_341_en.pdf. Accessed on September 15, 2013.

of the United Kingdom. As to the risk posed by GM crops and foods to the environment, the residents of no nation provided majority support for the view that GM crops and foods are safe for the environment, although the Czechs (41 percent), Slovaks (35 percent), and Hungarians (32 percent) were most supportive of the view, the Swedes (10 percent), Cypriots (12 percent), Greeks (14 percent), and Lithuanians (14 percent) were most critical of that view ("Biotechnology," questions QB4a.7, QB4a.2, and QBa4.9).

Regulation of Genetically Modified Crops and Foods in the European Union

Although the development of GM crops and foods has been a matter of some concern to many countries around the world, the responses to that concern have differed sharply from region to region. That fact is perhaps most clearly in evidence in the comparison of attempts to regulate GM food and crops in the United States and the European Union.

The American approach to the regulation of GM foods and crops was formulated to a large extent in the 1980s and early 1990s, under the administrations of President Ronald Reagan and George H. W. Bush. This approach was based on three primary principles. First, the regulations would focus on the specific products of genetic engineering, such as rDNA cotton and corn, and not on the general process by which these products were made. Second, the general assumption underlying regulation would be that GM substances would be regarded as safe unless there was competent scientific information to indicate otherwise. Third, existing regulatory agencies were adequate and sufficient for carrying out whatever regulatory activities were necessary. Recall that regulation of GM substances was distributed by the Coordinated Framework for Regulation of Biotechnology Products of 1986 among just such agencies, primarily the Food and Drug Administration, the Environmental Protection Agency, and the U.S. Department of Agriculture Animal and Plant Health Inspection Service. (For a complete history of this issue, see Marden 2003.)

The approach to the regulation of GM products in the European Union as a whole, as well as in individual nations, was different from that in the United States in two fundamental ways. In the first place, the European Union decided to focus its regulatory efforts on the process by which GM crops and foods were produced, tested, and marketed rather than on the individual products. Second, it was considerably more skeptical about the safety of these products, acting on the assumption that there might be good reason to err on the side of caution in regulating the products. This point of view is reflected in a philosophy that has long underlain much of the EU regulatory effort, the precautionary principle. The *precautionary principle* states that some new product or process should not be approved for use if the safety associated with the product or process is unknown or in serious dispute. Thus, a company that wanted to test or market a GM product in the European Union had first to prove beyond reasonable doubt that it was safe to use.

(For more on the comparison between the American and European approach to regulation, see Lynch and Vogel 2001.)

The European Union's earliest forays into the field of GMO regulation came in 1978, when the EC proposed a directive requiring that all researchers in member states submit proposals for any work on GMOs to it for final approval. The proposed directive reflected the significant level of concern about genetic engineering present in the United States at the same time, following the Asilomar conference by three years. The EC proposal was withdrawn only two years later without ever taking effect as European government officials (like those in the United States) began to feel somewhat more comfortable with rDNA research and began to worry instead about possible consequences on the competitiveness of European research if regulations were too severe (Shaffer and Pollack 2004).

At that point, EU regulators shifted their attention primarily from research to the release of GM organisms into the environment and the labeling of GM products. Among the first regulations adopted by the European Union was Directive 90/219/EEC of April 23, 1990. This directive required member states to adopt legislation that would ensure that GMOs introduced into the environment could not escape and travel into an adjoining state. It made provisions for notifications of member states about the release of GM organisms and distinguished between two general classes of GMOs, those that were known to be relatively safe, and those that were known to be unsafe or whose safety was in doubt ("Contained Use of Genetically Modified Micro-organisms").

For a few years, Council Directive 90/219/EEC and its amendments (especially 90/220/EEC) seemed to provide a satisfactory, if somewhat uneasy, solution for dealing with research and development on GM crops and foods. Then, in 1996, a series of events occurred in close proximity to each other to disrupt that compromise. In March of that year, the British government announced that more than 150,000 cows in Great Britain had been infected with bovine spongiform encephalopathy (BSE), popularly known as mad cow disease, a condition thought to be associated with Creutzfeldt–Jakob disease in humans. The importation of British beef to the Continent was almost immediately banned, and the general public became wary of the effectiveness of food regulations in protecting human health and that of domestic animals (Shaffer and Pollack 2004, 21).

This event was followed closely by a number of other adverse events that raised further doubts about the effectiveness of existing EU regulation of crops and foods. In December 1996, Scottish researchers announced the birth of the first cloned mammal, the sheep Dolly, and at almost the same time, the United States and Canada filed a complaint with the World Trade Organization (WTO) that the EU ban on the importation of hormone-treated beef was an illegal restrain on trade. EU food regulation policies were, thus, under attack from a variety of fronts: scientific, economic, political, and ethical.

Ironically, just at the time that doubts were being raised about the effectiveness of EU regulatory procedures, the EC had begun to grant approval to the importation and sale of GM foods. The first such action was taken in April 1996 (only a month after announcement of the BSE epidemic) when the EC approved the sale of GM soy beans. The action was taken in response to a request by the United Kingdom for such approval and in spite of the fact that every other EU state had voted to oppose the approval. The action reflected a somewhat unusual aspect of the EU regulatory procedure, in which a request by a single member state had to be approved by the EC, even though every other state opposed the action. The EC took a similar action only a few months later when it approved the sale of GM corn in January 1997. That action was also opposed by all member states except the requesting nation, in this case, France (Shaffer and Pollack 2004, 24).

The fragmented view on GM crops and foods in the European Union is reflected in these actions and in the further steps taken by individual member states. Those steps were permissible under the so-called safeguard clause in EU GM regulations. That clause allows individual member states to "provisionally restrict or prohibit the use and/or sale" of a GM product if it regards that product as harmful to human health or the environment ("GMOs in a Nutshell"). Over the years, various nations have invoked the safeguard clause for various products and reasons. As of early 2014, those nations include Austria, France, Germany, Greece, Hungary, and Luxembourg ("Rules on GMOs in the EU—Ban on GMOs Cultivation").

In January 1997, two events occurred that further clarified the EU position on GM foods and crops. The first event was the release of a new regulation by the EC, Regulation 258/97, more commonly known as the *Novel Foods Regulation*. This regulation was designed to define what a "novel food" was, and how it was to be regulated in the European Union. The concept of a novel food was hardly new, as it could and had been applied to a host of foods not native to the European continent whose safety may or may not have been known, but it clearly focused more specifically on crops and foods that had been genetically modified and whose safety was often in doubt. The regulation defined novel foods as any product "not hitherto . . . used for human consumption to a significant degree within the Community" ("Regulation [EC] No 258/ 97"). Significantly, it included both foods that had been genetically modified and foods produced from but not containing GMOs. As an example, some popular oils were being produced from GM crops, but they no longer contained any traces of GMOs (Shaffer and Pollack 2004, 20).

Two features of the regulation were of particular interest. In the first place, the principle of *substantial equivalence* was introduced as a guiding feature for determining the safety of novel foods. In a somewhat circular definition, the principle of substantial equivalence states that any new food or product that is substantially equivalent to an existing food or product can be treated in the same way as the known and/or conventional food in terms of its safety for human consumption.

So the task facing a company wanting to introduce a novel food in the European Union (or the United States, for that matter) was to show that one could not detect any real difference between the new food and other foods like it already in use.

The second feature of the Novel Foods Regulation was the restatement of the safeguard clause, which allowed any nation member of the European Union to prohibit the importation and/or sale of any substance that it had reason to believe might be harmful to its citizens. As pointed out earlier, this feature has become a powerful tool for EU nations that had misgivings about the safety of any type of GM product that has otherwise been approved for use elsewhere in the Union. Indeed, an example of that became available almost immediately when the second major event of January 1997 took place, the approval by the EC of the sale of GM maize in the Union.

The controversy arose when the French government requested approval for the use of a GM form of maize, Bt176, produced by the Syngenta company. After review by the EC, the French request was approved and distributed to the other 14 members of the Union. All 14 nations either opposed the EC recommendation or abstained from voting. According to the rules by which the EU works, however, these actions were insufficient to prevent the French from proceeding with the use of Bt176 maize. Eventually, three nations, Austria, Germany, and Luxembourg, invoked the safeguard clause against the importation and sale of Bt176 maize within their borders ("Austria Bans Monsanto's GM Oilseed Rape").

The Cartagena Protocol

The issue of GMOs was one of concern not only in the United States and the European Union but in many other parts of the world as well. That concern was expressed in a number of ways in a variety of settings. For example, discussions among nations about protection of Earth's biodiversity dating to the late 1980s came to fruition at the May 1992 Nairobi Conference for the

Adoption of the Agreed Text of the Convention on Biological Diversity (CBD). The document presented at that time laid out some general principles about the importance of biodiversity on the planet and a number of steps needed to ensure that biodiversity would be maintained in the face of an expanding human presence in the natural world. By June 4, 1993, 186 nations had signed that treaty, and it officially came into effect on December 29, 1993, after the 30th ratification. As of 2013, 192 nations and the European Union—every member of the United Nations except Andorra, South Sudan, and the United States—have ratified the treaty ("The Convention on Biological Diversity").

One of the most contentious issues in the negotiations over the CBD was how best to deal with GMOs (referred to in the treaty as *living modified organisms* [LMOs]). In fact, as is often the case, it required a number of international meetings to get a statement about GMOs into a form in which it could become part of the CBD. That point was finally reached at a meeting in Cartagena, Colombia, in January 2000. That document, now known as the *Cartagena Protocol*, is officially a part of the CBD. Its purpose is to protect biodiversity by establishing rigorous rules by which GMOs can be transferred from one nation to another. As of the end of 2013, 166 nations had ratified the protocol. A group of six nations that have withheld their support for the treaty, the so-called Miami Group consists of nations that are either responsible for the production of the great majority of GM foods and crops or major exporters of those crops and foods (Argentina, Australia, Canada, Chile, the United States, and Uruguay) (Rajamani 2013). (For a complete description of the Cartagena Protocol, see Mackenzie et al. 2003.)

A Shift in Emphasis

The debate over the Cartagena Protocol came at a time when the European Union was beginning to feel a squeeze on its policies about the regulation of GM crops and foods. On the one hand, nations that were moving forward aggressively with the production of GM foods and crops, such as (primarily) the United States, were trying to convince the Europeans to relax their restrictions on the importation of GM products. As a simple economic reality, they wanted to increase the marketplace for some of their major GM producers, such as Monsanto and Syngenta. On the other hand, individual nations were becoming more resistant to any liberalization in the rules controlling the production, testing, release, transport, and sale of GM products. More and more nations were choosing the safeguard clause as a way of ignoring EC efforts to mollify the United States and other members of the Miami Group.

As a way of dealing with these conflicting pressures, the EC began a reanalysis of its viewpoint on GM products, eventually producing a new statement of its position in a White Paper on Food Safety and a White Paper on the Precautionary Principle, both released in 2000. These papers recommended a restructuring of the EU approach to GM regulation with an eye to satisfying its critics on both sides of the debate. That compromise turned out to be unsatisfactory to both the Miami nations, which did not abandon their demand for greater access to European markets for their GM products, nor to individual European nations, some of whom became even more insistent that they would not allow GM crops, seeds, or foods within their boundaries.

A key development in this controversy occurred in May 2003, when the United States filed a complaint with the WTO, arguing that the EC regulatory policies constituted an illegal act of protectionism against trade from itself and other Miami countries. (A year later, Argentina and Canada joined the United States in this complaint.) In February 2006, the WTO ruled against the European Union in this dispute, saying that the region's ban on the importation of GM foods was illegal under international trade rules. The dispute between Argentina, Canada, and the United States on the one hand

and the European Union on the other dragged on, however, for nearly a decade. After extended discussion, Canada and the European Union reached an agreement in July 2009 and Argentina and the European Union, in March 2010. Discussions between the United States and the European Union lingered on into November 2012, however, when the WTO finally ruled that the EC bans on the importation of GM products was indeed illegal and ordered the European Union to remove those bans. In the end, the force of international trade had made its mark on European efforts to restrict the introduction and use of GM products to the continent ("EU and Argentina Settle WTO Case on Genetically Modified Organisms"; "EU GMO Ban Was Illegal, WTO Rules").

Current Status of Regulation of Genetically Modified Organisms in Europe

After three decades of legal maneuvering, the European Union has evolved a system for regulating GM seeds, crops, and foods available on the Continent. This process is quite precise and very detailed. Each GM crop or food is considered de facto to be a "new food" that must be tested to be sure that it is safe for human consumption and will not cause harm to the natural environment. Testing of a new GM product is carried out by the Panel on Genetically Modified Organisms of the European Food Safety Authority (EFSA). The EFSA then transmits its findings to the Standing Committee on Genetically Modified Food and Feed and Environmental Risk of the European Commission, which then accepts or rejects the EFSA recommendation. The EC also has the option of passing the recommendation on to its Council of Agricultural Ministers, which may make its own determination on the products or return the recommendation to the EC for promulgation. When a product passes all these hurdles, it may be officially approved for use in the European Union, although further roadblocks are also possible (Davison 2010; "GMOs in a Nutshell").

The most common of those additional hurdles is invoking of the safeguard clause by one or more member states. When that happens, the EC is required to investigate the complaint made by the nation or nations invoking the safeguard clause. It may then change its mind and revoke the original authorization or conclude that the authorization was legitimate and ask the invoking state to withdraw its objections. As noted earlier, as of early 2014, six states had invoked the safeguard clause against GM products that had been approved by the EC: Austria, France, Germany, Greece, Hungary, and Luxembourg.

As of early 2014, 47 products had been approved as a result of this process, virtually all of them intended for human or animal food or for the production of other foods. Of these, 27 were varieties of maize, eight of corn, seven of soybeans, three of oilseed rape, and one each of potato and sugar beet. A number of other products were moving through the regulatory pipeline and were subject to approval (or rejection) in the near future.

Authorization for the use of GM crops in the European Union is governed by 2001/18/EC, on the deliberate release of GMOs into the environment. According to that directive, GM seeds must be thoroughly tested to make sure that they pose no harm to the environment. That restriction applies also to plants imported from outside the European Union, which could conceivably be planted and grown on the Continent. As of early 2014, only two crops had been approved for use in the European Union under this direction. The first was a modified form of maize known as MON810, developed by the Monsanto company and approved for use against the European corn-borer caterpillar in 1998. That crop is now widely grown in Spain, where it is planted on more than 80,000 hectares (200,000 acres) of land. Smaller areas have also been planted in the Czech Republic, Germany, and Portugal ("Maize").

The second approved crop is a type of GM potato called *Amflora*, developed by the German company BASF. The varietal was developed not for human consumption but for use in the production of industrial starch used in the textile, paper, adhesive, and other industries. It was licensed in 2010 in a move that one of the world's most famous scientific journals called "a new dawn for transgenic crops in Europe" (Butler 2010). The company had been trying for 13 years to earn approval for its products. Only two years later, however, the company withdrew the product from the market and decided against its further promotion largely because of lack of public acceptance of the plant. At the time it discontinued sale of the potato, it had been planted to 150 hectares (370 acres) in the Czech Republic, 80 hectares (200 acres) in Sweden, and 15 hectares (37 acres) in Germany in 2010 and 2 hectares (4 acres) in Germany in 2011 ("Amflora—a Potato for Industrial Applications").

A Shift in Emphasis: European Regulations on Labeling

By the end of the 1990s, it had become apparent that the European Union was losing its battle to limit, prohibit, or effectively control the importation and use of GM crops and foods on the continent. At that point, the EC apparently began to shift its emphasis with regard to GMO crops and foods within the union. It decided, instead, to focus on the labeling of GMO crops and foods or food products containing GMOs. The philosophy appeared to be that if the organization could not restrict the use of GM crops and foods, it could at the very least let consumers know which products contained GMOs.

The first step in this new initiative was a provision of Regulation (EC) 258/97 (article 8) on novel foods and their ingredients. The purpose of that article was to ensure that consumers were aware of any food whose "composition, nutritional value or nutritional effects, or intended use of the food" made the food "no longer equivalent to an existing food or food ingredient." Among the properties that would produce such a change in a food product was, according to part 1(d) of the article, "the presence of an organism genetically modified by techniques of genetic modification, the non-exhaustive list of which is laid down in Annex I A, Part 1 of Directive 90/220/ EEC" ("Regulation [EC] No 258/97," Article 8). The regulation then went on in Article 9 to provide additional detail as to the steps that had to be followed to place into the marketplace a product containing a GMO. For example, the release of a GMO-containing product was required to be accompanied by, at least:

> a copy of the written consent, if any, from the competent authority, to the deliberate release of the genetically modified organisms for research and development purposes provided for in Article 6 (4) of Directive 90/220/EEC, together with the results of the release(s) with respect to any risk to human health and the environment;

and

> the complete technical dossier supplying the relevant information requested in Article 11 of Directive 90/220/ EEC and the environmental risk assessment based on this information, the results of any studies carried out for the purposes of research and development or, where appropriate, the decision authorizing the placing on the market provided for in part C of Directive 90/220/EEC. ("Regulation [EC] No 258/97," Article 9)

These labeling regulations were gradually refined over the following decade. Only a year later, for example, the EC adopted an amendment to 258/97, adding a number of GM products that were not covered by that document, primarily GM maize and soybeans. Regulation 1139/98 was very specific as to which products were to be covered by labeling regulations, and what kinds of working were required in the labeling system. In Article 2 of the regulation, for example, it provided that

> where the food consists of more than one ingredient, the words "produced from genetically modified soya" or "produced from genetically modified maize", as appropriate, shall appear in the list of ingredients provided for by Article 6 of Directive 79/112/EEC in parentheses immediately after the name of the ingredient concerned. Alternatively, these words may appear in a prominently displayed footnote to the list of ingredients, related by means of an asterisk (*) to the ingredient concerned. Where an ingredient is already listed as being produced from soya or maize the words "produced from genetically modified" may be abbreviated to "genetically modified"; if the abbreviated form of words is used as a footnote, the asterisk shall be directly attached to the word "soya" or "maize". Where either form of words is used as a footnote, it shall have a typeface of at least the same size as the list of ingredients itself. ("Council Regulation [EC] No 1139/98," Article 2, 3[a])

The EC went one step further in its labeling efforts with the adoption in 2000 of Regulation 50/2000. That regulation focused on a category of food products that had been expressly excluded from previous regulations, namely food additives and flavoring. Regulation 50/2000 corrected that omission by requiring that

> The words "genetically modified" shall appear in the list of ingredients immediately after the indication of the additive or flavouring in question. Alternatively, this wording may appear in a prominently displayed footnote to the list of ingredients, linked to the additive or the flavouring concerned by an asterisk (*). It shall be printed in a font

that is at least of the same size as that used for the list of ingredients itself. ("Commission Regulation [EC] No 50/2000 of 10 January 2000," Article 4, 2)

One of the interesting issues with which the EC has had to deal involves products offered for sale to the public that were produced from GM crops but which no longer contain any detectable amount of GM product. For example, the vast majority of corn now produced comes from GM seed. Some of that corn is used to produce corn oil that is used to make other food products or used directly for human and animal consumption. The production of the corn oil from GM corn, however, destroys essentially all the corn protein that would contain GM DNA. So is the corn oil available for sale at the corner grocery a GM product or not?

The EC position on this matter has long been that any food product derived from a GM substance must be labeled if there is any detectable amount of DNA or protein remaining from the original substance present in the final product ("GM Food & Feed—Labelling").

Yet one more step in the regulatory process was adopted by the EC in 2003. Regulation 1830/2003 deals with rules for the traceability, as well as the labeling, of GM substances. The purpose of this regulation is threefold: First, it provides regulators with a way of locating and tracing the movement of all GMO products through the supply chain, from production of seeds, to planting and growth, to processing, to marketing of the products to consumers. This chain of evidence applies not only to products that contain GM elements at the point of sale but also to processed foods in which the original modified DNA may have been destroyed or lost and also to the seeds from which such crops are grown. Second, it allows regulators to check information provided on the labels of GM foods to make sure that it accurately matches the information associated with the marked products. Third, it makes it possible to monitor the effects of GM crops and foods on the environment and human health and to order recalls of harmful products from the marketplace ("Traceability and Labelling of GMOs").

Since the 2003 action by the EC, the European Union, at many levels of its structure, has continued to struggle with the issue of the labeling and regulation of GM products. As of early 2014, it still faces a number of unresolved questions as to how most effectively to allow the use of GM products while maintaining the safety of human health and the natural environment, given the availability of those products. For an excellent overview of this issue, see the University of Massachusetts at Amherst International Dimensions of Ethics Education in Science and Engineering Case Study on this topic (Peterson and White 2010, with special attention to the appendices that accompany this document).

Regulation of Genetically Modified Products throughout the World

Questions about research on, development of, testing and production of, and marketing and regulation of GM seeds, crops, and foods often focus strongly on the situation in the United States and the European Union. That situation should not be surprising since the United States is by far the largest producer of research and production of GM products and, with the European Union, the largest consumer of such products in the world. However, that does not mean that other nations are not involved and interested in many of the same issues with which the United States and the European Union have had to deal over the past three decades or more.

Outside of the United States, the largest producers of GM crops are Brazil, Argentina, India, and Canada. Table 2.2 summarizes data for nations that grow GM crops, the type of crops most commonly grown, and the amount of land devoted to GM crops. As the table shows, the United States produces about 40 percent of all GM crops grown in the world, Brazil about 21 percent, and Argentina about 14 percent, with the

Table 2.2   Global Area of Biotech Crops in 2012: By Country (million hectares)

Rank	Country	Total Area**	Crop(s)
1	United States*	69.5	Maize, soybean, cotton, canola, sugarbeet, alfalfa, papaya, squash
2	Brazil*	36.6	Soybean, maize, cotton
3	Argentina*	23.9	Soybean, maize, cotton
4	Canada*	11.6	Canola, maize, soybean, sugarbeet
5	India*	10.8	Cotton
6	China*	4.0	Cotton, papaya, poplar, tomato, sweet pepper
7	Paraguay*	3.4	Soybean, maize, cotton
8	South Africa*	2.9	Maize, soybean, cotton
9	Pakistan*	2.8	Cotton
10	Uruguay*	1.4	Soybean, maize
11	Bolivia*	1.0	Soybean
12	Philippines*	0.8	Maize
13	Australia*	0.7	Cotton, canola
14	Burkina Faso*	0.3	Cotton
15	Myanmar*	0.3	Cotton
16	Mexico*	0.2	Cotton, soybean
17	Spain*	0.1	Maize
18	Chile*	<0.1	Maize, soybean, canola
19	Colombia	<0.1	Cotton
20	Honduras	<0.1	Maize
21	Sudan	<0.1	Cotton
22	Portugal	<0.1	Maize
23	Czech Republic	<0.1	Maize
24	Cuba	<0.1	Maize
25	Egypt	<0.1	Maize
26	Costa Rica	<0.1	Cotton, soybean
27	Romania	<0.1	Maize
28	Slovakia	<0.1	Maize
	Total	170.3	

*Eighteen biotech mega-countries growing 50,000 hectares, or more, of biotech crops.

**Rounded off to the nearest hundred thousand.

Source: James, Clive. 2012. *Global Status of Commercialized GM/Biotech Crops for 2012: ISAAA Brief 44.* Ithaca, NY: ISAAA. Used by permission.

rest of the world accounting for the remaining 25 percent of GM crops.

Thus, concerns about gaining access to world markets for GM crops and foods are largely those of a small handful of nations, the vast majority of nations have to deal with a quite different issue: What should be their policies about GM products? Should they even be permitted to be grown? Should they be allowed to be marketed? What regulations are needed to ensure the safety of human health and the natural environment in their countries?

As has been the case with the European Union, many nations have gone through a period of attempting to find the right answers to these questions for their own unique situations. Sometimes the nature of the questions and the possible answers to those questions are very different in some nations than they are in the United States and the European Union. In developing nations, for example, many experts believe that the availability of engineered crops may make it possible for nations to vastly increase their agricultural output, offering one important way of dealing with the overwhelming problem of hunger common in many developing nations (more about this topic in a later section of this chapter).

The issue of dealing with GM products for most nations, then, has come down to the same topic as it has in the European Union: How can GM seeds, crops, and foods best be regulated to provide for the safety of citizens and protection of the environment? The following section outlines some of the positions taken by various countries of the world.

In perhaps the most comprehensive and complete (although now somewhat dated) study of this issue, Guillaume P. Gruère of the Organisation de Coopération et de Développement Économiques and S. R. Rao of the Indian Ministry of Science and Technology found that nations could be categorized as to the kind of labeling policies they had and the degree of enforcement they used with those policies. Among the nations with the strictest policies were Australia, China, the European Union, Japan, New Zealand, Norway, Russia, Saudi Arabia, South

Korea, Switzerland, and Taiwan. Nations that had GM labeling policies but failed either to enforce them stringently or to enforce them at all included Brazil, Chile, Croatia, Ecuador, El Salvador, Indonesia, Mauritius, Serbia, Sri Lanka, Thailand (partially), Ukraine, and Vietnam. A number of nations that had indicated their intentions to introduce labeling regulations, but had not done so as of 2007, included Bolivia, Cameroon, Colombia, Egypt, Ethiopia, Georgia, India, Israel, Ivory Coast, Jamaica, Malaysia, Namibia, Nigeria, Paraguay, Peru, Philippines, Singapore, Uganda, UAE, Uruguay, and Zambia. Philippines had indicated that its labeling policy would be voluntary. Nations that already had voluntary labeling policies were Canada, Hong Kong, South Africa, and the United States (Gruère and Rao 2007, Table 1, 52).

Nations that had decided to label GM products also used a variety of policies and practices in this regard. For example, some nations followed the practice in the European Union of focusing regulating and labeling of processes by which GM crops and foods are produced and sold. The two other entities beside the European Union would follow this practice are Brazil and China. All other nations follow the model of the United States by regulating and labeling individual products. These nations tend to prepare a list of GM foods that have been tested or otherwise evaluated and then approved for distribution and use. Nations in this category include Australia, Indonesia, Japan, New Zealand, Russia, Saudi Arabia, South Korea, and Taiwan. Nations also differ with regard to the so-called *threshold level* at which regulations become effective. These threshold levels are the percentage of GM material that can be detected by laboratory analysis. The threshold levels that various countries have selected for their boundaries of regulation range from a high of 5 percent in East Asian nations such as Indonesia, Japan, and Taiwan to a low of 0 percent in China, 0.9 percent in Russia (as it is in the European Union), and 1 percent in Australia, Brazil, New Zealand, and Saudi Arabia (Gruère and Rao 2007, Table 2, 53).

Genetically Modified Crops and Foods: Pro and Con

More than four decades after the technology for producing GMOs was first developed, a dispute still rages worldwide about that technology. Proponents of rDNA research claim that GM seeds, crops, and foods are safe to use for human health and the natural environment and that they can bring unimagined benefits in dealing with some of the world's most serious ongoing problems, such as hunger and disease. Critics argue that such claims are overblown, that the safety of GM products is still an unresolved issue, and that, at the very least, GM substances should be adequately labeled so that consumers at all levels of the food chain will know when they are using GMO products and the extent to which they are present in crops and foods. The next section provides a detailed review of these issues.

The pros and cons of the use of GM products can generally be classified into three major categories: potential benefits and harm to the agricultural system, potential benefits and harm to human health, and potential benefits and harm to the natural environment.

Potential Benefits to the Agricultural System

Proponents of genetic modification of crops often point out that this process is really not so very different from the centuries-old process of hybridization, in which a farmer attempts to produce better crops by manipulating the genetic information available in existing plants. For example, he or she might try to produce a new type of apple by crossbreeding one type of apple with better taste with a second type that is especially resistant to frost. By crossbreeding the two types of apples over many generations, the farmer might be able to produce precisely the new type of apple he or she desires.

The advantage provided by rDNA procedures is that the farmer (or researcher) can take advantage of a much wider range of genetic properties in her or his research than is readily available in the natural world. To get that better tasting, frost-resistant apple, for example, the farmer or researcher may have difficulty finding the precise species or varietal with the properties needed to crossbreed into the new varietal. He or she may have to wait many generations until just the right result is obtained, or in some cases, the desired product may not even be possible if the appropriate parent plants do not exist in nature. With genetic engineering, the farmer or researcher can use genes from any or all possible apple species and varietals, as well as genes from totally unrelated species (e.g., a tobacco plant) or even genes that have been invented and produced synthetically in the laboratory. With this vastly wider range of possibilities, a much greater variety of agricultural products can be made than is possible with traditional crossbreeding procedures.

It is just this general principle, of course, that underlies the development of some of the most popular genetically engineered crops available today. Plants that have been engineered to contain the Bt gene that produces an insecticidal protein, for example, are normal cotton, corn, soybean, or some other type of plants to which has been added one or more genes from totally different organisms. The engineered plants then have an entirely new trait that reduces the need for using pesticides during the plant's growing season. The same is true for plants that have been engineered to be resistant to herbicides, such as Monsanto's Roundup Ready herbicides and Bayer CropScience's Liberty herbicides. Engineered plants of this kind provide, at least in theory, a huge advantage for farmers who have to use much smaller amounts of herbicides, an important money-saving advantage.

Bt-enhanced and herbicide-resistant plants are only one category of engineered plants possible by this process. Researchers are also exploring other changes in plants that can improve their survivability or improve their value as crops. As an example, the single most serious environmental problem facing farmers worldwide is an inadequate supply of fresh water for growing plants. In a number of regions, water resources are becoming more saline (salty), often as a result of increased annual temperatures and/or increased drought conditions. In such instances, plants that do not grow well in saline conditions tend to die out, and farmers may lose large portions of their crops.

One approach to dealing with this problem is to engineer plants that are more resistant to saline conditions. One way to do that is to remove one or more genes from plants that are normally more resistant to saline conditions (e.g., those that grow in and around salt water) and insert them into otherwise saline-sensitive plants. A number of attempts have been made in this direction, with greater or lesser success. Part of the challenge appears to be that saline resistance is not a function of a single gene in most cases, and identifying the groups of genes responsible for saline resistance and then successfully inserting them into a plant genome is a distinct challenge (see, for example, Agarwal et al. 2013; Peleg, Apse, and Blumwald 2011; Turan, Cornish, and Kumar 2012).

Another target of researchers is the development of heat-resistant plants. Climate scientists continue to predict that Earth's annual average temperature will continue to climb for the foreseeable future, suggesting that the planet's warmest regions will experience even more severe weather, adding yet another stress to plants growing there. One approach to dealing with this problem is to engineer plants so that they are better able to withstand the heat shock caused by rising temperatures. As an example of this line of research, plant molecular biologist L. Curtis Hannah, at the University of Florida, has been exploring ways of producing two genes known as Sh2 and Bt2 that code for the production of enzymes known as ASPases in plants. These enzymes are inactivated at elevated temperatures, causing death in plants. Hannah suggests that plants that carry the modified genes for these proteins will be able to withstand higher temperatures and, therefore, survive and thrive at the higher annual temperatures that climatologists predict will occur in Earth's future ("Heat-Tolerant Crops Could Prevent Future Starvation and Help Preserve Biofuels").

Yet another trait for which crops are being genetically modified is frost resistance. Recall from Chapter 1 that one of the first commercial GM crops was Frostban strawberry, a plant engineered to survive at temperatures that normally caused a plant to freeze. Efforts continue to develop frost-resistant plants in the mid-2010s, at least partly because one possible effect of global climate change may involve changes in frost seasons to which plants are not adapted. In 2006, for example, researchers at the Victorian AgriBiosciences Centre at La Trobe University in Australia transplanted a gene from a form of hair grass that occurs in Antarctica (*Deschampsia antarctica*) into wheat plants that were later found to be significantly more resistant to frost than were nonengineered plants. Government and industry representatives have been sufficiently interested in this development to provide significant funds for further research on the procedure. In October 2013, for example, the Australian Grains and Development Council (AGDC) announced that it would more than double its investment in the development of frost-resistant wheat over the next five years, from AUS $1.2 million to AUS$3 million ("GRDC Ups the Ante in Search for Frost Tolerant Crops"; see also Frederiks et al. 2012).

Proponents of the use of GM crops often point to the special benefits such crops can bring to developing nations, where the rate of population growth is generally high and hunger and nutrition are common problems. Most, if not all, of the approaches outlined earlier can be used for crops such as maize, soybeans, and cotton in developing nations. A 2003 publication by the United Kingdom's Nuffield Council on Bioethics has pointed out some of the benefits of extending the use of GM crops in developing nations. Some of the case studies presented in that publication include the following ("Possible Benefits of GM Crops in Developing Countries"):

- The expanded use of Bt cotton in China. The Nuffield report pointed to studies that indicated that pesticide use in areas where the GM cotton was planted fell by as much as 50 kilograms per hectare, a reduction of between 60 and 80 percent in comparison with pre-GM use. The report said that the savings thereby achieved were realized in particular by an estimated 3.5 million farmers who tended relatively small farms of less than 2 hectares (5 acres). (Also see Pray et al. 2002.)

- The development of dwarf varieties of rice for India. The rice historically grown on the Indian subcontinent tends to have long stems that are somewhat easily broken and damaged in wind storms and other inclement weather. Researchers have developed a dwarf form of the rice plant by inserting a gene from the common weed *Arabidopsis thaliana*, which codes for dwarfism in some plants. (For more on this technology, see Peng et al. 1999.)

- Virus-resistant sweet potatoes in Kenya. Sweet potatoes are the second most important food crop in Kenya, after maize. Yet crop yields tend to be very low, about half of the world average for the crop. One problem is that the plant is subject to a number of agents that reduce growth or kill plants, including a number of fungi and viruses. Since the early 1990s, the government of Kenya, in conjunction with Monsanto, has been working to develop virus-resistant strains of sweet potato that will significantly increase yields of the crop. (For more, see Odame, Kameri-Mbote, and Wafula 2002.)

A number of studies have been conducted attempting to quantify the gains to agricultural made by the use of GM crops. One of the most important of those is a 2012 report, *GM Crops: Global Socio-economic and Environmental Impacts 1996–2011*, the eighth in a series of annual reviews of the social and economic impact of the use of GM crops worldwide. The 2012 report mentioned a number of benefits resulting from the adoption of GM crops by farmers, including (all data from Brookes and Barfoot 2013):

- Direct global farm income benefit resulting from the use of GM crops in 2011 was $19.8 billion. This amount is the equivalent of having added 6.3 percent to the value of global production of the four main crops of soybeans, maize, canola, and cotton (9).

- In the period from 1996 to 2011, farm incomes have increased by $98.2 billion as a result of using GM crops. About half of that amount ($48 billion) has resulted from more effective treatment of weeds and pests and the remaining amount from decreased costs of production (9).

- Genetic modification of plant traits resulted in an increase of 110 million tonnes (120 million tons) of soybeans over the period of the study, 195 million more tonnes (215 million tons) of corn, 15.8 million tonnes (17.4 million tons) of cotton, and 6.6 million tonnes (7.3 million tons) of canola (Table 5, 13).

- Economic gains resulting from the use of GM crops has been greatest in the United States, Argentina, Brazil, India, and China. It has also been significant in developing countries, where, in the period between 1996 and 2011, farmers have achieved 51.2 percent of total global gains resulting from GM crop use (Table 3, 12).

- At the same time, the net cost to farmers in developing countries was much less (14 percent of the total economic gain) than it was in developed countries (21 percent of total economic gain) (Table 4, 12).

Some observers point out that the data presented here do not tell the whole story about the use of GM crops. In at least some cases, the hazards involved in using such crops can have significant negative impact on agricultural economics. One issue often mentioned is the fact that the introduction of herbicide-resistant crops has not necessarily or even commonly resulted in a reduction in the amount of herbicides used by farmers. A study by the organization Food & Water Watch in 2013, for example, found that in the United States, the amount of at least two popular herbicides, glyphosate and 2,4-D, increased significantly between the late 1990s, when herbicide-resistant crops were first made available, and 2012, the latest year for which data were available. Specifically, total herbicide use on corn, cotton, and soybean crops dropped by 42 million pounds (15 percent) between 1998 and 2001, but then it began to rise. Between 2001 and 2010, that number rose to 81.2 million pounds (an increase of 26 percent) (*Superweeds: How Biotech Crops Bolster the Pesticide Industry* 2013, 2).

The reason for this increase, according to Food & Water Watch, was the rapid increase in the amount of herbicide-resistant weeds resulting from the use of glyphosate and 2,4-D on herbicide-resistant crops. The growth of these "superweeds" resulted in a 10-fold increase in the amount of glyphosate used on corn, cotton, and soybeans between 1996 and 2012, from 15 million pounds to 159 million pounds, and the use of 2,4-D increased over the same time period by 90 percent (*Superweeds: How Biotech Crops Bolster the Pesticide Industry* 2013, 2).

The development of superweeds, and the concomitant cost to farmers of using additional herbicides, has outweighed the supposed economic benefits of using herbicide-resistant crops, in Food & Water Watch's view. The cost of GM corn seeds is about $40 higher per acre than non-GM corn seeds, and these costs nearly tripled between 1998 and 2013. However, the added costs of using additional herbicides to treat superweeds have added even more to farmers' expenses. Summarizing a number of studies conducted on this issue, Food & Water Watch concluded that the costs to farmers posed from treating superweeds ranged from $12 per acre (2 percent of the value of the crop) for Tennessee soybean farmers to $50 per acre (7 percent of the value of the crop) for a range of cotton farmers

(*Superweeds: How Biotech Crops Bolster the Pesticide Industry* 2013, Table 1, 10). (The Food & Water Watch study closely matches a similar long-range study of the use of herbicides conducted by Charles Benbrook (2012) at Washington State University.) The issue of the economic benefit of GM crops for farmers is obviously not entirely resolved.

Potential Benefits to Human Health

Plants and animals can both be engineered to provide a range of health benefits for humans. The example that is perhaps most often mentioned in this regard is the case of Golden Rice, discussed in Chapter 1. Other types of biofortification are also possible. *Biofortification* refers to the process by which the nutritional value of a plant or animal is increasing by genetic engineering or some other synthetic process. An example of current research in this area is the BioCassave Plus Programme (BC+), originally funded by the Bill and Melinda Gates Foundation in 2005. Cassava is the primary staple food for more than 250 million people in Africa and millions of others worldwide. The plant is, however, deficient in essential nutrients, providing, for example, less than 30 percent of the recommended daily amount of protein. The goal of the BC+ program is to develop mechanisms for genetically modifying the cassava plant to enrich the concentration of protein, iron, zinc, vitamin A, and other nutrients. Field tests in Puerto Rico and Nigeria in the second half of the first decade of the twenty-first century have focused on cassava genetically enhanced for improved β-carotene, iron, zinc, and protein and cassava lines with low cyanogens, increased shelf life, and virus resistance. Researchers have estimated that successful development of crops such as vitamin A–enhanced cassava could save up to $1.4 billion in health costs in Nigeria and $81 million in Kenya (Sayre et al. 2011).

Rice and cassava are by no means the only food crops being studied for possible biofortification by genetic means. One review of the field has noted that research is ongoing on other crops, such as the genetic engineering of carrots to increase calcium content, of lettuce with zinc to prevent organ disorders, of tomatoes to improve folate content, and of lettuce to increase tocopherol and resveratrol composition, as a way of reducing risk for coronary disease and arteriosclerosis (Silva Dias and Ortiz 2012).

Biofortification by genetic means might appear to have a number of advantages. Still, some critics have raised a number of objections to the practice. In the first place, such crops and food products sometimes look and even taste somewhat different from their natural cousins. These differences may give farmers pause in raising such crops and cause hesitation in getting consumers to eat them. Another complaint that is sometimes raised is that the increased emphasis on improving the nutritional quality of basic foods such as maize, rice, and cassava may tend to reduce the dietary variety for millions of people, with possible long-term nutritional issues that are still not entirely understood (Johns and Eyzaguirrea 2007).

Potential Benefits to the Natural Environment

Many of the arguments for the benefits of GM crops and foods to agriculture and human health also translate into potential benefits to the natural environment. For example, increasing the productivity of crops not only provides a benefit to human health and nutrition but also means that farmers may need to press less marginal land into cultivation. Marginal land is defined as low-quality land on which crops can be grown only at relatively high costs that may be only slightly less than the value of products obtained on the land. As population grows in a given region, food demand also increases. The only way of meeting increased food demands at the present time is to find land currently not used for—or well adapted to— agriculture. In many cases, that situation may mean draining swamps, cutting down forests, irrigating desert regions, and otherwise disrupting the natural environment, often with a host of ecological consequences. The use of GM crops, then, may not only increase the per-acre output of food but also protect some of the most sensitive and most essential components of an ecological system.

As noted earlier, the use of GM crops may also reduce farmers' dependence on chemical fertilizers and pesticides that can have devastating and unwanted effects on the natural environment. As the Food and Agriculture Organization of the United Nations has noted,

> Genetically engineered resistance to pests and diseases . . . is already happening. Farmers are growing maize, cotton and potatoes that no longer have to be sprayed with the bacterial insecticide *Bacillus thuringiensis*—because they produce its insecticidal agent themselves. Scientists are developing trees that have a lower content of lignin, a structuring constituent of woody plant cells. This could reduce the need for noxious chemicals in pulp and paper production. ("Weighing the GMO Arguments: For")

GM plants might also be used on land that is normally not otherwise productive. As noted earlier, they can be engineered to grow on land that is too dry, too wet, too salty, too hot, or too cold.

A quite different contribution that genetic engineering might make to the environment is the development of new or more abundant biofuels, organic materials that can be burned directly or converted to another form for use as a fuel. Biofuels are an increasingly important factor in most future assessments of a nation's energy equation. Currently, biofuels make up only 7.1 percent of all fuels burned in the United States and less than 1 percent worldwide ("U.S. Bioenergy Statistics"). Currently, they cannot compete economically with fossil fuels or most other renewable fuels. However, it may be possible to change the genetic structure of some types of plants to alter that fact, vastly increasing the types, efficiencies, and quantities of plants that can be used as energy sources (Stecker 2013).

Potential Harm to Human Health

Opponents of the genetic modification of seeds, crops, and foods tend to focus primarily on two concerns: How might such products affect human health and how might they damage the natural environment? With regard to the first question, critics of GM products are faced with a very large body of scientific evidence suggesting that GM foods have no demonstrable or measurable effects on human health. A number of highly regarded studies appear to confirm this contention. Among the strongest statements in this regard are the following:

- American Association for the Advancement of Science (AAAS): "the World Health Organization, the American Medical Association, the U.S. National Academy of Sciences, the British Royal Society, and 'every other respected organization that has examined the evidence has come to the same conclusion: consuming foods containing ingredients derived from GM crops is no riskier than consuming the same foods containing ingredients from crop plants modified by conventional plant improvement techniques'" ("AAAS Board of Directors: Legally Mandating GM Food Labels Could 'Mislead and Falsely Alarm Consumers'").

- The main conclusion to be drawn from the efforts of more than 130 research projects, covering a period of more than 25 years of research and involving more than 500 independent research groups, is that biotechnology, and in particular GMOs, is not per se more risky than, for example, conventional plant breeding technologies (*Decade of EU-Funded GMO Research (2001–2010)*).

- There is broad scientific consensus that genetically engineered crops currently on the market are safe to eat. After 14 years of cultivation and a cumulative total of 2 billion acres planted, no adverse health or environmental effects have resulted from commercialization of genetically engineered crops (Ronald 2011).

- Bioengineered foods have been consumed for close to 20 years, and during that time, no overt consequences on human health have been reported and/or substantiated in the peer-reviewed literature ("Report 2 of the Council on Science and Public Health [A-12]").

- In contrast to adverse health effects that have been associated with some traditional food production methods, similar serious health effects have not been identified as a result of genetic engineering techniques used in food production (Committee on Identifying and Assessing Unintended Effects of Genetically Engineered Foods on Human Health et al. 2004, R9–R10).

In the face of statements such as these, a number of observers have argued essentially that the debate over the safety of GM foods is over. In fact, British author, journalist, and environmental activist Mark Lynas made just that statement in January 2013. He apologized to his readers for having attacked GM foods for so many years, saying that "We no longer need to discuss whether or not it [GM food] is safe—over a decade and a half with three trillion GM meals eaten there has never been a single substantiated case of harm. You are more likely to get hit by an asteroid than to get hurt by GM food" (Kloor 2013).

Still, a substantial number of critics remain very much unconvinced that the debate is over. They continue to present evidence that additional research is needed and that there are sound reasons for believing that GM foods may be responsible for a host of risks to human health. For example, researchers at the University of Minnesota Food Policy Research Center issued a report in October 2012 arguing that significant questions remain about the safety of GM foods. That report said that "[s]cientific studies testing whole GE food show some mixed results so statements about all GE foods being safe or unsafe are unwarranted." A fundamental reason for this uncertainty, the report went on, was that "[w]hole-food feeding studies for GE safety assessment are tricky, as plant varieties are diverse in chemical composition and the effect of the introduced genes or changes caused by them are hard to tease out" (Kuzma and Haase 2012).

Even a cursory examination of the print and electronic literature shows that concerns about the safety of GM foods are ongoing. Those concerns are generally based on three fundamental questions: Are some GM food products actually toxic to humans and other animals; do they pose a risk to the nutritional needs of humans and other animals; and are GM foods allergenic to a significant portion of the human population? A number of individuals and organizations with varying degrees of professional expertise argue that GM foods do or may pose a significant threat to human health. For example, a committee of the American Academy of Environmental Medicine (AAEM) reviewed the published evidence about the biological effects of GM foods on humans and other animals came to the conclusion that

There is more than a casual association between GM foods and adverse health effects. There is causation as defined by Hill's Criteria in the areas of strength of association, consistency, specificity, biological gradient, and biological plausibility. The strength of association and consistency between GM foods and disease is confirmed in several animal studies. (Dean and Armstrong 2009) (Note: The so-called Hill's Criteria is a set of measures that can be used to determine whether two factors are associated simply by association or by a cause-and-effect relationship.)

Some of the specific conditions mentioned in the AAEM report were infertility; failure of the immune system; accelerated aging; dysregulation of genes associated with cholesterol synthesis, insulin regulation, cell signaling, and protein formation; and changes in the liver, kidney, spleen, and gastrointestinal systems. At the conclusion of their report, the AAEM authors recommended that additional tests be conducted on the safety of GM foods and, until further information becomes available, that physicians advise their patients to avoid GM foods to the extent possible.

A number of articles have been written and reports issued reviewing and summarizing the purported health effects of GM foods on human health. As an example, a team of Indian researchers published an article in 2011 in which they reviewed a large body of scientific research and came to the conclusion that "GMOS are inherently unsafe." Among the "unique dangers" they identified were:

- Toxic reactions in the digestive tract
- Liver damage
- Higher death rates and organ damage in experimental animals
- Reproductive failure and higher infant mortality rates
- Immune reactions and allergenicity (Verma et al. 2011, 7–8)

An example of the type of problem that might arise from the consumption of GM foods was reported online by a team of Chinese researchers in late 2011. Those researchers discovered the presence of so-called microRNA (miRNA) in the blood and organs of humans, where it is not normally found. They pointed out that the miRNA had apparently been transferred from rice to humans and then survived the digestive process to attack human cells. Since they were discovered early in the twenty-first century, miRNAs have been found to disrupt a variety of cell functions, resulting in a variety of health conditions that include some types of cancer, diabetes, and

Alzheimer's disease. Opponents of the consumption of GM foods point out that scientists clearly do not yet know what the health effects might be of foreign genes introduced into plants that work their way into the human (or other animal) body, where they may constitute a significant hazard to health. (The original report is Zhang et al. 2012, with commentary on the article at Levaux 2012.)

The debate over the safety of GM foods goes somewhat beyond a disagreement as to what the research shows. Opponents of genetic engineering of plants sometimes argue that the research cited by supporters of GMO crops and foods use unfair and dishonest mechanisms for advancing their case. The fundamental problem, according to one critic of GM foods, is that "the industry is unregulated, and when companies say their foods are safe, their views are unquestioned." Agribusinesses like Monsanto, he says, will stop at nothing to develop and promote the use of their GM products. As a consequence, he goes on, they are guilty of all kinds of errors, such that

> their studies are substandard, adverse findings are hidden, and they typically "fail to investigate the impacts of GM food on [a variety of bodily functions]. . . . In addition, industry-funded studies creatively avoid finding problems or conceal any uncovered. They cook the books by using older instead of younger more sensitive animals, keep sample sizes too low for statistical significance, dilute the GM component of feeds used, limit the duration of feeding trials, ignore animal deaths and sickness, and engage in other unscientific practices. (Lendman 2008; also see Smith 2007; for an extended review of studies on health and nutritional effects of GM foods, see Magaña-Gómez and Calderón de la Barca 2009)

Questions have also been raised about the potential allergic effects of GM foods. One of the most famous episodes in the history of GM food testing—and one that is still cited by opponents of GM foods today—involved the introduction of a Brazil nut protein into soybeans in an effort to improve the nutritional value of that crop. During the testing of the GM crop, researchers found that some consumers of the modified soybean experienced an allergic reaction to the GM product. Upon making this discovery, further research on the GM soybean was discontinued, and it was never made commercially available ("The Safety of Genetically Modified Foods Produced through Biotechnology" 2003).

Critics point out that GM foods may produce allergic reactions in humans in one of three ways:

1. They may cause allergic reactions in individuals who are already allergic to the introduced protein or to other proteins similar to it.

2. An introduced gene may alter the expression of existing genes in the host plant, making it allergic in circumstances where it had previously not had that effect.

3. An introduced gene and the protein for which it codes may create a new allergy in humans who consume that product.

Proponents of GM foods and crops and many neutral observers tend to repeat the mantra that "no allergic reactions to GM food by consumers have been confirmed" (see, for example, Cenčič and Krygier 2007, 232). Critics of GM foods simply do not buy that statement, however, and offer a number of studies that seem to suggest the reverse of that situation. As an example, a study conducted by Indian researchers found that individuals who had been exposed to GM cotton carrying the gene for the Bt protein exhibited obvious allergic reactions. The researchers concluded that

All the evidence gathered during the investigation shows that [Bt engineered cotton] has been causing skin, Upper [*sic*] respiratory tract and eye allergy among persons exposed to cotton. The symptoms vary from mild, moderate to very severe to the extent that one woman had to be admitted for 9 days as a result of allergy. (Gupta et al. 2005)

Potential Harm to the Natural Environment

Opponents of GM seeds and crops offer a number of examples of ways in which these products can harm the natural environment. First, they point out that genes present in any plant, natural or genetically modified, can escape from that particular plant and travel into other members of the same or different species. The transfer of genes from one organism to another by such a process, or any other process other than traditional reproduction, is called *horizontal gene flow* (or *horizontal gene transfer*). Plants that are pollinated by the wind or by insects are especially at risk for this effect, because the pollination process can carry genes over relatively great distances, allowing GM pollen to interact with non-GM plants. One review of these effects mentioned a number of specific examples of the process that have already been observed, including:

- Contamination of an organic canola farm in West Australia by pollen blown in from a nearby GM-planted farm
- Contamination of up to 5 percent of non-GM rapeseed in Canada by cross-pollination from GM crops
- Spontaneous growth of GM cotton and soybeans in Costa Rica from GM seeds blown in from areas planted with those seeds
- Widespread contamination of virtually all agricultural land in Canada by at least some minimal amount of GM canola seed
- Contamination of as much as 30 percent of all U.S. long-grain rice plantings with GM rice varietals

The transfer of herbicide-resistant genes from engineered plants to weeds, discussed earlier in this chapter, is another example of this type of gene transfer that may be possible in nature.

Proponents of GM seeds and crops suggest that this problem can be avoided by constructing a buffer zone around areas where GM crops are planted. One problem with this suggestion is that it is not clear how wide a buffer zone has to be in order to protect native plants from pollen drift. One study conducted on this question found that the width required was quite large. The Japanese province of Hokkaido, for example, requires a buffer zone of 300 meters, 10 times the size required by the Japanese Ministry of Agriculture, Forestry and Fisheries. Studies found, however, that native plants were contaminated with GM pollen at distances of up to 600 meters for rice plants and 1,200 meters for sugar beets. Buffer zones of this size would, in many cases, effectively prevent the growing of GM crops in most areas ("Buffer Zones Can Not Prevent GMO Cross Pollination"; "Cross-Fertilization by Airborne Pollen Found at Surprisingly Large Distances").

Opponents of GM crops and seeds also point out that the insertion of a foreign gene into a plant can have extensive effects on the genetic composition of that plant, beyond that which is planned and expected by researchers. They point out that information on possible plant mutations is simply not available, and it is a risky enterprise to attempt in-the-field experiments on the insertion of genes without knowing the possible effects that change will produce (Smith 2005).

The response to this argument is that, yes, inserting genes into a plant does have extensive effects on that plant's genome. However, that type of change has been going on for centuries, ever since humans began crossbreeding plants. Furthermore, as one reviewer has pointed out, as of late 2013, "not a single ill effect has ever been demonstrated to be the result of DNA alteration in a food or feed plant" ("Any DNA Insertion Can Cause a Mutation").

Critics raise questions also about the possibility that genes injected into a crop plant might accidentally activate so-called *sleeper genes*. A sleeper gene is a gene that is usually inactive in a plant but that can be turned out by the introduction of an abnormal substance or event (e.g., unusually high temperatures or drought conditions) into the plant's environment. Scientists simply do not know at this point whether engineered genes can act as activators of this kind, setting off changes in a plant's biochemistry about which researchers may know little or nothing.

Questions have also been raised about the potential consequences resulting from horizontal gene flow from cultivated transgenic plants into the wild, followed by their incorporation into wild plants of the same or other species. Such a scenario is fraught with a number of questions, such as whether such transfers can actually occur and, if so, how easily and how often; how the incorporation of genes would affect the physical characteristics of the wild plants; what environmental advantages and disadvantages the GM wild plants would have in comparison with their non-GM cousins; and how such events are likely to affect the diversity of a biological community. One of the potential problems posed by some researchers is that the growth of new GM plants in the wild produced by gene transfer could result in the loss of native, non-GM plant species that have grown up within a biome with the ability to withstand particular environmental stresses. The loss of those species, then, could result in a less diverse and less vigorous biological community than existed before the gene transfer. (For an excellent discussion of this issue, see Lu 2008.)

Generally speaking, many of these arguments can be subsumed under a common theme: It is fairly clear that genes that have been introduced into domestic crops by genetic engineering are capable of escaping into the wild, and no one knows precisely how this process is likely to affect the genotypes and phenotypes of natural plants thus infected or how, if at all, they will affect the general ecological structure of an area. And the general response to that query is that humans have been altering organisms for many centuries (as with hybridization), and those changes have not produced problems at the level of either individual species or ecological systems. (For an extended discussion of this topic, see Andersson and de Vicente 2010; Boškovic et al. 2010.)

Potential Social and Economic Harm

The introduction of GM crops and foods has had impacts on human society that go far beyond those of agriculture, human health, the environment, and other primarily scientific issues. Particularly over the past decade, a number of observers have been asking how GM crops and foods have changed the economics of food production, the social characteristics of the agricultural endeavor, the politics of food production, and related issues. Some information about those issues is now available.

As noted earlier, one of the strongest arguments for the use of GM seeds and crops is the benefits such products will have for farmers. It is also possible that those products may cause farmers problems that they would not otherwise have in growing traditional, non-GM crops. For example, the cost of purchasing GM seed is often higher than the cost of non-GM traditional seed. For example, the Organic Center maintains a Seed Premium-Farm Income Database that tracks the cost of crop seeds from 1975 to the current year. Figures from that database showed that the price of conventional corn seed in 2010 was $152.90 per bag, compared to $170.10 per bag for organic seed, $270.25 per bag for GM seed, and $320.00 per bag for a specialty GM seed called *SmartStax*. Comparable prices for soybean seeds were $36.50 per bag for conventional seed, $48.56 per bag for organic seed, $59.52 per bag for GM seed, and $70.43 per bag for Roundup Ready seed. The comparison was even more dramatic for cotton seed, which sold for $118.65 per hundred-weight for conventional seed and $700.35 per hundred-weight for GM seed. (For more details on this issue, see Benbrook 2009.)

Such a pattern makes sense because the cost of developing GM seeds and plants is high, and corporations only naturally want to make back their expenses of development along with a reasonable profit. Although this is true, the reality is that GM seed may be too expensive for smaller farmers, especially those living in developed countries who may simply not be able to afford such seeds.

Biotechnology companies have also developed mechanisms for ensuring that, to the extent possible, farmers use only engineered seeds that they purchase from one of the major producers (Monsanto, Syngenta, DuPont, Bayer, and BASF). Even if farmers growing conventional, non-GM crops accidentally use seed blown in from adjacent farms that use GM seeds, they can be sued by biotechnology companies for infringement of patent rights on those seeds. And to close the circle on their control of GM seeds and crops, biotechnology companies have developed a technology known as *genetic use restriction technology* (GURT). GURT can be used for the production of so-called *suicide seeds* that can be grown for a crop in one year but whose own seeds are sterile and unable to be used for growing crops in later years (Dimech 2002). Monsanto claims that it has not sold such seeds, nor does it plan to do so, even though the technology is available ("Monsanto Sells Terminator Seeds").

Labeling of Genetically Modified Foods in the United States

Many critics of GMO have taken a second approach in their opposition to GM foods: They have suggested or demanded that any such foods made available for sale to consumers be so labeled. At the beginning of 2014, more than 60 nations worldwide had some type of laws or regulations along these lines. Those nations included Australia, Brazil, China, Russia, South Africa, Turkey, and the member states of the European Union (Kingston 2013). As discussed earlier, the European Union has struggled for many years to resolve the issue as to whether or not to require the labeling of GM foods, at what stage of their use to do so, what the nature of a label should be, and a host of other issues relating to the labeling process. (For a good overview of the EU labeling regulations, see "Labeling of GMO Products.") Although the United States has a complex system for approving research on, development of, and sale of GM foods, there are no federal labeling laws or regulations.

This difference between the way the European Union and the United States approach the labeling of GM foods reflects significant differences in public attitudes about GM foods in the two regions, as noted earlier. As recently as 2012, public opinion polls showed that about 20 percent of Americans viewed GM foods "not favorably," compared to 61 percent of Europeans who held a similar view in a poll held two years earlier (Kreibohm 2013, 3). For this reason, efforts to produce federal legislation on the labeling of GM foods in the United States has gone essentially nowhere.

Activists have been forced, therefore, to pursue their case for the labeling of GM foods at the state and local level. Each year over the past decade, labeling laws have been introduced into dozens of state legislatures, always without success. During 2013, for example, 26 state legislatures considered at least one bill (and some more than a half dozen bills) requiring the labeling of GM products, the great difference being that two of those bills were, for the first time, passed ("State Labeling Initiatives"). The first of those bills was passed by the Connecticut legislature and signed by Governor Dannel P. Malloy in June 2013. The bill was written in such a way, however, that it would not take effect until four other states, one of which shares a boundary with Connecticut, took similar action. Within a matter of days, the Maine legislature passed a similar bill, with similar provisions. Thus, two states technically have GM food labeling laws, although those laws may not go into effect for a while (Artz 2013).

Activists have also placed initiatives on state ballots requiring the labeling of GM foods. The first such initiative was

California's Proposition 37, requiring the labeling of all food products that contained any type of GMO. After intense and expensive campaigning, that initiative failed in the November 2012 election by a margin of 53 percent to 47 percent. A second attempt was made in the state of Washington a year later, when voters were presented with Initiative 522. Once again, the proposal was defeated at the polls by a vote of 55 percent to 45 percent. Like the California campaign, the Washington contest was dominated by national and international out-of-state interests, such as the Grocery Manufacturers Association, Monsanto, DuPont Pioneer, Dow AgroSciences, and Bayer CropScience in support of the "no" side of the vote and Dr. Bronner's Magic Soaps, Center for Food Safety Action Fund, Mercola.com Health Resources LLC, Organic Consumers Association, and Presence Marketing, Inc., on the "yes" side. The total investment by the two sides was about $22 million for the "no" side and $7 million for the "yes" side (Behrson 2013).

Pros and Cons of Labeling

Proponents of mandatory GM food labeling often put forward a relatively straightforward argument. They suggest that many people remain unconvinced by claims of pro-genetic engineering that GM foods are safe to eat and safe for the environment. They argue that such individuals should, at the very least, be allowed the right to decline to purchase GM foods. The only way they can do that, they continue, is for foods to be labeled to indicate whether or not they contain GM foods.

Other arguments in favor of labeling can be made also. For example, more than 60 nations require the labeling of GM foods, and opinion polls suggest that a large fraction of the American populace (if not a majority) approves of food labeling. What harm is there, then, in providing that same option to the American population? Also, it is possible that individuals who do not eat meat for one reason or another might be exposed to genes from meat products by eating GM foods. Such individuals should have the right to avoid such products. (For one of the many statements in favor of GM food labeling, see Bronner 2013.)

Critics of mandatory food labeling counter such arguments with a number of opposing views. In the first place, requiring the labeling of GM foods for all practical purposes acknowledges that such foods do pose a risk to human health or the natural environment. However, opponents say, that concern has been disproved over and over again by countless numbers of research studies over the years. Also, the desire to offer consumers a greater degree of choice by labeling GM foods may be admirable in the abstract, but it has turned out not to be true in real life. Some studies have showed that the additional costs of handling labeled GM foods have prompted many retailers to stop stocking such items and prevented consumers from purchasing them (see, for example, Carter and Gruère 2003).

Opponents of labeling also point to the huge cost that would be involved with the handling of labeled foods, from the design and printing of labels, to the production of separate batches of products, to the transportation and storage of additional food items, to the stocking and merchandising separate versions of what is essentially the same product. Finally, they take note that worries about the presence of animal genes in GM foods are unfounded, because no animal genes are now used in the production of such foods. (For summary statements in opposition to mandatory GM food labeling, see, for example, Editors of Scientific American 2013; Sunstein 2013, with many responses to the blog.)

Conclusion

One of the points raised by critics of the production and consumption of GM seeds, crops, and foods is that this technology is still very new. Many of the potential problems they see with the technology may not be manifested for years or decades.

At this early point, they say, humans should exercise caution as to their use of GM products. Such concerns are unreasonable, proponents of GM products say. Humans cannot hold off forever to take advantage of new technologies on the basis of possible harmful results many years or decades into the future. With this diversity of basic assumptions, one can only assume that the debate over GM products will continue long into the future.

References

"AAAS Board of Directors: Legally Mandating GM Food Labels Could 'Mislead and Falsely Alarm Consumers'." http://www.aaas.org/news/releases/2012/1025gm_statement.shtml. Accessed on November 25, 2013.

Agarwal, Pradeep K., et al. 2013. "Bioengineering for Salinity Tolerance in Plants: State of the Art." *Molecular Biotechnology* 54(1): 102–123.

"Amflora—a Potato for Industrial Applications." GMO Safety. http://www.gmo-safety.eu/science/potato/263.amflora-potato-industrial-applications-starch-potatoes-renewable-raw-material.html. Accessed on October 21, 2013.

Andersson, Meike S., and M. Carmen de Vicente. 2010. *Gene Flow between Crops and Their Wild Relatives*. Baltimore: Johns Hopkins University Press.

"Any DNA Insertion Can Cause a Mutation." Academics Review. http://academicsreview.org/reviewed-content/genetic-roulette/section-2/2-1-dna-insertion/. Accessed on November 30, 2013.

Artz, Kenneth. 2013. "Connecticut, Maine Pass GMO Labeling Laws." http://news.heartland.org/newspaper-article/2013/07/12/connecticut-maine-pass-gmo-labeling-laws. Accessed on December 1, 2013.

"Austria Bans Monsanto's GM Oilseed Rape." GM Watch. http://gmwatch.org/latest-listing/1-news-items/137-austria

-bans-monsantos-gm-oilseed-rape. Accessed on October 13, 2013.

Bartley, Nancy. 2006. "2 Charged in Arson at Oregon Tree Farm." *Seattle Times*. http://community.seattletimes .nwsource.com/archive/?date=20060224&slug=eco24m. Accessed on September 11, 2013.

Baskin, Yvonne. 1987. "Testing the Future." The Alicia Patterson Foundation. http://aliciapatterson.org/stories/ testing-future. Accessed on September 11, 2013.

Behrson, Pamela. 2013. "Data Release: WA GMO Labeling Initiative—$22M from 57 NO Contributors; $7.7M from 10,500+ YES Contributors." MapLight. http://maplight .org/data-release/data-release-wa-gmo-labeling-initiative -22m-from-57-no-contributors-77m-from-10500-yes-. Accessed on December 1, 2013.

Benbrook, Charles. 2009. *The Magnitude and Impacts of the Biotech and Organic Seed Price Premium*. The Organic Center. http://www.organic-center.org/reportfiles/ SeedPricesReport.pdf. Accessed on November 30, 2013.

Benbrook, Charles M. 2012. "Impacts of Genetically Engineered Crops on Pesticide Use in the U.S.—the First Sixteen Years." *Environmental Sciences Europe* 24: 24. http:// www.enveurope.com/content/pdf/2190-4715-24-24.pdf. Accessed on September 9, 2013.

"Biotechnology." Eurobarometer 73.1. Brussels: TNS Opinion & Social. http://ec.europa.eu/public_opinion/archives/ebs/ ebs_341_en.pdf. Accessed on September 15, 2013.

Bonny, Sylvie. 2008. "How Have Opinions about GMOs Changed Over Time? The Situation in the European Union and the USA." *CAB Reviews: Perspectives in Agriculture, Veterinary Science, Nutrition and Natural Resources* 3(093). http://icon.slu.se/ICON/Documents/Publications/BONNY _How%20have%20opinions%20about%20GMOs%20 changed%20over%20time_CAB%20rev%202008%20 %20PAV3093.pdf. Accessed on September 15, 2013.

Boškovic, Jelena V., et al. 2010. "Assessing Ecological Risks and Benefits of Genetically Modified Crops." *Journal of Agricultural Sciences* 55(1): 89–101.

Bronner, David. 2013. "5 Reasons to Get on the Soapbox for GMO Labeling." *Huffington Post.* http://www.huffington post.com/david-bronner/five-reasons-to-get-on-the-soap box_b_4183815.html. Accessed on December 1, 2013.

Brookes, Graham, and Peter Barfoot. 2013. *GM Crops: Global Socio-economic and Environmental Impacts 1996–2011.* Dorchester, UK: PG Economics, Ltd. https://www.landes bioscience.com/journals/gmcrops/2013GMC0001R.pdf. Accessed on November 30, 2013.

"Buffer Zones Can Not Prevent GMO Cross Pollination." GM Watch. http://www.gmwatch.org/index.php/news/archive/ 2008/9542-buffer-zones-can-not-prevent-gmo-cross -contamination. Accessed on November 30, 2013.

Butler, Declan. 2010. "A New Dawn for Transgenic Crops in Europe?" *Nature.* http://www.nature.com/news/2010/100309/ full/news.2010.112.html. Accessed on October 21, 2013.

Carter, Colin A., and Guillaume P. Gruère. 2003. "Mandatory Labeling of Genetically Modified Foods: Does It Really Provide Consumer Choice?" *AgBioForum.* http://www .agbioforum.org/v6n12/v6n12a13-carter.htm. Accessed on December 1, 2013.

Cencič, Avrelija, and Krzysztof Krygier. 2007. "Miscellaneous Hazards." In Frank Devlieghere, Pieternel Luning, and Roland Vehe, eds. *Safety in the Agri-food Chain*, 223–248. Wageningen, the Netherlands: Wageningen Academic Publishers.

"Commission Regulation (EC) No 50/2000 of 10 January 2000." *Official Journal of the European Communities.*

http://faolex.fao.org/docs/pdf/eur19091.pdf. Accessed on October 30, 2013.

Committee on Identifying and Assessing Unintended Effects of Genetically Engineered Foods on Human Health, Board on Life Sciences, Food and Nutrition Board, Board on Agriculture and Natural Resources, Institute of Medicine, and National Research Council of the National Academies. 2004. *Safety of Genetically Engineered Foods: Approaches to Assessing Unintended Health Effects.* Washington, DC: The National Academies Press.

"Consumer Insights Regarding Food Biotechnology." International Food Information Council Foundation. http://www.food.insight.org/Resources/Detail.aspx?topic =Consumer_Insights_Regarding_Food_Biotechnology. Accessed on September 15, 2013.

"Contained Use of Genetically Modified Micro-organisms." Europa. http://europa.eu/legislation_summaries/other/l21157_en.htm. Accessed on September 23, 2013.

"The Convention on Biological Diversity." Convention on Biological Diversity. https://www.cbd.int/convention/. Accessed on October 13, 2013.

"Council Regulation (EC) No 1139/98 of 26 May 1998 Concerning the Compulsory Indication of the Labelling of Certain Foodstuffs Produced from Genetically Modified Organisms of Particulars Other than Those Provided for in Directive 79/112/EEC." ec.europa.eu/food/fs/gmo/legal_oj/reg1139-98_en.pdf. Accessed on May 7, 2014.

Crawford, Mark. 1987. "California Field Test Goes Forward." *Science* 236(4801): 511.

"Cross-Fertilization by Airborne Pollen Found at Surprisingly Large Distances." *BioJournal.* http://www5d.biglobe.ne.jp/~cbic/english/2008/journal0805.html. Accessed on November 30, 2013.

Davison, John. 2010. "GM Plants: Science, Politics and EC Regulations." *Plant Science* 178(2): 94–98.

Dean, Amy, and Jennifer Armstrong. 2009. "Genetically Modified Foods." American Academy of Environmental Medicine. http://www.aaemonline.org/gmopost.html. Accessed on November 26, 2013.

A Decade of EU-Funded GMO Research (2001–2010). Directorate-General for Research and Innovation. European Union. http://ec.europa.eu/research/biosociety/pdf/a _decade_of_eu-funded_gmo_research.pdf. Accessed on November 25, 2013.

Dimech, Adam. 2002. "Terminator." http://www.adonline.id .au/terminatorseeds/. Accessed on November 30, 2013.

Editors of Scientific American. 2013. "Labels for GMO Foods Are a Bad Idea." *Scientific American.* http://www.scientific american.com/article.cfm?id=labels-for-gmo-foods-are-a -bad-idea. Accessed on December 1, 2013.

"EU and Argentina Settle WTO Case on Genetically Modified Organisms." Press Releases Database. http://europa.eu/ rapid/press-release_IP-10-325_en.htm. Accessed on October 13, 2013.

"EU GMO Ban Was Illegal, WTO Rules." EurActiv.com. http://www.euractiv.com/trade/eu-gmo-ban-illegal-wto -rules-news-216529. Accessed on October 13, 2013.

"Four Arrested in 1999 New Year's Eve Agricultural Hall Arson." [Michigan State University] Agriculture. http:// special.news.msu.edu/ag_hall/index.php. Accessed on September 11, 2013.

Frederiks, T. M., et al. 2012. "Current and Emerging Screening Methods to Identify Post-Head-Emergence Frost Adaptation in Wheat and Barley." *Journal of Experimental Botany* 63(15): 5405–5416.

Galbraith, Kate. 2013. "Attitudes on Crops Are Modifying." *New York Times.* http://www.nytimes.com/2013/07/11/

business/energy-environment/11iht-green11.html?ref
=geneticallymodifiedfood&_r=0. Accessed on
September 15, 2013.

"GM Food & Feed—Labelling." European Commission.
http://ec.europa.eu/food/food/biotechnology/gmfood/
labelling_en.htm. Accessed on October 30, 2013.

"GMOs in a Nutshell." Health and Consumers, European
Commission. http://ec.europa.eu/food/food/biotechnology/
qanda/d1_en.htm. Accessed on September 23, 2013.

"GRDC Ups the Ante in Search for Frost Tolerant Crops."
Grains Research and Development Council. http://www
.noodls.com/view/FD98A689C5269EC870AEA385A1
B316A7263D6D7D. Accessed on October 31, 2013.

"Greenpeace Protestors Paint Field of Genetically Altered
Soybeans." AP News Archive. http://www.apnewsarchive
.com/1996/Greenpeace-Protesters-Paint-Field-of-Genetically
-Altered-Soybeans/id-7f3397419d2a1a90ca894cbb2f6f796a.
Accessed on September 11, 2013.

Gruère, Guillaume P., and S. R. Rao. 2007. "A Review of
International Labeling Policies of Genetically Modified
Food to Evaluate India's Proposed Rule." *AgBioForum* 10
(1): 51–64.

Gupta, Ashish, et al. 2005. "Impact of Bt Cotton on Farmers'
Health (in Barwani and Dhar District of Madhya Pradesh)."
Investigation Report, Oct–Dec 2005. http://www.docstoc
.com/docs/123222095/BT-Health-Report-NBA-JSA.
Accessed on November 26, 2013.

"Heat-Tolerant Crops Could Prevent Future Starvation
and Help Preserve Biofuels." National Science Foundation.
http://www.nsf.gov/discoveries/disc_summ.jsp?cntn
_id=114642&org=NSF. Accessed on October 31,
2013.

Johns, Timothy, and Pablo B. Eyzaguirrea. 2007.
"Biofortification, Biodiversity and Diet: A Search for

Complementary Applications against Poverty and Malnutrition." *Food Policy* 32(1): 1–24.

Jukes, Thomas. 1987. "The Nonsense about Frostban." *The Scientist.* http://www.the-scientist.com/?articles.view/articleNo/8658/title/The-Nonsense-About-Frostban/. Accessed on September 11, 2013.

Kingston, Hudson B. 2013. "64 Countries around the World Label GE Food." http://www.pccnaturalmarkets.com/sc/1305/countries_label_ge.html. Accessed on December 1, 2013.

Kloor, Keith. 2013. "Greens on the Run in Debate over Genetically Modified Food." The Grid. http://www.bloomberg.com/news/2013-01-07/green-activist-reverses-stance-on-genetically-modified-food.html. Accessed on November 25, 2013.

Kreibohm, Linnea. 2013. "Who's Afraid of GMOs? Understanding the Differences in the Regulation of GMOs in the United States and European Union." Issue Brief 44. American Institute for Contemporary German Studies. The Johns Hopkins University. http://www.aicgs.org/site/wp-content/uploads/2013/08/Issue-Brief-44_GMOs1.pdf. Accessed on December 1, 2013.

Kuzma, Jennifer, and Rachel Haase. 2012. *Safety Assessment of Genetically Engineered Foods: US Policy & Current Science.* University of Minnesota Food Policy Research Center. http://www.foodpolicy.umn.edu/prod/groups/cvm/@pub/@cvm/@fprc/documents/content/cvm_content_411776.pdf. Accessed on November 26, 2013.

"Labeling of GMO Products: Freedom of Choice for Consumers." GMO Compass. http://www.gmo-compass.org/eng/regulation/labelling/. Accessed on December 1, 2013.

Lendman, Stephen. 2008. "Potential Health Hazards of Genetically Engineered Foods." GlobalResearch.

http://www.globalresearch.ca/potential-health-hazards-of -genetically-engineered-foods/8148. Accessed on November 26, 2013.

Levaux, Ari. 2012. "The Very Real Danger of Genetically Modified Foods." *The Atlantic.* http://www.theatlantic.com/ health/archive/2012/01/the-very-real-danger-of-genetically -modified-foods/251051/. Accessed on November 26, 2013.

Lu, Bao-Rong. 2008. "Transgene Escape from GM Crops and Potential Biosafety Consequences: An Environmental Perspective." http://www.icgeb.org/~bsafesrv/pdffiles/ Bao-Rong.pdf. Accessed on November 30, 2013.

Lynch, Diahanna, and David Vogel. 2001. *The Regulation of GMOs in Europe and the United States: A Case-Study of Contemporary European Regulatory Politics.* New York: Council on Foreign Relations Press.

Mackenzie, Ruth, et al. 2003. *An Explanatory Guide to the Cartagena Protocol on Biosafety.* Gland, Switzerland, and Cambridge, UK: IUCN. http://www.cbd.int/doc/books/ 2003/B-01669.pdf. Accessed on May 20, 2014.

Magaña-Gómez, Javier A., and Ana M. Calderón de la Barca. 2009. "Risk Assessment of Genetically Modified Crops for Nutrition and Health." *Nutrition Reviews* 67(1): 1–16.

"Maize." GM Compass. http://www.gmo-compass.org/eng/ grocery_shopping/crops/18.genetically_modified_maize_eu .html. Accessed on October 21, 2013.

Marden, Emily. 2003. "Risk and Regulation: U.S. Regulatory Policy on Genetically Modified Food and Agriculture." *Boston College Law Review* 44(3): 733–787.

Mccomber, J. Martin. 1999. "Ecoactivists Go after Wrong Target." *The Seattle Times.* http://community.seattletimes .nwsource.com/archive/?date=19991129&slug=2998261. Accessed on September 11, 2013.

Medina, Carolina, et al. 2004. "U.S. Consumer Attitudes toward Food Biotechnology." Paper prepared for

presentation at the Southern Agricultural Economics
Association Annual Meeting, Tulsa, Oklahoma,
February 18. http://ageconsearch.umn.edu/bitstream/
34626/1/sp04me01.pdf. Accessed on September 15, 2013.

"Monsanto Sells Terminator Seeds." Monsanto. http://www
.monsanto.com/newsviews/Pages/terminator-seeds.aspx.
Accessed on November 30, 2013.

Naimon, Jonathan S. 1991. "Using Expert Panels to Assess
Risks of Environmental Biotechnology Applications: A Case
Study of the 1986 Frostban Risk Assessments." In Morris A.
Levin and Harlee S. Strauss, eds. *Risk Assessment in Genetic
Engineering*, 319–353. New York: McGraw-Hill. Inc.

Odame, Hannington, Patricia Kameri-Mbote, and David
Wafula. 2002. "Innovation and Policy Process: Case of
Transgenic Sweet Potato in Kenya." *Economic and Political
Weekly* 37(27): 2770–2777.

"Opposition Decreasing or Acceptance Increasing?" GMO
Compass. http://www.gmo-compass.org/eng/news/stories/
415.an_overview_european_consumer_polls_attitudes
_gmos.html. Accessed on September 15, 2013.

Peleg, Zvi, Maris P. Apse, and Eduardo Blumwald. 2011.
"Engineering Salinity and Water-Stress Tolerance in Crop
Plants: Getting Closer to the Field." *Advances in Botanical
Research* 57: 405–443.

Peng, J., et al. 1999. " 'Green Revolution' Genes Encode
Mutant Gibberellin Response Modulators." *Nature* 400
(6741): 256–261.

Peterson, M. J., and Paul A. White. 2010. "The EU–US
Dispute over Regulation of Genetically Modified
Organisms, Plants, Feeds, and Foods—Case Summary."
International Dimensions of Ethics Education in Science
and Engineering Case Study Series. http://scholarworks
.umass.edu/cgi/viewcontent.cgi?article=1007&context
=edethicsinscience. Accessed on October 30, 2013.

Pew Initiative on Food and Biotechnology. http://www.pew health.org/projects/pew-initiative-on-food-and-biotechnology -85899367237. Accessed on September 15, 2013.

"The Pew Initiative on Food and Biotechnology." 2006. The Mellman Group. http://www.pewtrusts.org/uploadedFiles/ wwwpewtrustsorg/Public_Opinion/Food_and_Biotechnology/ 2006summary.pdf. Accessed on September 15, 2013.

"Possible Benefits of GM Crops in Developing Countries." Nuffield Council on Bioethics. http://www.nuffield bioethics.org/gm-crops-developing-countries/gm-crops -developing-countries-possible-benefits-gm-crops -developing-co. Accessed on October 31, 2013.

Pray, Carl E., et al. 2002. "Five Years of Bt Cotton in China—the Benefits Continue." *Plant Journal* 31(4): 423–430.

"Protestors around the World March against Monsanto." *USA Today*. http://www.usatoday.com/story/news/world/2013/ 05/25/global-protests-monsanto/2361007/. Accessed on September 11, 2013.

Rajamani, Lavanya. 2013. "The Cartagena Protocol—a Battle over Trade or Biosafety?" Third World Network. http:// www.twnside.org.sg/title/lavanya-cn.htm. Accessed on October 13, 2013.

"Regulation (EC) No 258/97 of the European Parliament and of the Council of 27 January 1997 Concerning Novel Foods and Novel Food Ingredients." http://eur-lex.europa.eu/ LexUriServ/LexUriServ.do?uri=CONSLEG:1997R0258: 20090120:EN:PDF. Accessed on October 13, 2013.

"Report 2 of the Council on Science and Public Health (A-12)." American Medical Association. http://www .ama-assn.org/resources/doc/csaph/a12-csaph2-bio engineeredfoods.pdf. Accessed on November 25, 2013.

"Report on Genetically Modified Organisms in Monterey County, California." http://ag.co.monterey.ca.us/assets/

resources/assets/132/Report%20on%20GMOs%20in% 20Monterey%20Co%20CA.1.3.11.pdf?1296753661. Accessed on September 11, 2013.

Ronald, Pamela. 2011. "Plant Genetics, Sustainable Agriculture and Global Food Security." *Genetics* 188(1): 11–20.

"Round-Up Ready Corn under Attack in California." III Publishing. http://www.iiipublishing.com/politics/gmnews .htm. Accessed on September 11, 2013.

"Rules on GMOs in the EU—Ban on GMOs Cultivation." Health and Consumers, European Commission. http://ec .europa.eu/food/food/biotechnology/gmo_ban_cultivation _en.htm. Accessed on September 23, 2013.

"The Safety of Genetically Modified Foods Produced through Biotechnology." 2003. *Toxicological Sciences* 71(1): 2–8.

Sayre, Richard, et al. 2011. "The BioCassava Plus Program: Biofortification of Cassava for Sub-Saharan Africa." *Annual Review of Plant Biology* 62: 251–272.

The Seed Premium-Farm Income Database. The Organic Center. http://organic-center.org/reportfiles/ SeedPricesDatabase.pdf. Accessed on November 30, 2013.

Shaffer, Gregory C., and Pollack, Mark A. 2004. *Regulating between National Fears and Global Disciplines: Agricultural Biotechnology in the EU*. New York: New York University School of Law. http://centers.law.nyu.edu/jeanmonnet/archive/ papers/04/041001.pdf. Accessed on September 23, 2013.

Silva Dias, João, and Rodomiro Ortiz. 2012. "Transgenic Vegetable Breeding for Nutritional Quality and Health Benefits." *Food and Nutrition Sciences* 3: 1209–1219.

Smith, Jeffrey M. 2005. "Scrambling and Gambling with the Genome." Institute for Responsible Technology. http:// www.responsibletechnology.org/gmo-dangers/Scrambling -and-Gambling-with-the-Genome-July-2005. Accessed on November 30, 2013.

Smith, Jeffrey M. 2007. *Genetic Roulette: The Documented Health Risks of Genetically Engineered Foods.* Fairfield, IA: Yes! Books.

"State Labeling Initiatives." Center for Food Safety. http://www.centerforfoodsafety.org/issues/976/ge-food-labeling/state-labeling-initiatives. Accessed on December 1, 2013.

Stecker, Tiffany. 2013. "New Enzyme May Lead to Cheaper Biofuels." *Scientific American.* http://www.scientificamerican.com/article.cfm?id=new-enzyme-may-lead-to-cheaper-biofuels. Accessed on November 25, 2013.

Sunstein, Cass R. 2013. "Don't Mandate Labeling of Gene-Altered Food." Bloomberg View. http://www.bloomberg.com/news/2013-05-12/don-t-mandate-labeling-for-gene-altered-foods.html. Accessed on December 1, 2013.

Superweeds: How Biotech Crops Bolster the Pesticide Industry. 2013. Washington, DC: Food & Water Watch, July 2013. Available online at http://documents.foodandwaterwatch.org/doc/Superweeds.pdf. Accessed on November 1, 2013.

"Traceability and Labelling of GMOs." Europa: Summaries of EU Legislation. http://europa.eu/legislation_summaries/environment/nature_and_biodiversity/l21170_en.htm. Accessed on October 30, 2013.

Turan, Satpal, Katrina Cornish, and Shashi Kumar. 2012. "Salinity Tolerance in Plants: Breeding and Genetic Engineering." *Australian Journal of Crop Science* 6(9): 1337–1348.

Tuttle, Jeff. 1999. "Group Claims Responsibility for Corn Crop Damage." Institute for Agriculture and Trade Policy. http://www.iatp.org/news/group-claims-responsibility-for-corn-crop-damage. Accessed on September 11, 2013.

"U.S. Bioenergy Statistics." United States Department of Agriculture. Economic Research Service. http://www.ers.usda.gov/data-products/us-bioenergy-statistics.aspx#.UpPOesQqh8F. Accessed on November 25, 2013.

U.S. Congress, Office of Technology Assessment. 1987. *New Developments in Biotechnology—Background Paper: Public Perceptions of Biotechnology.* OTA-BP-BA-45. Washington, DC: U.S. Government Printing Office. http://digital.library .unt.edu/ark:/67531/metadc39888/m1/10/?q=food. Accessed on May 7, 2014. Also available at http://www .princeton.edu/~ota/disk2/1987/8721/. Accessed on May 7, 2014.

"Vandals Uproot Plants Used in Bacteria Test." 1987. *New York Times.* May 27. http://www.nytimes.com/1987/05/27/ us/vandals-uproot-plants-used-in-bacteria-test.html?n=Top %2fReference%2fTimes%20Topics%2fSubjects%2fT %2fTests%20and%20Testing. Accessed on September 11, 2013.

Vaughan, Adam. 2012. "Public Concern over GM Food Has Lessened, Survey Shows." *Guardian.* http://www.the guardian.com/environment/2012/mar/09/gm-food-public -concern. Accessed on September 15, 2013.

Verma, Charu, et al. 2011. "A Review on Impacts of Genetically Modified Food on Human Health." *Open Nutraceuticals Journal* 4: 3–11.

"Weighing the GMO Arguments: For." Food and Agriculture Organization of the United Nations. http://www.fao.org/ english/newsroom/focus/2003/gmo8.htm. Accessed on November 25, 2013.

Wilson, Kimberly A. C. 2013. "Genetically Engineered Sugar Beets Destroyed in Southern Oregon." Oregon Live. http:// www.oregonlive.com/pacific-northwest-news/index.ssf/ 2013/06/genetically_engineered_sugar_b.html. Accessed on September 11, 2013.

Zhang, Lin, et al. 2012. "Exogenous Plant MIR168a Specifically Targets Mammalian LDLRAP1: Evidence of Cross-Kingdom Regulation by microRNA." *Cell Research* 22: 107–126.

Introduction

This chapter provides individuals with an opportunity to write brief essays on some specific aspects of genetically modified (GM) foods. Those essays cover a wide variety of topics, from recent developments in the technology of genetic engineering to reasons to support or oppose the expanded use of GM foods in the United States and other parts of the world.

A Sledgehammer or a Dart?: Sandy Becker

I do not mind eating genetically modified (GM) foods. I have probably done it for years without noticing it, since until recently there has not been any law here in Connecticut demanding that they be labeled. As a biologist, I am not aware of any studies showing that eating GM foods can harm me. However, I am worried about what may happen during the process of growing them.

There are basically three major categories of GM crops. There are those modified to be immune to weed killers, so the farmer can douse his or her crop with an herbicide to kill weeds, without harming the crop. There are those modified to be poisonous to

A harvester works through a field of genetically modified corn near Santa Rosa, California. GM corn now makes up well over 90 percent of all corn crops grown in the United States. (AP Photo/Rich Pedroncelli)

common insect pests, so the farmer does not have to douse the crop with insecticides. And there are those modified to be immune to various microbe-caused diseases. The advantages of each of these traits are pretty obvious.

Bt corn, for example, contains an inserted gene from a naturally occurring soil bacterium (*Bacillus thuringiensis*, hence the Bt) that is highly toxic to caterpillars: for example the European corn borer, whose larvae feed on both the stalks and the ears of corn. The evidence so far, of which there is a lot, indicates that it is not at all toxic to us. However, it is a sledge-hammer approach, toxic to the caterpillars of other moths and butterflies as well. I have some concerns about killing *every* caterpillar that takes a bite of Bt corn. One person's hated pest is another person's beloved endangered species. Monarch but-terfly caterpillars eat milkweed, which farmers consider a weed. Should I be concerned that the Bt gene in GM corn could spread to milkweed and poison the caterpillars of monarch butterflies?

Probably not. The process of genetically modifying plants is so difficult and complex that I am not too worried about the inserted genes jumping to another nearby plant on their own. So I will worry a little less about the monarch caterpillars. However, it is entirely plausible to imagine that the inserted genes could end up being transferred to a closely related wild species that can cross-pollinate with the GM crop. This process has been suspected in Mexico. Wild maize growing in the vicinity of Bt corn has been found to contain the Bt gene, although data from various studies disagree—some claim it has happened; some say it has not. But if this has happened, what butterfly larvae may feed on wild maize and be poisoned?

I would prefer to use a dart, not a sledgehammer, to kill agri-cultural insect pests. If we really want to be sure we are poison-ing only the insect pest we are aiming for, there may be a better weapon available soon: RNA interference (RNAi). Like a well-thrown dart, this technique could target a specific pest for destruction. How does RNAi work? (No, it is not a newfangled football play.) Remember that any protein an organism needs must be first transcribed from the gene into messenger RNA, which functions as a template to make the protein. If the RNA is destroyed, the protein cannot be made, and if it is a crucial protein, the cell will die without it. RNAi can precisely target a specific protein, in a specific insect pest.

RNAi was discovered in the 1990s and is most likely a defense against some viral infections. When replicating, some viruses consist of double-stranded RNA—the two matching nucleic acid strands stuck together like a closed zipper, as DNA (the "double helix") normally is. Messenger RNA transcribed from a gene is single stranded. Thus, the cells of most organisms recognize that there is something fishy about double-stranded RNA—it should not be there. A defense against these invaders has been evolved: RNAi. When a cell notices double-stranded RNA, the cell chops it into short chunks, which then work with other cellular machinery to destroy all matching RNAs. If the invading double-stranded RNA belongs to a virus, the cell can destroy it in this way.

Researchers often use RNAi to "turn off" a given gene so they can see what happens to the cell without it. However, if a curious researcher introduces double-stranded RNA belonging to a gene critical to the cell itself, the cell will destroy the messenger RNA for its own important gene and will not survive. It is very difficult to introduce double-stranded RNA into the cells of mammals, but it is very easy to get it into insects—you just feed it to them. So, if a plant can be genetically modified to produce a double-stranded RNA crucial to the survival of an insect pest, for example, the corn rootworm, the worms that feed on the corn will die. The worms eat the corn containing the RNA, and the worms' own cellular machinery destroys the "invader." However, in this case, the "invader" is RNA responsible for a protein crucial to the worm's cells, and the worm dies when it is destroyed.

These double-stranded RNAs can be engineered to be exquisitely specific to just one species of insect pest, so no other (possibly beneficial) insects are at risk. RNAi-containing GM crops are not in the fields yet, but several companies are hard at work getting them ready for commercial use.

In science, it is not possible to prove things harmless. Failure to find evidence of harm may only mean we did not look hard enough yet. I am still concerned about possible harm to the environment from growing GM crops, but I suspect the rising human population that needs to be fed will keep them around for some time.

Sandy Becker is a molecular biologist at Wesleyan University in Connecticut. She has not created any GM plants but has made some GM mouse stem cells.

Genetic Engineering in Agriculture: Uncertainties and Risks: Debal Deb

Genetic engineering (GE) transfers genes across the natural reproductive barrier across species—even across taxonomic kingdoms—so that genes from viruses, bacteria, fungi, or animals are inserted into a plant cell and vice versa. This is a brilliant tool of gene mixing, enabling biologists to "create" novel organisms never found in nature.

Genetic engineers have transferred genes from the firefly to tobacco, to create a novel tobacco plant that glows in the dark. This novel genetically modified (GM) tobacco was created for purely scientific curiosity, but different crops have also been developed to yield agronomic benefits. With a view to protecting crop plants from insect pests, genes coding for a class of insecticidal toxins from the soil bacterium *Bacillus thuringiensis* (shortened as "Bt") have been transferred to common plants to create Bt crops.

Another group of GM crops is created explicitly for promoting agrochemical business. A prominent example is Monsanto company's Roundup Ready™ crops, which are designed to withstand the assault from the company's proprietary herbicide Roundup™, so the farmers can freely apply this herbicide to their farms, without harming the GM herbicide tolerant (GMHT) crop from the same company.

Uncertainties in Genetic Engineering

The process of gene transfer across natural taxic barriers is fraught with uncertainties on molecular, organismal, and ecological levels. The different sources of uncertainty, which render the claims of GE to precision untenable, are as follows.

Molecular Level

"Gene silencing" or gene expression failure is common when more than one transgene is inserted into the GM plant (Qin, Dong, and von Arnim 2003; de Sadeleer 2012). If the Bt transgene in the Bt corn is silenced, the insecticidal Bt toxin is not produced in the crop tissues, so no pest insects will be controlled.

Conversely, a transgene may be "overexpressed," so that the cell manufactures an unregulated excess of gene products, which may interfere with other unrelated signaling pathways. This may disrupt many cellular biochemical pathways (Nakai et al. 2013; Scheel 2002).

In transformants that are homozygous for a transgene, "co-suppression" of the genes may occur. The native genes in the GMO may become inactivated when a homologous transgene is inserted into an ectopic position of the genome (Meyer 1988).

Finally, the transgene may be expressed differently in different tissues and organs. "Variable expression" of the transgene would result in another unintended effect: If the Bt gene is expressed in the roots and leaves of Bt cotton plant, but not in its bolls, then the pest bollworms will remain unaffected by the Bt toxin, causing cotton production failure. This is what happened in several states of India, causing Bt cotton yield loss (Sahal and Rahman 2003).

A specific transgene may behave differently in different host crops, for unknown reasons. Thus, Bt toxin is known to exude from the roots of Bt corn and Bt rice, but not of Bt cotton, Bt canola, and Bt tobacco (Saxena et al. 2004).

Organismal Level

The introduction of a transgene usually alters the gene expression patterns of the whole cell. The native genes, small RNA molecules (e.g., siRNA [small interfering RNA]), and different proteins in the GM plant cells may coordinate in unpredictable manners, resulting in either co-suppression, silencing, or overexpression of the transgene and certain native genes, leading to unpredictable effects on the organism's growth and reproduction. For instance, overexpression of a gene involved in pectin synthesis has no effect in tobacco but caused premature leaf shedding in apple trees (Atkinson et al. 2002). Golden Rice plants showed unexplained alterations in morphology, such as shorter stature, later flowering, and lesser panicle density than the non-GM cultivars (Datta et al. 2003).

"The problem is that currently there is no way to predict the resultant changes in protein synthesis" (Schubert 2002). For instance, retinoic acid (RA), retinol (vitamin A), and its derivatives are involved in some signaling events that control mammalian cell development (Gronemeyer and Miturski 2001). GM plants (e.g., Golden Rice) making vitamin A may also produce RA derivatives in the biochemical pathways of the human consumer. These derivatives would then act as agonists or antagonists in the organism's developmental pathways, causing direct toxicity or abnormal embryonic development.

Ecosystem Level

If the transgene products of a GM crop are toxic, it would necessarily kill off at least some organisms. Of course, Bt crops are intended to kill phytophagous insects. There is a growing body of experimental evidence that GM crops have unintended, deleterious effects on nontarget organisms (O'Callaghan et al.

2004). Bt toxin may have adverse effects on several insect taxa (Marvier et al. 2007). Bt toxin runoff from the farm into water bodies may have deleterious effects on various aquatic organisms (Rosi-Marshall et al. 2007).

Even when a GM crop is not designed to kill anything, increased herbicide application associated with GMHT crop cultivation leads to the elimination of broadleaved plants, butterflies, and birds (Bohan et al. 2005). The use of Roundup herbicide also kills off tadpoles of both aquatic and terrestrial frogs (Costa et al. 2008; Relyea 2005).

Suppression or elimination of a target or nontarget insect population—whether by chemical or biotechnological means—may trigger secondary extinction of several species in the agroecosystem, thereby disrupting the ecosystem functioning (Deb 2009), much of which is not yet fully understood. Furthermore, short-term elimination of pests may result in undesirable effects of pest outbreaks in the long term (Reilly and Elderd 2014).

Bt toxin resistance has been recorded in many insect populations (e.g., diamondback moth [Tabashnik and Carrière 2004; Zhao et al. 2000] and cotton bollworm [Morin et al. 2003]). Neither organic Bt spray nor Bt crops can control the resistant pests, which would compel farmers to apply more pesticides, driving cascades of ecological destruction.

Health Risks

A series of GM crops are being developed as panacea for nutritional security. GM "Golden Rice" fortified with β-carotene and iron is also promoted as the solution to undernutrition in the global South. However, GE cannot reduce vitamin A deficiency, unless (1) intestinal disease like diarrhea is absent and (2) the diet also contains triglycerols and zinc (Castenmiller and West 1998; Nutting et al. 2002). Clearly, micronutrient deficiency is a public health problem, requiring multiple approach, such as safe drinking water supply and access to food diversity. A wide range of food plant diversity in the South is known to be 10 to 200 times richer in β-carotene than is the Golden Rice. The leaves of *Amaranthus spinosus, Ipomoea aquatica,* Indian mustard, and taro yam tuber are examples (West and Poortvliet 2014), which prove investing in Golden Rice is unnecessary. There are traditional rice landraces (a local plant or animal species that has been improved by traditional agricultural methods) that are richer in iron than the iron-fortified GM rice so far developed (Anandan et al. 2011).

Besides, regular consumption of β-carotene and its derivatives may have adverse health effects. RA, derived from β-carotene, is biologically active at concentrations several orders of magnitude lower than retinol. Thus, excess RA or its derivatives are dangerous, particularly to infants and during pregnancy (Schubert 2008).

Transgenic endotoxins are manufactured in the GM plant, wherever the genes are expressed, round the clock. The long-term health effects of transgenic endotoxins are yet unknown, because there has been no long-term rigorous experiment with GM foods. The biotech corporations do not allow any publication of adverse effects of their proprietary crops ("Do Seed Companies Control GM Crop Research?" 2009).

A published study that demonstrated serious health effects on rats was conducted by Séralini et al. (2012), whose paper was nevertheless retracted a year later by a newly appointed associate editor of the journal, who is an ex-Monsanto employee ("Open Letter on Retraction and Pledge to Boycott Elsevier" 2013).

In the absence of conclusive evidence, the rational option is to adopt the precautionary principle (PP) until some future experiments prove the GM foods, case by case, to be safe beyond doubt.

The Precautionary Principle

When introducing a new drug, vaccine, or food product, it is a universal norm to follow the PP, which aims to reduce the Type II error in experiments. Type I error consists of rejecting the null hypothesis ("no effect") when it is actually true. Type

II error is the error of accepting the null hypothesis when it is actually false. Either error may result from sampling error, faulty observation, or spurious analyses. Now suppose we erroneously accept the null hypothesis of "no harm from a GM food" when it is actually harmful. The consequence would be dangerous— consumers who will eat the food may fall sick, even die. By the time more rigorous experiments may prove the null hypothesis to be false, it will be too late. This is exactly what happened in the late 1980s with L-tryptophan food supplements (Mayeno and Gleicha 1994) and in the early 1990s with GM soya containing a gene from Brazil nut (Nordlee et al. 1996).

Conversely, if we commit Type I error, and stop eating the GM food until future experiments prove the null hypothesis to be correct, we will have, at worst, postponed the benefits of eating the food. It is therefore safer to reduce Type II error than Type I error and delay accepting the null hypothesis until it is conclusively proven to be true.

Conclusions

There is a growing body of evidence of unforeseen behavior of transgenes in GMOs and their unpredictable impacts on the environment and human health. Therefore, application of the PP to GE research is imperative before the commercial release of GM crops. Putative nutritional benefits from GM foods are unrealistic and unlikely to outweigh the risks. Besides, micronutrient contents in GM food crops, developed to fight nutrient deficits, are far less than in many food plants, which render the costly technology unnecessary.

References

Anandan, A., et al. 2011. "Genotypic Variation and Relationships between Quality Traits and Trace Elements in Traditional and Improved Rice (*Oryza sativa L.*) Genotypes." *Journal of Food Science* 76(4): H122–H130.

Atkinson, Ross G., et al. 2002. "Overexpression of Polygalacturonase in Transgenic Apple Trees Leads to a Range of Novel Phenotypes Involving Changes in Cell Adhesion." *Plant Physiology* 129(1): 122–133.

Bohan, David A., et al. 2005. "Effects on Weed and Invertebrate Abundance and Diversity of Herbicide Management in Genetically Modified Herbicide-Tolerant Winter-Sown Oilseed Rape." *Proceedings of the Royal Society: Biological Sciences* 272(1562): 463–474.

Castenmiller, J. J., and C. E. West. 1998. "Bioavailability and Bioconversion of Carotenoids." *Annual Review of Nutrition* 18: 19–38.

Costa, M. J., et al. 2008. "Oxidative Stress Biomarkers and Heart Function in Bullfrog Tadpoles Exposed to Roundup Original." *Ecotoxicology* 17(3): 153–163.

Datta, Karabi, et al. 2003. "Bioengineered 'Golden' Indica Rice Cultivars with ß-carotene Metabolism in the Endosperm with Hygromycin and Mannose Selection Systems." *Plant Biotechnology Journal* 1(2): 81–90.

de Sadeleer, Nicolas, ed. *Implementing the Precautionary Principle: Approach from the Nordic Countries, EU and USA.* London: Routledge, 2012.

Deb, Debal. 2009. "Biodiversity and Complexity of Rice Food Webs: An Empirical Assessment." *The Open Ecology Journal* 2: 112–129.

"Do Seed Companies Control GM Crop Research?" 2009. *Scientific American.* http://www.scientificamerican.com/article/do-seed-companies-control-gm-crop-research/. Accessed on May 8, 2014.

Gronemeyer, H., and R. Miturski. 2001. "Molecular Mechanisms of Retinoid Action." *Cell & Molecular Biology Letters* 6(1): 3–52.

Marvier, Michelle, et al. 2007. "A Meta-Analysis of Effects of Bt Cotton and Maize on Nontarget Invertebrates." *Science* 316(5830): 1475–1477.

Mayeno, A. N., and Gerald J. Gleicha. 1994. "Eosinophilia-Myalgia Syndrome and Tryptophan Production: A Cautionary Tale." *Trends in Biotechnology* 12(9): 346–352.

Meyer, Peter. 1988. "Stabilities and Instabilities of Transgene Expression" In Keith Lindsey, ed. *Transgenic Plant Research*, 263–277. London: Harwood.

Morin, Shai, et al. 2003. "Three Cadherin Alleles Associated with Resistance to Bacillus Thuringiensis in Pink Bollworm." *Proceedings of the National Academy of Sciences of the United States of America* 100(9): 5004–5009.

Nakai, Yusuke, et al. 2013. "Overexpression of VOZ2 Confers Biotic Stress Tolerance but Decreases Abiotic Stress Resistance in Arabidopsis." *Plant Signaling and Behavior* 8 (3): e23358.

Nordlee, J. A., et al. 1996. "Identification of a Brazil-Nut Allergen in Transgenic Soybeans." *New England Journal of Medicine* 334(11): 688–692.

Nutting, D. F., et al. 2002. "Nutrient Absorption." *Current Opinion in Gastroenterology* 18(2): 168–175.

O'Callaghan, M., et al. 2004. "Effects of Plants Genetically Modified for Insect Resistance on Nontarget Organisms." *Annual Review of Entomology* 50: 271–292.

"Open Letter on Retraction and Pledge to Boycott Elsevier." 2013. http://www.i-sis.org.uk/Open_letter_to_FCT_and _Elsevier.php. Accessed on March 20, 2014.

Qin, H., Y. Dong, and A. G. von Arnim. 2003. "Epigenetic Interactions between Arabidopsis Transgenes: Characterization in Light of Transgene Integration Sites." *Plant Molecular Biology* 52: 217–231.

Reilly, James R., and Bret D. Elderd. 2014. "Effects of Biological Control on Long-Term Population Dynamics: Identifying Unexpected Outcomes." *Journal of Applied Ecology* 51(1): 90–101.

Relyea, Rick A. 2005. "The Lethal Impact of Roundup on Aquatic and Terrestrial Amphibians." *Ecological Applications* 15(4): 1118–1124.

Rosi-Marshall, E. J., et al. 2007. "Toxins in Transgenic Crop Byproducts May Affect Headwater Stream Ecosystems." *Proceedings of the National Academy of Sciences of the United States of America* 104(41): 16204–16208.

Sahal, Suman, and Shakeelur Rahman. 2003. "Mahyco–Monsanto's Bt Cotton Fails to Perform." *Current Science* 85 (4): 426.

Saxena, Deepak, et al. 2004. "Larvicidal Cry Proteins from *Bacillus thuringiensis* Are Released in Root Exudates of Transgenic *B. thuringiensis* Corn, Potato, and Rice but Not of *B. thuringiensis* Canola, Cotton, and Tobacco." *Plant Physiology and Biochemistry* 42(5): 383–387.

Scheel, Dierk. 2002. "Signal Transduction Elements." In Kirsi-Marja Oksman-Caldentey and W. H. Barz, eds. *Plant Biotechnology and Transgenic Plants*, 363–376. New York: M. Dekker.

Schubert, D. 2002. "A Different Perspective on GM Food." *Nature Biotechnology* 20(10): 969.

Schubert, D. R. 2008. "The Problem with Nutritionally Enhanced Plants." *Journal of Medicinal Food* 11(4): 601–605.

Séralini, G. E., et al. 2012. "Long Term Toxicity of a Roundup Herbicide and a Roundup-Tolerant Genetically Modified Maize." *Food and Chemical Toxicology* 50(11): 4221–4231.

Tabashnik, Bruce E., and Yves Carrière. 2004. "Bt Transgenic Crops Do Not Have Favorable Effects on Resistant Insects." *Journal of Insect Science* 4(4): 1–3.

West, C. E., and E. J. Poortvliet. "The Carotenoid Content of Foods with Special Reference to Developing Countries." International Science and Technology Institute, Inc. http://pdf.usaid.gov/pdf_docs/PNABR428.pdf. Accessed on March 20, 2014.

Zhao, J. Z., et al. 2000. Development and Characterization of Diamondback Moth Resistance to Transgenic Broccoli Expressing High Levels of Cry1c. *Applied Environmental Microbiology* 66(9): 3784–3789.

Debal Deb is chair of the Centre for Interdisciplinary Studies, Barrackpore, India.

The U.S. Government Should Not Require Genetically Modified Food Labels: Phill Jones

In the United States, the Food and Drug Administration (FDA) has the authority to ensure the safety and wholesomeness of most foods. Over 20 years ago, the FDA was asked to consider if foods produced from genetically modified (GM) crops should be required to display special labeling to reveal that fact to consumers. The FDA's authority comes from the Federal Food, Drug, and Cosmetic Act, and according to the act, the FDA can only require information on a label that is accurate and material. In a 1992 policy statement, the FDA said that "the agency does not believe that the method of development of a new plant variety (including the use of new techniques including recombinant DNA techniques) is normally material information . . . and would not usually be required to be disclosed in labeling for the food."

The FDA's announcement that the agency would not require GM food labels sparked protests. Yet activists seem to overlook that mandatory GM food labeling is incompatible with the FDA's regulation system. The FDA uses a science-based approach to evaluate the safety of foods produced from new plants. FDA scientists focus on the characteristics of food and its components rather than the fact that a new method (e.g., genetic engineering) was used at some point to produce the food. Mandatory GM labeling would force a shift in the FDA's approach from science-based regulation to a regulatory system based in political and social criteria, such as consumer curiosity.

Nevertheless, GM food label campaigners continue to promote a labeling requirement, using flawed justifications.

Mandatory Genetically Modified Food Labels Would Incorrectly Indicate a Risk

Advocates for GM food labeling claim that labels would enable consumers to avoid health risks probably associated with GM foods. Mandatory labeling would validate this idea of a health risk, an idea discredited by many scientific and medical organizations. During 2012, for example, the Board of Directors of the American Association for the Advancement of Science commented on efforts to require labels for foods produced from GM crops. "These efforts are not driven by evidence that GM foods are actually dangerous," the board said. "Indeed, the science is quite clear: crop improvement by the modern molecular techniques of biotechnology is safe" (American Association for the Advancement of Science 2013). Officials of the FDA, the American Medical Association, the U.S. National Research Council, the World Health Organization, and the European Union also have stated that GM foods do not present unique risks.

According to the FDA, foods developed by genetic engineering do not create greater safety concerns than foods developed by traditional plant breeding. This is a point often overlooked by advocates of GM food labeling: Humans have genetically modified agricultural plants for thousands of years using conventional plant breeding techniques.

Mandatory Genetically Modified Food Labels Would Increase the Cost of Food

Promoters of mandatory labeling argue that the cost of GM food labels would be small—just a matter of adding information to existing food labels. This is incorrect.

During 2012, Northbridge Environmental Management Consultants, a private research company, investigated possible consequences of California's Genetically Engineered Foods Mandatory Labeling Initiative. After analyzing experiences with GM labeling in other parts of the world and consulting with business experts, Northbridge concluded that food companies would comply with a GM labeling law by substituting other ingredients for GM ingredients in their products. "This means that companies would change the way in which they source ingredients or manufacture their products," Northbridge stated, "in order to avoid labeling their products with a vague and potentially frightening warning that conveys little meaningful information."

In this scenario, food companies would face the costs of manufacturing products that do not contain GM ingredients. These costs arise from the need to verify the absence of GM ingredients by tracking food components starting with companies that sell seeds and continuing to farmers, grain storage companies, transport firms, food processors, and food product distributors. In addition, conventional (non-GM) crops can require more pesticides, herbicides, and water, which also increase cost. Northbridge estimated that a GM food labeling law would cost a Californian household at least an additional $350 to $400 per year (Northbridge Environmental Management Consultants 2012). Others have estimated the cost of mandatory GM food labeling at 10 percent of a person's food bill.

Consumer Choice Does Not Justify Mandatory Genetically Modified Food Labeling

Mandatory labeling advocates often urge that consumers have the right to know. The most important point about the "right to know" is that it does not exist. Theoretically, the FDA could require GM labels to satisfy consumer curiosity. However, the FDA has stated that the agency does not have the authority to mandate labeling based solely on a consumer's right to know the method of food production if the agency considers the final food product to be safe.

Consumers have the right to choose food products that do not have ingredients from GM plants. Today, anyone who wants to avoid GM ingredients can purchase food products certified as "organic." In addition, the FDA wrote guidelines for companies that want to voluntarily label their food products to inform consumers that they do not use ingredients produced using biotechnology.

Mandatory GM food labeling would actually reduce consumer choice. During the late 1990s, the European Union required GM food labels based on perceived consumer demand. Soon, retailers refused to sell products with the labels, fearing that they would lose customers. GM food products almost disappeared from European markets. If the FDA required GM labels, this would lead to a similar decreased choice for U.S. consumers.

According to law professors Gary E. Marchant and Guy A. Cardineau (2013), this outcome represents the true goal of mandatory GM food labeling campaigns. "[T]he organizers and funders of the GM labeling campaigns have developed a strategy to leverage GM labeling to eliminate GM crops from the United States," they wrote. "It is a campaign funded almost entirely by the organic food industry, which realizes its future growth is limited by the strong preference for GM crops by farmers."

References

American Association for the Advancement of Science. 2013. "Statement by the AAAS Board of Directors on Labeling of Genetically Modified Foods." http://www.aaas.org/news/releases/2012/media/AAAS_GM_statement.pdf. Accessed on October 15, 2013.

Food and Drug Administration. 1992. "Foods Derived from New Plant Varieties." Federal Register 57: 22984–23005.

Marchant, G. E., and G. A. Cardineau. 2013. "The Labeling Debate in the United States." GM Crops and Food 4(3): 126–134. http://www.ncbi.nlm.nih.gov/pubmed/23982076. Accessed on October 15, 2013.

Northbridge Environmental Management Consultants. 2012. "The Genetically Engineered Foods Mandatory Labeling Initiative: Overview of Anticipated Impacts and Estimated Costs to Consumers." http://www.noprop37.com/files/Prop.-37-Will-Raise-Grocery-Bills-400-Annually.pdf. Accessed on October 15, 2013.

Phill Jones earned a PhD in physiology/pharmacology and a JD. He worked 10 years as a patent attorney, specializing in biological, chemical, and medical inventions. As a freelance writer, he writes articles and books in the areas of general science, agbiotech, forensic science, medicine, and history.

Health Problems Linked to Genetically Modified Crops: Rashmi Nemade

Humans have been genetically altering foods and crops for millennia from simple crossbreeding and crude irradiation or chemical mutagenesis to modern laboratory genetic modification techniques. At the present time, the impact of simply altering the genetic makeup of a plant does not seem harmful in and of itself, but very little research has been done on the long-term effects on humans.

What we do know is that there are some very serious problems that genetically modified foods (GMFs) are already causing on a large scale. Humans have never been able to genetically modify plants as rapidly and as widely as is currently being done. In fact, an approved GMF can be grown on millions of acres within just a few years. Whole fields (hectares) of the major foods we eat or wear are now genetically modified (wheat, corn, rice, soybean, and cotton). According to the United States Department of Agriculture's (USDA) Economic Research Service (ERS), biotechnology plantings as a percentage of total crop plantings in the United States in 2013 were about 90 percent for corn, 90 percent for cotton, and 93 percent for soybeans ("Genetically Engineered Varieties of Corn, Upland Cotton, and Soybeans, by State and for the Unites States, 2000–13" 2013).

Widespread GMFs allow us more freedom in how we grow our food. This means that we can now use more herbicides (poisons to kill weed) and pesticides (poisons to kill insect) that are harmful to not only the environment but human health as well.

Herbicides, Pesticides (human-cides?)

Weeds and insects are a nuisance in any garden or farm; they must be watched and pulled, or they will take over the garden or farm. Today, in industrial operations, most of our crops carry an herbicide-resistance gene, which allow farmers to spray their fields widely with heavy amounts of herbicides to control the weeds. As these herbicides kill all plants (good and bad), the plants with the resistance gene stay alive while all other plant matter dies. Now that the soil is contaminated and depleted of its natural plant matter—microorganisms and smaller plants that help crops grow—we need more fertilizer, yet another chemical to boost our food production. After some time, weeds begin to modify their genome too—a natural process of evolution whereby these weeds adapt to their environment; over time, the weeds become resistant to the herbicides. Currently, agriculture is battling an unexpected outcome of this way of farming—superweeds—so stronger and stronger herbicides are needed to grow our food.

The same is true of insects and pesticides. Insects are becoming resistant to insecticide genes in genetically modified plants, as well as the sprayed pesticides. The methods GMF companies use to pest-proof their crops are also killing beneficial bugs, such as bees and butterflies. Spraying herbicides, pesticides, and fertilizers have another outcome—they drift. They can drift for thousands of miles and impact crops and people in faraway places.

Initially, GMFs sound like a revolution with the promise of preventing a world food crisis because of its ability to grow more crops in less space with much more speed, but once the pests and weeds develop immunity, farmers have little choice except to spray ever-increasing amounts of herbicides and pesticides, effectively raising chemical pollution levels. Slowly these chemical pollution levels will start to destroy our environment and make us sick.

In fact, as there is no national registry for herbicides and pesticides in the United States, farmers are not required to report chemical releases. Thus, we have no idea how many tons of chemicals are used on, for example, the 59 million acres of U.S. wheat. What we do know is that in counties where wheat is grown, there are significantly lower rates of conception, higher rates of birth defects, cognitive delays, and autism (Steingraber 2011, 92–93).

Our foods now contain, for the first time in humanity's history, unprecedented quantities of chemicals. And the health impacts are not theoretical, yet to be seen, or suspected; they are proven in doctor's offices, clinics, hospitals, health records, and laboratory reports all over the country. The rising rates of diabetes, obesity, digestive disorders, inflammatory bowel disease, colitis, autism spectrum disorders (ASD), attention deficit disorders (ADD), autoimmune diseases, sexual dysfunction, sterility, asthma, cancers, and so on are all modern phenomena, which have soared with the use of GMFs (Mercola 2012).

Around the world, countries are watching this issue unfold and explode in the United States. Despite the promises of higher food yields, countries in Asian and Africa where millions of people go hungry and have widespread malnutrition are refusing to import GMFs (Freedman 2013, 82). Numerous countries—including China and the European Union—require labeling of genetically engineered foods, but the United States (the largest producer of GM crops) still has no such laws (several states are considering such bills). This makes it incredibly difficult for people to choose whether or not they want to consume GMFs, as many folks are not even aware when they are eating a GM product. As so much of our corn and soy is genetically modified, GMFs are in just about every prepackaged food. Thus, there is a good chance Americans are eating a lot more GMOs than they realized.

As consumers our best defense is education that comes through labeling, so that we can make our own choices. The reality is that we do not need to wait for research, but we already know the health impacts from using chemicals on our foods, so GMFs are already causing enough trouble to prove they are not worth our while.

References

Freedman, David H. 2013. "Are Engineered Foods Evil?" Scientific American 309(3): 80–85.

"Genetically Engineered Varieties of Corn, Upland Cotton, and Soybeans, by State and for the Unites States, 2000–13." 2013. USDA Economic Research Service. http://www.ers .usda.gov/data-products/adoption-of-genetically-engineered

-crops-in-the-us.aspx#.Ug0OJZLCZ8F. Accessed on August 15, 2013.

Mercola, Joseph. 2012. "Decade-Long Feeding Study Reveals Significant Health Hazards of Genetically Engineered Foods." http://articles.mercola.com/sites/articles/archive/2012/08/07/genetically-engineered-foods-hazards.aspx#_edn1. Accessed on May 8, 2014.

Steingraber, Sandra. 2011. *Raising Elijah: Protecting Our Children in an Age of Environmental Crisis.* Philadelphia: Da Capo Press.

Rashmi Nemade is passionate about the environment and its impact on food safety and health. She is an advocate for education on these topics for a healthier and improved future. She holds a PhD in molecular genetics and is a freelance scientist-writer and consultant.

Genetically Modified Organisms: Tony Owen

Growing up, I was taught "you are what you eat," and I took it to heart, always preferring whole grains and plenty of fruits and vegetables. In the late sixties1960s to late 1970s, I had an organic market garden, and my three daughters got their treats in the rows of peas to the extent that we never had enough for our customers. The markets we sold to were unaware of "organic" and were simply pleased to get a source of local produce, which sold well. One time the store manager pointed to a tiny slug on a bunch of handsome Swiss chard. I popped it in my mouth and said, "There's no poison on the leaf!" He was astonished and my girls said, "Eeeww!" when I told the story at the dinner table, and I could never get them to ignore the occasional aphid on their broccoli. I do believe their good health (they are now in their 40s) originates in what food they grew up on. Today, every mouthful of food I eat is organic, not because I reject GMOs but because I support the soil conservation and diversity of pollinators associated with organic cultivation.

I had the privilege, at a meeting of organic farmers in San Francisco, of making the motion to create a California Certified Organic Farmers Association, and the motion was carried. Later, when the U.S. Department of Agriculture solicited input as to what could be labeled organic, I voted to exclude GMOs, as I believed that was what my customers would expect, not because I had any reservations about the technology.

I believe that opposition to GMOs is a political point of view rather like climate-change skepticism and is not based on science. GM crops, like apples and oranges, bear no resemblance to one another and have in common only the technology by which they were developed. All modern crops have been genetically modified from primitive precursors, and the non-GMO sort simply used crossbreeding as molecular biology was unknown. Monsanto has made much opposition by its heavy-handed efforts to protect its intellectual property. I hope this does not lead to throwing out the technological baby with the anticorporate bath water. All present crops were developed to appeal to farmers. Perhaps things would have been different had consumers been the target as with high vitamin and mineral content coupled with legacy flavor. If the clamor for GM labeling succeeds, it might take off. You could have a choice between a tomato bred for shipping and handling and one with the high vitamin C content of a guava and the flavor of the old timers.

Most research is carried out around the world to develop disease resistance in subsistence crops like cassava. Recently, a Golden Rice crop in the Philippines was vandalized by those who share the same self-righteous motivation as those who bomb abortion clinics. Sea levels are rising, and only genetic engineering can deliver crops that can withstand the occasional drenching with salt water. Growers in many parts of the world (think Florida or Bangladesh) will face hazards like these, and a few genes from salt marsh hay may save their crops. The first major intersection of genetic engineering and foodstuffs occurred in 1987 with the first tests of a modified version of the bacterium Pseudomonas syringae on strawberry fields in California. The bacterium, which commonly lives on the surface of crops, normally produces a protein that allows ice to more easily begin crystallizing, causing damage to the host plant. However, the strain of P. syringae used in the experiment had been engineered without the gene needed to produce the protein in hopes of reducing frost-induced crop loss. Though the data looked positive following the trial, they could not be fully trusted due to environmental activists destroying some of the test crops in protest of the experiment.

In many parts of the world, fears abound over potential health problems and the prospect of environmental catastrophe, all stemming from the production and consumption of GM foods. Although the paranoia is gradually decreasing, a lot of misinformation is still thrown about regarding genetic engineering and GM foods.

GM foods have been consumed by millions with no documented health effects. A suggestion that a protein in StarLink corn caused an allergic reaction in 28 people eating taco shells made partly from the corn was discredited by the U.S. Centers for Disease Control and Prevention (CDC) when it was pointed out that the protein would have been completely denatured in the high temperature used in cooking the shells and their blood contained no trace of the protein in question.

Studies of pest resistance and weeds acquiring herbicide resistance as has occurred in conventional crops is also present in GMOs. It is a natural effect of evolution, and a quick development of new strains of pest resistance in crops can easily be met with genetic engineering while herbicide resistance in weeds is amenable with crop rotation and other cultivation techniques.

The real promise in my view is the creation of new varieties of crops such as perennial grains that require little or no tillage and fix their own nitrogen like legumes. The contamination of ground water, streams, lakes, and even the ocean itself with the nitrate runoff from farms is a huge problem that affects everything from human health to the biodiversity of our coastal areas where dead zones occur. The rising sea level, as mentioned, will also put novel demands on food production where novel solutions are the only practical response.

In a world where millions of people believe that the world is only 6,000 years old or that humans are not the generator of global warming, skepticism of the scientific consensus is so common as to adversely affect our education and indeed our very future. It is a shame that children can graduate from high school and not be aware of, or even disbelieve, facts that have a direct and very important bearing on their futures.

Closely examined, objections to GMOs do not withstand rigorous scientific scrutiny, and the use of this very valuable technology is imperative in the future we all share.

Tony Owen is 77 years old and was born in Kahuku, Oahu, Hawaii, in October 1936. He has three daughters and four granddaughters. He is currently involved in 3D modeling and animation.

Genetically Modified Foods in Developing Countries: Santosh Pandey

Sustainable agriculture and food security are critical foundations that underpin human society. Sustainable agriculture refers to the ability of a farm to produce crops indefinitely and profitably, without damaging the ecosystem. As agriculture by its very nature is one of the most expensive and environmentally harmful practices carried out by humans, the need to balance profitability and environmental stewardship is a significant economic and scientific challenge. The use of transgenic plants offers great promise for the integration of improved varieties into traditional cropping systems because improved plant lines can be generated quickly and with relative precision once suitable genes for transfer have been identified (Ferry and Gatehouse 2009).

Today, the majority of GMO crops are grown in developed countries and address the needs of commercial farmers. However, farmers in developing countries are increasingly beginning to adopt GMO crops. Crop losses from insects and other pests can be staggering, resulting in devastating financial loss for farmers and starvation in developing countries. The use of pesticides in food causes various harmful health effects. GMO foods promise to meet the needs of the developing countries in a number of ways. GMO crops could address these problems, where other breeding techniques have failed. Pest resistance, disease resistance, as well as cold, drought, herbicide, and salinity tolerance of the GMO crops could be a magic wand that can achieve sustainable agriculture and free the developing world from poverty, hunger, and malnutrition. Similarly, plants could be genetically modified to produce vaccines or other medicines. Potatoes have been modified to produce edible vaccines against *Escherichia* coli bacteria that cause diarrhea. This would allow cheap and easy distribution of the vaccine ("The Use of Genetically Modified Crops in Developing Countries").

Not all GMO plants are grown as crops. Plants such as poplar trees have been genetically engineered to clean up heavy metal pollution from contaminated soil (Whitman 2000). Scientists now can not only mix genes from two different plants but also mix a gene of a plant with the gene of an animal. It will not be surprising if scientists develop elephant-sized chickens or pumpkin-sized tomatoes. Cow milk has a lot of nutrients, but it lacks the antibiotic elements found in human milk. The scientists are now developing a new breed of cows whose milk contains the antibiotic components found in human milk. Malnutrition is common in Third World countries, where impoverished peoples rely on a single crop such as rice for the main staple of their diet. However, rice does not contain adequate amounts of all necessary nutrients to prevent malnutrition. If rice could be genetically engineered to contain additional vitamins and minerals, micronutrient deficiencies could be alleviated (Bimba 2013).

GMO technology is not free from controversies. The technology demands a rigorous control and meticulous use of the scientific methods for obtaining new breeds. Even a slight mistake in the experiment might result in the nightmarish incidents. The criticism of agribusiness in developing countries is for pursuing profit without concern for potential hazards, and the criticism of governments is for failing to exercise adequate regulatory oversight. Those who had the most to gain, multinational biotech companies, propounded a very convincing message through well-funded mass media that biotechnology was the miracle that would solve world famine, reduce reliance on pesticides, or cure the diseases of humankind (Smith 2003).

Concerns about GMO foods in developing countries include environmental hazards, human health risks, and economic concerns. The major environmental concern about GMOs is the reduced effectiveness of pesticides and different unintended harm to other organisms. Also genetically engineered crops can cross-pollinate with certain forms of weeds, resulting in "super weeds" that are herbicide resistant or that, over time, certain species of insects will also become resistant to pesticides (Pandey 2014). The potential cross-pollination of GM seeds onto non-GM crops is also a concern to farmers, particularly those farmers who certify their crops as non-GM or organic crops. The farmers of many developing countries have the practice of saving seed between harvests rather than buying new seed each year. It is suggested that the introduction of GM crops will force farmers to buy seed. Some people feel that the effects of GM crops on human health (bioethics) are not yet adequately understood. Different allergenic symptoms have been observed as a result of the consumption of some GM foods. As genes make proteins, and proteins are potential allergens, one cannot exclude the possibility that genetic engineering of foods may introduce proteins into foods that will cause sensitivities and allergic reactions in some portion of the population (Abraham 2009).

In developing countries, there is also an ethical obligation to explore the potential of GMO crops responsibly. The impact of human action on nonhuman animals is controversial because some people deny that animals can be harmed at all. In his article "Ethical Perspectives on Food Biotechnology," Michigan State University ethicist Paul B. Thompson suggested that agricultural biotechnology has become caught up in several long-standing moral and political debates, as well as having introduced a few new wrinkles on its own (Brunk and Coward 2009).

Yields of almost all crops are significantly lower in developing countries than developed countries. Most people believe that GMO foods will eliminate the need for political, social, or economic change or that they will simply "feed the developing world." Others argue that genetic modification is "unnatural," and the use of organic farming methods, integrated pest management, and mixed cropping would be a more appropriate solution than the use of GM technology. GMO foods have the potential to solve hunger and malnutrition problems and to help protect and preserve the environment by increasing yield and reducing reliance upon chemical pesticides and herbicides. Conversely, acceptance of this technology without paying attention to the legal conditions may distress the economy of poor farmers in developing countries. To solve this, scientists are drafting guidelines on the experiment and their risks so far as humans are concerned. International and regional treaties, conventions, and protocols are being drafted to regulate the production of GM foods and seeds.

References

Abraham, Samuel. 2009. "Genetics and Genetically Modified Organisms." In Conrad Brunk and Harold Coward, eds. *Acceptable Genes? Religious Traditions and Genetically Modified Foods,* 19–37. Albany: SUNY Press.

Bimba, D. H. 2013. Main Agenda. Face to Face. 13. Nepal Forum of Environmental Journalists.

Brunk, Conrad, and Harold Coward, eds. 2009. *Acceptable Genes? Religious Traditions and Genetically Modified Foods.* Albany: SUNY Press.

Ferry, Natalie, and Angharad M. R. Gatehouse, eds. 2009. *Environmental Impacts of Genetically Modified Crops.* Oxfordshire, England: CAB International.

Pandey, Santosh. 2014. "The Lesser Evil." República. http://www.myrepublica.com/portal/index.php? action=news_details&news_id=69341. Accessed on March 13, 2014.

Smith, Jeffrey M. 2003. *Seeds of Deception: Exposing Industry and Government Lies about the Safety of the Genetically Engineered Foods You're Eating.* Fairfield, IA: Yes Books.

Thompson, Paul B. 2009. "Ethical Perspectives on Food Biotechnology." In Conrad Brunk and Harold Coward, eds. *Acceptable Genes? Religious Traditions and Genetically Modified Foods,* 39–61. Albany: SUNY Press.

"The Use of Genetically Modified Crops in Developing Countries." Nuffield Council on Bioethics. http://www .nuffieldbioethics.org/sites/default/files/GM%20Crops %20Discussion%20Paper%202004.pdf. Accessed on March 13, 2014.

Whitman, Deborah B. 2000. "Genetically Modified Foods: Harmful or Helpful?" ProQuest. http://www.csa.com/ discoveryguides/gmfood/overview.php. Accessed on March 13, 2014.

Santosh Pandey is a food journalist and student of food technology at the Central Campus of Technology, Tribhuvan University, Dharan, Nepal.

Genetically Modified Crops in Africa: Fear of the Unknown?: Elizabeth Shoo

According to estimates from the United Nations, 223 million people in sub-Saharan Africa suffer from malnutrition. One of the causes is long periods of drought, which lead to poor harvests of staple foods such as maize and millet. For years, African politicians have called for the introduction of genetically modified (GM) plants as a means to combat the decline in yields. Their hope is that drought- and pest-resistant crops will benefit African small-scale farmers who make up the majority of the population. At an African Agriculture Conference in 2012, 24 African countries said they were in favor of allowing the use of GM crops.

However, just like everywhere else in the world, there is a heated debate on whether GM crops should be grown in Africa, a decision that each country has to make on its own.

So far, the commercial use of genetically engineered seeds is permitted only in South Africa, Egypt, Sudan, and Burkina Faso. South Africa was the first country to introduce commercially grown GM crops in 1997 and is now one of the top producers of GM maize, soybeans, and cottonseed oil.

Not only politicians but also researches have shown their support for GMOs. In its annual Africa Agriculture Status Report of 2013, the Kenyan-based Alliance for a Green Revolution in Africa (AGRA) urged African countries to be more open toward GM crops. "There is growing public opposition to GM crops in Africa that is best described as a fear of the unknown," the report states ("Africa Agriculture Status Report" 2013). In an effort to take away this fear from farmers and policy makers in Africa, AGRA researchers insist that GMOs are safe. "It is important to point out that GM crops have been subject to more testing worldwide than any other new crops, and have been declared as safe as conventionally bred crops by scientific and food safety authorities worldwide."

The opinion that African countries should not completely resist the introduction of GM food is shared by Calestous Juma, professor of the Practice of International Development at Harvard University.

"Too often the biotechnology decisions made in Africa are politically motivated and do not reflect the balance of scientific evidence," he points out. Therefore, he suggests that African countries should have presidential offices for science and technology, which would "allow African leaders to act strategically and analytically, adopting agricultural biotechnologies when and where it makes sense to do so" (Juma and Gordon 2014).

Arid regions above all would profit from GM seeds, Juma said. U.S. agriculture giant Monsanto has already developed drought-tolerant maize seeds, named Water Efficient Maize for Africa (WEMA). On its website, Monsanto advertises that WEMA could feed an additional 21 million people in Africa. The corn is being grown conventionally at the moment, but field tests for the GM version are underway in Mozambique, Tanzania, and Uganda. Monsanto already grows trial crops of GM cotton, sugar cane, tomatoes, and bananas in eight African countries, including Kenya, Tanzania, Mozambique, and Uganda. In South Africa, farmers can buy Monsanto's GM corn and cotton seeds and sow them on their fields. More than half of the corn planted there is the GM variety.

Even though South Africa started growing GM crops more than 15 years ago, there is still a large opposition toward these crops. Demonstrations against GM companies like Monsanto take place regularly, with farmers and activists wanting the companies' GM products to be banned from their country. The hesitation and resentment is present all over Africa. In 2012, various civil society organizations called out African governments to completely ban the growing, importing, and exporting of GMOs on the African continent. In their joint petition to ban GMOs, the civil society organizations clearly stated why they are against

GMOs. Their main concern is the safety of GM foods. They urge African governments to conduct independent tests. They are worried about the "patenting of life forms and privatization of agriculture, which has led to the dependence by farmers, rural communities and indigenous people on external private and monopolistic seeds suppliers." And they air their concern about the impact of industrial and GM based agriculture on biodiversity and climate change.

One of the prominent opponents of GMO is Million Belay, coordinator of the pan-African platform Alliance for Food Sovereignty in Africa (AFSA). AFSA promotes biodiversity and ecological land management in Africa and fights against the use of GM seeds. "By pushing just a few varieties of seed that need fertilizers and pesticides, agribusiness has eroded our indigenous crop diversity," he writes in an article for the Guardian, adding that seed variety is the solution to hunger and malnutrition. There is a danger of having just one or a few types of seeds, he adds. "If northern governments genuinely wish to help African agriculture, they should support the revival of seed-saving practices, to ensure that there is diversity in farmers' hands" ("GM Crops Won't Help African Farmers").

Even African governments are moving from policies that support seed variety to those that favor single seeds. The Council of Ministers of the Common Market for Eastern and Southern Africa (COMESA) in September 2013 approved controversial new seed trade regulations. According to the rules, only standardized, certified seeds may be sold among the 19 member states. The seeds are patented and must guarantee consistent results over a long period of time, ruling out further use of traditional seeds. Small farmers could no longer jointly collect seeds and sell the unpatented variety. The agreement would also pave the way for major agricultural companies that have GM seeds on offer. The COMESA members are free to decide, however, whether they want to introduce GM seeds.

The ruling has not yet gone into force, but when it does, many small farmers are bound to be affected. "Ownership would be transferred to companies, and that would actually mean the life of the people would be controlled by few interest groups and big companies like Monsanto," Belay warned.

Just three companies are responsible for more than 50 percent of the worldwide sale of seeds: Monsanto, Syngenta from Switzerland, and DuPont, another U.S. giant.

The debate on whether or not Africa should embrace GM technology will continue, and in the end, each country will decide for itself. Influences from Western powers will play a role. Even then, there are two equally probable outcomes: If African leaders look toward the United States, where GM foods are allowed, they might be in favor of them. On the other hand, if they take the European Union as an example, they could rule against GM crops because the European Union prohibits GM foods for human consumption.

References

"Africa Agriculture Status Report: Focus on Staple Crops." 2013. http://reliefweb.int/sites/reliefweb.int/files/resources/agrafinalaugust20akim.pdf. Accessed on February 9, 2014.

"GM Crops Won't Help African Farmers." http://www .theguardian.com/global-development/poverty-matters/ 2013/jun/24/gm-crops-african-farmers/print. Accessed on March 9, 2014.

Juma, Calestous, and Katherine Gordon. 2014. "Leap-Frogging in African Agriculture: The Case of Genetically Modified Crops." http://www.brookings.edu/~/media/ Research/Files/Reports/2014/foresight%20africa%202014/ 06%20foresight%20african%20agriculture%20juma %20gordon.pdf. Accessed on March 9, 2014.

Elizabeth Shoo is a Tanzanian journalist working for DW, Germany's international broadcaster. She is based in Bonn,

Germany, and mainly reports about political, social, and economic issues in Europe and Africa.

Accepting Genetically Modified Crops in India: Sweta

The Green Revolution of the 1960s has no doubt made India self-sufficient in the production of food grains. Introduction of high-yielding varieties of seeds and excessive use of chemical fertilizers were the major factors for this change. However, in the last few decades, the extensive use of chemical pesticides and fertilizers has led to increasing health hazards and depletion of overall soil quality. Now, there is a need for second green revolution in India. Different experts have different opinions on this topic. Some support organic farming, whereas others strongly feel that use of genetically modified (GM) crops can boost India's food production to a level of second green revolution. Here we are going to discuss about GM food.

GM or transgenic crops express foreign genes that confer resistance to viruses, insects, herbicides, or postharvest deterioration and accumulation of useful modified storage products. These advances form the basis of a chemical free and economically viable approach for pest and disease control.

One of the most hotly debated topics in India remains GM foods. No doubt these foods possess a lot of potential to enhance our food security. However, various concerns with direct relevance to our agricultural system have been raised. The conservative assumptions underlying regulations in India is that all GM crops are potentially hazardous, and the obstacles range from legal and regulatory hurdles, economic factors, and social concerns.

Let us start with 2012 when the Parliamentary Committee on Agriculture clearly asked the government of India to establish a bar on the production of Bt brinjal (a type of eggplant) and immediately stop all ongoing field trials. The reason for this request was that the committee was convinced that there are several better options to enhance food security and increase food production in India than the use of GM crops. A ban on transgenic crops was also recommended by the committee as many farmers, especially those in the Vidarbha region of Maharashtra, were not able to shift the cultivation of cotton from transgenic varieties to farmer-friendly and traditional varieties due to nonavailability of seeds. The expert panel had merely talked about the apprehensions and concerns that society at large has toward GM crops.

In 2013, the Parliamentary Standing Committee on Agriculture and Technical Expert Committee (TEC) of the Supreme Court submitted their reports related to deliberate concerns over GM crops. The recommendations of the TEC called for the following:

• A ban on all the field trials and commercial releases of GM crops until the "major gaps in the regulatory system" are addressed and there is more accurate information regarding the safety of using Bt genes in food crops.

• A ban on all herbicide-tolerant crops because manual weeding generates employment in small farms and is feasible in India.

• A ban on GM crops whose point of origin is India.

There was no difference in the TEC's recent report from the earlier one that had recommended a 10-year ban on Bt gene–based technology in all food crops.

In fact the truth is that with the widespread adoption of Bt cotton, a genetically engineered crop that contains a bacterial protein harmful to certain insects, India has boosted its cotton production to a level of 500 kilograms/hectare in just six years, which was not possible before. People should understand that the cotton plant is producing natural insecticides in its tissues reducing the use of pesticides in cotton fields. This proves that

GM crops are eco-friendly. Bt cotton is the only crop permitted in India so far that is commercially cultivated.

In a recent development, Jayanthi Natarajan, minister of state for environment and forests, said that the field trials of 20 GM crops have been approved by the Indian government. In fact the field trials of three GM crops—mustard, corn, and cotton—have been initiated after getting a no-objection certificate (NOC) from the state governments. Other crops are waiting for NOC from the respective state governments.

Recently, the union agriculture minister, Sharad Pawar, backing the use of transgenic crops said that GM crops are preferred by farmers as they produce higher yields than do traditional varieties, as well as are being more disease resistant.

Further, he added that he is against any ban on GM crops as they reduce the use of harmful chemicals in the field, maintaining the quality of soil as well as saving the hard-earned money of farmers. However, there are a lot of people in India who remain convinced that GM crops are not only unsafe for consumption but also inappropriate for an agricultural economy as Bt seeds are more expensive than normal seeds.

Genetically Modified Crops: Possible Risks

Two most important factors that attract farmers greatly toward GM crops are the following:

1. High yield: Yield cannot be increased magically by inserting a gene. There are several factors that control yield, such as soil, water, and crop management practices. So, GM crops may prove to be a costly distraction over many sustainable agroecological and non-GM methods.

2. Insect resistance: Use of GM crops reduces pesticide use, but this gain is short-lived. Over time, the target pest develops resistance, and secondary pests often increase. We can

see this in Bt cotton, where pink ballworm developed resistance in less than a decade and sucking pests increased.

In a developing country like India, there is a need to create awareness and spread genuine information regarding GM crops. Different people have different views, and confusion arises here. GM food is an important topic for farmers as well as for the public to understand. We need to be more transparent about its benefits and potential risks. GM foods should be tested extensively and exhaustively before their commercialization. The queries of people on safety of GM crops should be cleared by not only talking but also presenting the scientific data available about their safety.

The Indian government has been struggling with different views on GM food for the past decade, but now it seems to be showing more commitment over the commercialization and field trials of GM crops. It may have realized the importance of being up-to-date in terms of modern technological innovation for a country to compete at the global level. The biggest challenge for the Indian government now is to come up with a good regulatory system and better communication on GM food.

Sweta is a freelance writer based in Gurgaon, India. She has done postgraduate work in genetics and plant breeding at Banaras Hindu University, Varanasi, and has a research paper published in World Journal of Agricultural Sciences.

A Growing World Demands New Food Technology: Susan Young

Not so long from now, the planet will be home to 9 billion people. To get nutritious food on all our plates in an environmentally sustainable way, we may need to lean on genetically modified foods (GMFs).

The United Nations estimates that the number of people on Earth is going to grow by nearly one-third in the next 35 years

("Revised UN Estimates Put World Population at over 9 Billion by 2050" 2009). Most of that baby boom will take place in developing countries where rising incomes are likely to lead to even greater demand for food. The growing population will need the world to produce 70 percent more food than it does now ("How to Feed the World 2050: The Technology Challenge" 2009). This task will be made all the more difficult with the expected impacts of climate change. Scientists predict that in the coming decades, droughts will become more common (Dai 2013) and crop-destroying pests will spread to new areas of the planet (Bebber 2013).

The United Nations has called on technology to address the increased pressures on food production and points to genetic engineering as a tool to "transfer desired traits between plants more quickly and accurately than it is possible with conventional plant breeding" ("How to Feed the World 2050: The Technology Challenge" 2009).

GMO crops are already grown in the United States and abroad, and most Americans have been eating GMOs for decades as they are common in processed foods (Byrne 2010; "Recent Trends in GE Adoption" 2013; Phillips and Corkindale 2002). One of the GM crops already grown in the United States is a variety of corn that makes its own pesticide. The strain was created by splicing into the corn genome a copy of a gene from bacteria that kill certain insects. Scientists report that this "in-plant" resistance has helped farmers protect their crops and apply less insecticide than in years before the transgenic strain was available (Brookes and Barfoot 2010; Pilcher et al. 2002).

Genetic engineering may be able to help other crops resist damage and disease. Plant breeder and geneticist Walter De Jong thinks that genetic engineering could help potato farmers grow their crops with fewer pesticides than are needed to care for typical potato plants. As reported by science journalist Amy Maxmen (2013), De Jong hopes to help develop a GM potato that resists potato blight, the plant disease that caused the Irish famine of the mid-1800s so that less pesticide is needed.

Genetic engineering might even save our favorite breakfast drink, orange juice, while avoiding big increases in pesticide use. Citrus greening, a disease caused by a bacterium that can kill orange trees, has recently spread from Asia to the United States and Brazil, the world's largest producers of orange juice. Fighting that disease, which is carried by an insect called a psyllid, has led to sharp increases in pesticide use, reports Amy Harmon in the *New York Times*: "Growers in Florida did not like to talk about it, but the industry's tripling of pesticide applications to kill the bacteria-carrying psyllid was, while within legal limits, becoming expensive and worrisome" (2013).

Genetic engineering could also address the challenges of climate change, which includes more frequent droughts. Although researchers have been able to create drought-tolerant crops with conventional breeding methods, genetic engineering can be faster and more direct. "Trying to create drought-tolerant crops is not going to be easy to do," Kent Bradford, director of the Seed Biotechnology Center at the University of California, Davis, told the *Los Angeles Times* (Lopez 2012). "We certainly need all the tools [available] to do that, and that includes conventional breeding and adding transgenic traits."

GM seed and herbicide manufacturer Monsanto developed a drought-resistant variety of corn that became available to farmers in 2013. Of 250 farmers who tested the GM crop in dry and water-limited land in Kansas, 72 percent said they had increased production, according to the *Midwest Producer* (Anderson 2013).

GM crops could also help infants and children in developing countries get proper nutrition. One of the most famous genetically engineered crops is Golden Rice. This plant developed to prevent vitamin A deficiency in children for whom rice is a staple of their diet. The World Health Organization estimates that as many as 500,000 children become blind every year because of vitamin A deficiency ("Micronutrient Deficiencies"). Around half of these children will die within a year of becoming blind because they are more at risk for common childhood infections.

To try to address this issue, scientists genetically engineered rice plants to produce β-carotene, which human cells convert into vitamin A, in their rice grains (Paine et al. 2005; Ye et al. 2000). This change could not have been made by traditional breeding, say scientists (Beyer 2010). In tests where people ate the rice, scientists eventually showed that one serving of Golden Rice can provide around 60 percent of a child's daily needs of vitamin A (Tang et al. 2012).

Despite its potential benefits, some groups oppose any use of GM crops. In the summer of 2013, a plot of Golden Rice grown as part of another trial in the Philippines was vandalized by GMO protestors (McGrath 2013). Still, the Golden Rice trials continue, and supporters of Golden Rice expect it to be available in the Philippines by 2016 (France-Presse 2013).

Many people are concerned that GM crops are a danger to human health and the environment. There are conflicting studies, and introducing a new crop into the environment can have unforeseen consequences. For instance, although some research has shown that GM corn leads to less pesticide use, others have shown that the absence of the targeted insect can lead to an abundance of another pest (Lu et al. 2010).

The future may need GMOs, but we will also need to carefully introduce these organisms into the environment and people's diets. Although people have been consuming GM crops for decades with no known ill effect on health, we should prudently expand the use of genome editing tools to protect human health and the environment and to make sure that everyone has a full plate.

References

Anderson, T. 2013. "Test Plots Show Favorable Results with DroughtGard." Midwest Producer. http://www.midwest producer.com/news/crop/test-plots-show-favorable-results

-with-droughtgard/article_41bb9896-b292-11e2-8243
-001a4bcf887a.html. Accessed on November 15, 2013.

Bebber, D. P. 2013. "Crop Pests and Pathogens Move
Polewards in a Warming World." *Nature Climate Change* 3:
985–988.

Beyer, P. 2010. "Golden Rice and 'Golden' Crops for Human
Nutrition." *New Biotechnology* 25(5): 478–481.

Brookes, G., and P. Barfoot. 2010. "Global Impact of Biotech
Crops: Environmental Effects, 1996–2008." *AgBioForum*
13(1): 76–94.

Byrne, P. 2010. "Labeling of Genetically Engineered Foods."
http://www.ext.colostate.edu/pubs/foodnut/09371.html.
Accessed on November 15, 2013.

Dai, A. 2013. "Increasing Drought under Global Warming in
Observations and Models." *Nature Climate Change* 3: 52–58.

France-Presse, Ag. 2013. "Genetically Modified 'Golden Rice'
Coming to Philippines by 2016." The Raw Story. http://
www.rawstory.com/rs/2013/11/05/genetically-modified
-golden-rice-coming-to-philippines-by-2016/. Accessed on
November 15, 2013.

Harmon, A. 2013. "A Race to Save the Orange by Altering Its
DNA." *New York Times.* http://www.nytimes.com/2013/
07/28/science/a-race-to-save-the-orange-by-altering-its-dna
.html?_r=2&. Accessed on November 15, 2013.

"How to Feed the World 2050: The Technology Challenge."
2009. http://www.fao.org/fileadmin/templates/wsfs/docs/
Issues_papers/HLEF2050_Technology.pdf. Accessed on
November 15, 2013.

Lopez, R. 2012. "As Drought Hits Corn, Biotech Firms See
Lush Field in GMO Crops." *Los Angeles Times.* http://
articles.latimes.com/2012/sep/17/business/la-fi-drought
-corn-research-20120917. Accessed on November 15, 2013.

Lu, Y., et al. 2010. "Mirid Bug Outbreaks in Multiple Crops Correlated with Wide-Scale Adoption of Bt Cotton in China." *Science* 328(5982): 1151–1154.

Maxmen, A. 2013. "GMOs May Feed the World Using Fewer Pesticides." NOVA Next. http://www.pbs.org/wgbh/nova/next/nature/fewer-pesticides-farming-with-gmos/. Accessed on November 15, 2013.

McGrath, M. 2013. " 'Golden Rice' GM Trial Vandalised in the Philippines." BBC News. http://www.bbc.co.uk/news/science-environment-23632042. Accessed on November 15, 2013.

"Micronutrient Deficiencies." World Health Organization. http://www.who.int/nutrition/topics/vad/en/. Accessed on November 15, 2013.

Paine, J. A., et al. 2005. "Improving the Nutritional Value of Golden Rice through Increased Pro-vitamin A Content." *Nature Biotechnology* 23(4): 482–487.

Phillips, P. W. B., and D. Corkindale. 2002. "Marketing GM Foods: The Way Forward." *AgBioForum* 5(3): 113–121.

Pilcher, C. D., et al. 2002. "Biotechnology and the European Corn Borer: Measuring Historical Farmer Perceptions and Adoption of Transgenic Bt Corn as a Pest Management Strategy." *Journal of Economic Entomology* 95(5): 878–892.

"Recent Trends in GE Adoption." 2013. http://www.ers.usda .gov/data-products/adoption-of-genetically-engineered -crops-in-the-us/recent-trends-in-ge-adoption.aspx#.UoZN XBDQw4k. Accessed on November 15, 2013.

"Revised UN Estimates Put World Population at over 9 Billion by 2050." 2009. http://www.un.org/apps/news/story.asp? NewsID=30159&Cr=family#.UoYmaBDQw4k. Accessed on November 15, 2013.

Tang, G., et al. 2012. "ß-Carotene in Golden Rice Is as Good as ß-carotene in Oil at Providing Vitamin A to Children." *American Journal of Clinical Nutrition* 96(3): 658–664.

Ye, X., et al. 2000. "Engineering the Provitamin A (Beta-carotene) Biosynthetic Pathway into (Carotenoid-Free) Rice Endosperm." *Science* 287(5451): 303–305.

Susan Young is a science writer currently living in Boston, Massachusetts. She earned a PhD in molecular biology by studying the origin of animals.

171,645
Public Comments
Opposing the Approval of
Genetically Engineered Salmon

Introduction

One way of understanding more about the development of genetically modified foods throughout history and around the world is by learning about the lives and work of individuals and organizations that have been involved in that subject. This chapter provides brief biographical sketches of a number of important men and women in the field as well as organizational sketches of groups that have supported that research or worked for or against its implementation in everyday life.

American Academy of Environmental Medicine

6505 E. Central Ave., #296
Wichita, KS 67206
Phone: (316) 684-5500
Fax: (888) 411-1206
Email: administrator@aaemonline.org
URL: http://www.aaemonline.org/

Wenonah Hauter of Food and Water Watch carries a box containing public comments opposing the Food and Drug Administration (FDA) approval of genetically engineered salmon before speaking at an FDA veterinary medicine advisory committee hearing on modified salmon in Rockville, Maryland on September 20, 2010. (AP Photo/Charles Dharapak)

The American Academy of Environmental Medicine (AAEM) was founded in 1965 under the name of the Society for Human Ecology (SHE). The driving force behind the organization was Theron Randolph, a specialist in allergy and immunology. Randolph noted that a number of his patients appeared to be developing allergic symptoms as the result of exposure to a variety of synthetic products in the environment, such as cosmetics, plastics, automotive fuels, exhaust fumes, and food additives. His attempts to encourage other physicians to join in the study of these interactions were largely ineffective, as most traditional allergists and immunologists were not willing to accept cause-and-effect relationships between human health conditions and environmental factors. In an effort to overcome this resistance, Randolph founded SHE in 1965. In 1985, SHE changed its name to its current title.

The fundamental principles on which AAEM is based were stated in an overview statement published by the association in 1992. That statement said that

Environmentally Triggered Illnesses (EI) result from a disruption of homeostasis by environmental stressors. This disruption may result from a wide range of possible exposures, ranging from a severe acute exposure to a single stressor to cumulative relatively low grade exposures to many stressors over time. The disruption can affect any part of the body via dysfunctioning of any number of the body's many biologic mechanisms and systems. The ongoing manifestations of Environmentally Triggered Illnesses are shaped by the nature of stressors and the timing of exposures to them, by the biochemical individuality of the patient, and by the dynamic interactions over time resulting from various governing principles such as the total load, the level of adaptation, the bipolarity of responses, the spreading phenomenon, the switch phenomenon, and individual susceptibility (biochemical individuality). (Quoted in *A Report on Multiple Chemical*

Sensitivity (MCS), http://www.health.gov/environment/mcs/toc.htm, accessed on December 8, 2013)

Today, the major focus of AAEM's activities is the education of physicians and the general public about the interrelationship of environment chemicals and human health. The association is accredited by the Accreditation Council for Continuing Medical Education (ACCME) to provide continuing education instruction to physicians on a number of such topics and by a variety of mechanisms. For example, the organization offers national and regional conferences on environmental health topics such as "Chronic Disease: Highlighting EMF Hypersensitivity, Lyme, Mycotoxicity, Autism, Cancer and Much More" (2013 annual conference), "Lifestyle Exposures Which Affect Human Health: First Line Therapy for Chronic Disease," "Environmental Causes of Inflammation and Pain—Integrative Solutions," and "Fatigue—The Modern Dilemma." AAEM also offers a series of courses online. Some titles recently available are "The Diagnosis and Treatment of Inhalant Allergies," "The Diagnosis and Treatment of Food Sensitivities," "The Diagnosis and Treatment of Chemical Sensitivities," and "The Metabolism: Nutrition and the New Endocrinology."

On the association's web page, the AAEM lists position papers on a number of topics essential to its mission and work. These position papers cover subjects such as radio frequency exposure limits, chemical sensitivities, the use of mercury in vaccines, the role of molds and mycotoxins in human health disorders, the use of fluorides in public water supplies, and government policy on the use of biologically identical compounds of estriol for women.

The issue of genetically modified (GM) foods is a reasonable topic with which the AAEM would be concerned. In general, the association has concerns about the safety of such foods, suggesting that they have not been adequately tested to ensure that they have no effects on human health. In a 2009 position paper, the association recommended that physicians encourage their patients to avoid GM foods whenever possible, to consider the possibility of GM foods as being a source of allergy among their patients, to expand the research currently being done on the safety of GM foods, and to promote a moratorium on the development and production of GM foods until better information is available about their safety.

Biological Regulatory Services

USDA APHIS BRS
4700 River Rd., Unit 147
Riverdale, MD 20737
Phone: (301) 851-3877
Email: biotechquery@aphis.usda.gov
URL: http://www.aphis.usda.gov/biotechnology/index.shtml

Biological Regulatory Services (BRS) is a division of the U.S. Department of Agriculture's Animal and Plant Health Inspection Service (APHIS). In 1986, the White House Office of Science and Technology Policy (OSTP) issued a directive that divided up responsibility for the regulation of genetically engineered organisms among three federal agencies: the Food and Drug Administration (FDA), Environmental Protection Agency (EPA), and APHIS. For example, the directive assigned responsibility for the approval of genetically engineered animal drugs to the FDA, for the approval of all contained uses to the EPA, and for the approval of genetically engineered plants and animals to APHIS. APHIS, in turn, assigned all responsibilities that it received from the directive to its specialized division in charge of all biotechnology issues, the BRS.

BRS has developed a strategic plan that contains four fundamental goals:

1. Strengthen safeguarding, which involves developing regulatory policies that are timely and commensurate with the risks posed by GM products

2. Strengthen incident and emergency preparedness and response, which involves the dissemination of information about BRS's role in managing and responding to emergencies, responding effectively to such emergencies, and developing partnerships with other entities for dealing with emergencies

3. Improve communication and outreach, which includes improving contacts with stakeholders in the public and private sector at all levels, from international to local communities

4. Create a highly effective organization, an objective directed at internal issues within BRS, such as hiring the best possible personnel, ensuring that adequate financing is available, and providing for the most supportive work environment possible

BRS carries out its regulatory responsibilities primarily in one of two ways, either through permits and notifications or through petitions. Permits and notifications are authorizations issued by BRS for the release of genetically engineered organisms that have the potential for causing harm to plants in the environment. These statements of approval specify the precise conditions under which importation, interstate transport, or release into the environment may occur such that no real threat to plants is likely to occur. Notifications are essentially comparable to permits, although they are processed online in a more streamlined fashion. Petitions are requests by the producers of GM organisms for deregulation of a particular product, based on a body of scientific evidence that shows that the organism poses no threat to plants in the environment and that it is essentially comparable to naturally occurring organisms to which it is related.

Once permits or notifications have been approved, the BRS has a detailed program of inspection and compliance to ensure that researchers and producers are following conditions stipulated in these documents. In case of an adverse event, researchers and producers are required to report to the agency about the event, providing all relevant details that will allow the agency to make a determination of its severity and of actions that may need to be taken. The agency itself also conducts inspections of field testing and other conditions in which GM organisms may be involved to ensure that permit and notification holders are complying with the terms of their agreement with the agency.

Details of the steps involved in the permit, notification, petition, and inspection aspects of the BRS's work are available on the agency's website at http://www.aphis.usda.gov/biotechnology/index.shtml. The website also contains a great deal of valuable background and reference material, such as a listing of all relevant legislation and administrative rules dealing with the release of GM organisms, a collection of recent relevant news and information, and a BRS library containing books, articles, and other materials on the agency's work.

Biotechnology Industry Organization

1201 Maryland Ave., SW, Suite 900
Washington, DC 20024
Phone: (202) 962-9200
Fax: (202) 488-6301
Email: info@bio.org
URL: http://www.bio.org

The Biotechnology Industry Organization (BIO) is the world's largest biotechnology trade organization, with more than 1,100 members worldwide. BIO is a 501(c)(6) nonprofit organization that provides advocacy, business advice, and communication services for its members. BIO members are drawn from every aspect of the biotechnology community, ranging from some of the largest companies in the world, including Amgen, Lilly, Merck, Pfizer, and Sanofi, to smaller companies such as Atossa Genetics, Blueprint Medicines, Okanagan Specialty Fruits, and Prosidion, Ltd. Many major academic institutions are also members, including Emory, Johns Hopkins, Northwestern, and Rush universities, as well as the universities of California (12 campuses), Illinois, Notre Dame, and Pittsburgh.

BIO maintains a very ambitious program of activities, one of the most important of which is advocating for the interests of all aspects of the biotechnology industry. It works on an international, national, and state level for the adoption of legislation, regulations, and other actions that promote biotechnological research and development. As of early 2014, it had two major initiatives: Unleashing the Promise of Biotechnology and International Biotech Policy. The former program involves the development of a comprehensive national strategy that will allow the biotechnology industry to move forward more aggressively, so as to achieve the potential of which it is capable. The second initiative involves drawing upon what the organization regards as the best policies currently in existence in nations around to world to produce a model that can be applied worldwide to produce the most favorable regulatory and political setting for the further development of biotechnology.

Much of BIO's work is organized into nine major areas: health care, emerging companies, food and agriculture, intellectual property, public policy, industrial and environmental, bioethics, international trade, and small business early stage investment. Most of these areas are further divided into more specialized topics. For example, the health care area is further divided into programs on biopharmaceutical manufacturing and distribution, biosimilars, drug discovery and development, Food and Drug Administration review, personalized medicine, Prescription User Fee Act, reimbursement and health policy, and vaccines and biodefense.

Another large category of the organization's activities is categorized as industry intelligence and analysis, through which BIO provides its members and other interested individuals and organizations with a host of valuable information about the status of the biotechnology industry. BIO backgrounders, for example, cover topics such as "How to Grow Jobs through Biotech Industry Development," "Current Uses of Synthetic Biology," "How Do Drugs and Biologics Differ?" "Background Information on Plant Biotechnology," and "2010: Awareness & Impressions of Synthetic Biology and Nanotechnology." The organization's monthly newsletter, *BIOtech Now*, is available free of charge on the BIO website at http://www.bio.org/articles/welcome-biotech-now.

BIO also provides a very large array of valuable publications, some of which are restricted for member use, but many of which are available online to the general public. The agriculture product database, for example, is an interactive resource in which one can find detailed information about production numbers for a number of important agricultural products from a variety of manufacturers in countries throughout the world. The industry intelligence and analysis page of the website also contains some useful reviews of industry best practices and access to the Battelle/BIO State Bioscience Industry Development, which presents some key findings about the status of the biotechnology industry in the United States. The same page lists a number of publications of general interest to the public, such as "Healing, Fueling, Feeding: How Biotechnology Is Enriching Your Life," "Biotechnology Solutions for Everyday Life," "Biotechnology . . . Fields of Benefits," "BIO Grassroots Handbook," and "Bioethics—Facing the Future Responsibly."

The organization also sponsors a variety of conferences, forums, and other meetings on topics of interest in biotechnology, as well as the annual BIO International Conference. Other such events are the annual BIO Investor Forum, the annual CEO and Investor Conference, irregular BioSafe meetings, and the World Conference on Industrial Biotechnology.

José Bové (1953–)

What do the French military, McDonald's, U.S. tariff policies, and GM soybean seeds have in common? The answer is José

Bové, a university trained biologist, sheep farmer, and politician from Aveyron in the Pyrénées region of France. Over the past two decades, Bové has organized or participated in a series of political actions on social, economic, and scientific issues that he sees of international significance.

José Bové was born in Talence, Gironde, France, on June 11, 1953. His parents are Luxembourg-born Joseph-Marie Bové and Colette née Dumeau Bové, specialists in the diseases of fruit trees. José lived the first seven years of his life in Berkeley, California, where his parents conducted their research at the University of California. He then returned to France, enrolling at a private Jesuit bilingual secondary school in Athis-Mons, a small town southeast of Paris. He was later expelled from the school for being "faithless." Although he did not return to school, he continued to study on his own and eventually took the national baccalaureate exam, the major college-entrance examination in France. He passed the exam in economics *avec mention* (with honors).

In 1970–1971, Bové moved to the Bordeaux region, where his parents had been working. He enrolled at the University of Bordeaux, thinking perhaps to major in philosophy. However, by that time, he had become so thoroughly involved in political actions that he withdrew from the university to devote all his time to those activities. While still a high school student, for example, he had participated in demonstrations on behalf of conscientious objectors and deserters.

His first political involvement in Bordeaux concerned the French government's decision to expand its military base on the Larzac plateau. In response to requests from peasants living in the area, Bové and a group of other activists moved into the Larzac area and began building a traditional stone sheep shelter, which they believed would disrupt plans to expand the military base. After working on the project for two years, Bové decided that he like the idea of being a sheep farmer and added that career to his work as a political activist.

In 1987, Bové combined his political and agricultural interests by forming an agricultural union called the *Confédération*

Paysanne. The goal of the organization was the promotion of human and environmental needs in the agricultural process, a goal achieved by focusing local farming activities on organic farming. The event that brought Confédération Paysanne its greatest notoriety took place in 1999 when the McDonald's organization decided to build a new franchise in the town of Millau in Bové's home region of Larzac. Members of the Confédération dismantled the half-built McDonald's building, resulting in a conviction of Bové that sent him to jail for six weeks. The McDonald's action was initiated not so much specifically against the American corporation itself as it was against what Bové and his colleagues saw as a bastardization of traditional attitudes toward food production and distribution, in which economic interest trumped all other concerns.

At about the same time as the McDonald's incident, Bové was also becoming increasingly agitated about the threats that he saw GM seeds, crops, and foods posing to French consumers. His position on GM products was that "[t]he greatest danger that genetically modified corn represents as well as other GM crops resides in the impossibility of evaluating the long term consequences and following the effects on the environment, animals, and humans." As usual, he expressed his beliefs and concerns with concrete political actions, destroying a stock of GM seeds at a site in France owned by Swiss biotechnology company Novartis in 1998 and destroying GM rice plants at an experimental laboratory in Montpellier in 1999. For these two crimes, Bové was sentenced to a total of 10 months in jail. At the same time, his fame as a political activist and opponent of GM crops and foods had spread worldwide, and he had become a hero for opponents of GM products everywhere.

Bové is as strongly in favor of labeling GM products as he is opposed to such products in general. He argues that the refusal to label GM foods is simply evidence for the control that multinational businesses have over the food industry and agriculture at every label of production, distribution, and sale.

In January 2007, Bové announced that he was a candidate for president of the French Republic. Although he did gain support from a number of French political leaders, he did poorly in the election, garnering 483,000 votes, about 1.32 percent of the popular vote cast in the election. Two years later, he ran for the European Parliament on the slate of Europe Écologie, a coalition of French environmentalist political parties. He won 16 percent of the popular vote in that election, a sufficient number for him to be elected.

Herbert Boyer (1936–)

In the history of DNA technology, the names of Herbert Boyer and Stanley N. Cohen will forever be paired with each other. In 1972, the two researchers were both attending a conference in Hawaii on plasmids, circular loops of DNA found in bacteria and protozoa. Over lunch, the two men found that they were engaged in very similar research projects. Cohen was studying the antibiotic properties of certain bacterial plasmids, whereas Boyer was studying methods for introducing cut DNA into precisely defined segments with ends that could be attached to other pieces of DNA. The two decided to collaborate and within four months had carried out one of the classic studies in the history of molecular biology. In these studies, they introduced specified pieces of DNA into a bacterial plasmid (using methods developed by Boyer) and then inserted the plasmid into bacteria (using methods developed by Cohen). The results of these experiments were bacteria whose DNA contained clearly defined segments of foreign DNA (genes) capable of synthesizing specific proteins. When those bacteria reproduced, they then became tiny "factories" for the production of those proteins, the earliest forerunners of contemporary industrial rDNA technologies.

Herbert Wayne Boyer was born in Derry, Pennsylvania, on July 10, 1936. He received his AB from St. Vincent College, in Latrobe, Pennsylvania, in 1968, and his MS and PhD (bacteriology) from the University of Pittsburgh in 1960 and 1963, respectively. He did his postdoctoral work at Yale University as a U.S. Public Health Service research fellow from 1963 to 1966. In 1966, Boyer left Yale to accept a position at the University of California at San Francisco (UCSF) as assistant professor of microbiology. He was promoted to associate professor of microbiology in 1971, associate professor of biochemistry in 1975, and full professor in the department of biochemistry and biophysics in 1976, a post he held until his retirement in 1991. Boyer also served as director of the graduate program in genetics from 1976 to 1981. He currently holds the title of emeritus professor of biochemistry and biophysics in the UCSF School of Medicine.

In 1976, Boyer and venture capitalist Robert A. Swanson founded the world's first corporation for the development of commercial products made with rDNA research, Genentech, Inc. Within its first year of operation, Genentech had produced the first commercial rDNA product, the hormone somatostatin. Boyer served as vice president of Genentech from its founding until his retirement from the company, also in 1991.

Among the honors given to Boyer are the Albert Lasker Award for Basic Medical Research (1980), Industrial Research Institute Achievement Award (1982), National Medal of Technology (1989), National Medal of Science (1990), Helmut Horten Research Award (1993), Lemelson-MIT Prize (1996), Biotechnology Heritage Award (2000), Albany Medical Center Prize (2004), Shaw Prize in Life Science and Medicine (2004), the Perkin Medal of the American section of the Society of Chemical Industry (2007), and Cold Spring Harbor Laboratory Double Helix Medal (2009). The graduate faculty at UCSF has created the Herbert W. Boyer Program in Biological Sciences in recognition of Boyer's contribution to the university. In 1990, Boyer and his wife Grace donated the single largest sum ever given to the Yale School of Medicine by an individual or family, $10,000,000. In recognition of that gift, the university named a new facility in the Boyers' honor, the Boyer Center for Molecular Medicine, in 1991.

Canadian Biotechnology Action Network

180 Metcalfe St., Suite 206
Ottawa, Ontario, K2P 1P5
Canada
Phone: (613) 241-2267, ext.25
Fax: (613) 241-2506
Email: info@cban.ca
URL: http://www.cban.ca/

The Canadian Biotechnology Action Network (CBAN) had its origins in informal meetings in 1999 among 23 environmental, social justice, and consumer groups that met to develop a common strategy for dealing with issues raised by the increasing use of genetic engineering in the development of crops and foods and in other areas. That information affiliation was successful in achieving a number of goals, including the prohibition of milk produced from cows treated with recombinant bovine growth hormone (rBGH) and abandonment by Monsanto of its plans to introduce genetically engineered wheat into the country. In 2006, participating groups decided to formalize its relationship with the creation of the CBAN under the auspices of Tides Canada. Tides Canada is a national charity that focuses on issues of importance to the people of Canada and their natural environment by connecting donors with worthy projects.

CBAN's current mission statement calls for the organization

to promote food sovereignty and democratic decision-making on science and technology issues in order to protect the integrity of the environment, health, food, and the livelihoods of people in Canada and around the world by facilitating, informing and organizing civil society action, researching, and providing information to government for policy development.

Among the organizations that currently make up CBAN are ACT for the Earth (Toronto), Canadian Organic Growers, Ecological Farmers of Ontario, Food Action Committee of Ecology Action Centre (Halifax), GE Free Yukon, GeneAction (Toronto), Greenpeace Canada, National Farmers Union, P.E.I. Coalition for a GMO-Free Province, Saskatchewan Organic Directorate, Society for a G.E. Free B.C., and Union Paysanne. The organization also receives support from a variety of commercial enterprises, including The Big Carrot Natural Foods (Toronto); Julie Daniluk, RHN, Daniluk Consulting; Eatmore Sprouts (British Columbia); ETC Group (Ottawa); Harmony Organic (Ontario); and Mumm's Sprouting Seeds (Saskatchewan).

CBAN activities are based on four primary objectives:

1. Facilitating collaborative campaigning at the local, regional, national, and international levels
2. Enabling individual Canadians to take strategic and effective action
3. Researching and monitoring new technologies and providing credible information
4. Challenging government to transparency, accountability, and democratic process

At the beginning of 2014, CBAN was pursuing four major projects: No GM Fish, Get GM Sweet Corn Out, Stop the GM Apple, and Stop Legalized Contamination from Unapproved GM Foods: "Low Level Presence." Each of these projects has been created in opposition to specific efforts by companies to introduce new GM products into Canada. The No GM Fish project, for example, was developed to oppose the request by a U.S. company, AquaBounty, to begin marketing a GM form of salmon that grows throughout the year rather than during only a certain season each year. The project consists largely of writing to the Canadian Minister of the Environment, expressing one's objection to the approval of this request.

The CBAN website is also a very rich source of information on a large variety of topics, such as agrofuels; corporate control of the food supply; environmental impacts of GM crops; specific GM products, such as apples, alfalfa, flax, potatoes, rice, wheat, cotton, corn, canola, soybeans, sugar beets, and fish; GE Free Zones; experimental work on GM goats, trees, and other organisms; human health risks; labeling issues; nanotechnology; patents; regulation and policy; synthetic biology; and terminator technology. It also provides some very useful information on tools that can be used by individuals and organizations to express their opposition to GM products, such as relevant articles, briefing notes, consumer guides, e-news, films, maps, pamphlets, factsheets, photos and graphics, reports, and workshops and presentations.

The organization also sponsors, cosponsors, and advertises a variety of events of interest to individuals who oppose the use of GM foods and crops in Canada. Some recent examples include the recently produced play *Seeds* about the legal battle between Saskatchewan farmer Percy Schmeiser and the Monsanto company; the showing of the film *GMO OMG*, dealing with issues of GM products in today's world; and a webcast featuring a panel of four food experts on the challenges of feeding a world of 9 billion people. A frequently asked questions section of the website also provides a brief but excellent general introduction to the issue of GM crops and foods.

Center for Food Safety

660 Pennsylvania Ave., SE, #302
Washington, DC 20003
Phone: (202) 547-9359
Fax: (202) 547-9429

Email: http://www.centerforfoodsafety.org/contact-us
URL: http://www.centerforfoodsafety.org

The Center for Food Safety (CFS) was founded in 1997 by attorney, environmental activist, and consumer advocate Andrew Kimbrell, who still serves as executive director of the organization. CFS was founded as a nonprofit organization for the purpose of working to protect human health and the natural environment by opposing the use of harmful food production technologies and by promoting organic and other forms of sustainable agriculture.

The center organizes its activities around 10 major themes: genetic engineering, seeds, pollinators and pesticides, animal cloning, food and climate, aquaculture, food safety, factory farms, organic and beyond, and nanotechnology. Two of these themes are further subdivided into more specific categories: genetic engineering into GE foods, GE food labeling, GE fish, GE animals, GE insects, and GE trees; and food safety into food safety (in general), food irradiation, rbGH, mad cow disease, and sewage sludge. For each of these topics, the CFS website provides detailed information about the issue and suggestions for ways in which consumers can become involved in actions to resolve specific issues. For each topic, there is also a list of publications and resources that include reports on the topic, legal actions taken with respect to the issue, policy statements by various organizations, testimony provided by CFS representatives and other individuals, and news about recent development with regard to the issue. The web page on aquaculture, for example, provides an essay defining and describing the process, a discussion of the forces responsible for the depletion of ocean resources, a description of the threats posed to the marine environment and marine wildlife, a review of human health risks posed by the practice of aquaculture, a description of special issues related to shellfish aquaculture, and a summary of regulation relevant to aquaculture practices. The usual list of publications and other resources is also included.

The center has also developed a number of initiatives to which members and interested readers are invited to participate. Examples of those initiatives include campaigns to get Lowe's and Home Depot to stop selling pesticides that are toxic to honeybees, to stop the development of genetically engineered fish, and to stop GE crop field tests; and petitions to get the Environmental Protection Agency more involved in efforts to protect honeybees, to urge the retailer Trader Joe's to stop selling meat containing antibiotics, and to convince the U.S. Department of Agriculture to ban the growing and sale of genetically engineered apples.

CFS also makes available to members and interested others a wide range of print and electronic publications in the form of fact sheets, newsletters, reports, policy statements, testimonials, and legal actions. Examples of fact sheet topics that are available are "Guide to Avoiding GE Fish," "Factory Farms: Antibiotics in Distiller Grains," "Pollinators & Pesticides," "Help the Honeybees: A List of Pesticides to Avoid," and "Genetically Engineered Foods: The Labeling Debate." The organization's primary newsletter is *Food Safety Now*. It also provides news electronically to subscribers on its True Food Network.

Among the reports available from the organization on its website are "Best Public Relations That Money Can Buy: A Guide to Food Industry Front Groups," "Genetic Engineered Food Labeling Laws Map," "Seed Giants vs. U.S. Farmers," "Pollinators & Pesticides: A Report by Center for Food Safety on Pollinator Health, Research, and Future Efforts for Pollinator Protection," and "Food Safety Review: Going Backwards: Dow's 2,4-D-Resistant Crops and a More Toxic Future."

Mary-Dell Chilton (1939–)

Chilton is best known for her research on the process by which *Agrobacterium* bacteria infect tobacco plants. Her team showed that a bacterium is able to transmit its DNA into the host plant genome and that, furthermore, removal of disease-causing genes from the bacterial DNA does not affect this process. The information gained from these studies demonstrated the feasibility of producing transgenic plants by inserting foreign genes into the genome of a host plant, giving it the ability to produce proteins not typically associated with the native plant. The experiments conducted by Chilton's team have now become classics in the field of genetic engineering of plants. In 2013, Chilton was awarded a share of the World Food Prize, widely recognized as one of the highest honors that can be granted for accomplishments in the invention, development, and application of new products through modern agricultural biotechnology.

Mary-Dell Chilton was born in Indianapolis, Indiana, on February 2, 1939. She was originally interested in astronomy and was a finalist in the 1956 Westinghouse Science Talent Search for building "a long telescope in a short tube." She planned to major in astronomy when she entered the University of Illinois at Champaign Urbana in 1956, but soon she found that her instructors did not take her seriously because she was a woman. She briefly transferred to physics but found that subject boring, so eventually decided to major in chemistry, earning her BSc in that subject in 1960 and her PhD, also in chemistry, in 1967. Chilton then accepted an appointment at the University of Washington, in Seattle, where she remained until 1979. It was at the University of Washington that she conducted much of her initial work on the production of transgenic plants.

In 1979, Chilton moved to Washington University in St. Louis, where she continued her research on the genetic modification of tobacco plants. After four years, she resigned her academic position to take a job with the CIBA-Geigy Corporation (now Syngenta Biotechnology, Inc.) in Research Triangle Park, North Carolina. At Syngenta, she has been involved in both research and administrative activities, serving as principal scientist, distinguished science fellow, and vice president of agricultural biotechnology. In addition to the World Food Prize, Chilton has been honored with a number of other awards, including the American Institute of Chemists Bronze Medal (1960), Rank Prize in Nutrition of the United Kingdom (1967), election to the National Academy of Sciences (1986), the David Gottlieb Medal of the University of Illinois (1986), the Hendricks Medal of the American Chemical Society (1987), election to the American Academy of Arts and Sciences (1993), election as a fellow to the American Academy of Microbiology (1994), the John Scott Award of the City of Philadelphia (2000), the Benjamin Franklin Medal in Life Sciences of the Franklin Institute in Philadelphia (2002), and the CSSA Presidential Award of the Crop Science Society of America (2011). In 2009, Washington University established the Mary-Dell Chilton Distinguished Professorship in Arts and Sciences in her honor. She has published well over 100 scientific papers in the field of the genetic modification of organisms.

Chilton had been married for more than two decades to Dr. Scott Chilton, professor of botany in the College of Agriculture and Life Sciences at North Carolina State University. He died unexpectedly in 2004. In her retirement years, Chilton is no longer involved with company projects, although she does continue to work in her laboratory at Syngenta, working on projects that interest her, no matter the future practical value they may or may not have.

Stanley N. Cohen (1935–)

Cohen and Herbert Boyer performed one of the classic experiments in the early history of DNA technology in the early 1970s when they found a way to insert a foreign gene into a plasmid, a double-stranded circular piece of DNA found in bacteria and protozoa. This technology allowed Cohen and Boyer to make duplicate copies (clones) of precise segments of DNA from any given source.

Stanley Norman Cohen was born in Perth Amboy, New Jersey, on February 17, 1935. His grandparents had emigrated from Eastern Europe and settled in Perth Amboy, where Cohen's parents were also born. In his autobiography, Cohen remembers Perth Amboy as a "wonderful paradigm of ethnic, religious, and racial diversity," in which he lived a very typical childhood and adolescence. He played basketball and football and worked in a variety of jobs during the week and sold magazine subscriptions on the weekend. He was torn between his interests in physics and biology in high school, but eventually he chose the latter and decided to become a geneticist.

He entered Rutgers University in the fall of 1952, where he majored in premedical studies. He was granted his BA in biological sciences in 1956, and then enrolled at the University of Pennsylvania School of Medicine, from which he received his MD in 1960. He then did his residency, internship, and medical research at a number of institutions, including University Hospital at the University of Michigan, Mt. Sinai Hospital in New York City, Duke University Hospital, and the National Institute of Arthritis and Metabolic Diseases. At some point during these studies, Cohen recognized the fact that he was more interested in the research side of medicine than in clinical work, so began to focus his postgraduate studies in the former field. His future was sealed when he was given a fellowship at the U.S. National Institutes of Health, where he was introduced to the new and growing field of molecular biology. After additional studies at the Albert Einstein College of Medicine in New York City, he accepted his first academic appointment as assistant professor of medicine at Stanford University, where he spent the remainder of his academic career. He was named professor of medicine in the Stanford School of Medicine in 1975, professor of genetics in the School of Medicine in 1977, and Kwoh-Ting Li Professor of Medicine in 1993, titles that he continues to hold. Cohen also served as trustee at the University of Pennsylvania and its Medical Center from 1989 through 2002. An award of excellence in biomedical research has been named in his honor at Pennsylvania.

Cohen and Boyer met at a conference in Hawaii on bacterial plasma and over lunch discovered that their research interests melded with each other beautifully. At the time, Cohen was studying methods for inserting plasmids into bacteria to study their ability to develop resistance to certain antibiotics. Boyer was working on the development of certain kinds of enzymes that cut DNA into precisely defined segments with "sticky" ends. The two combined their skills to develop a method for inserting precise DNA segments into plasmids and then inserting those plasmids into bacteria. The modified bacteria could, by this method, be "engineered" to produce any desired protein product specified by the inserted DNA and, in this regard, marked the beginning of industrial biotechnology based on rDNA molecules.

Cohen's research interests range over a wide array of topics, including the development and evolution of antibiotic resistance, the function of ribonucleic acids (RNA) in cells, and possible molecular mechanisms for the rise of neurological disorders in animals.

In his long and illustrious career, Cohen has received a number of awards and honors, including the Wolf Prize in Medicine (1971), Lemelson-MIT Prize (1996), Albert Lasker Basic Medical Research Award (1980), National Medal of Science (1988), National Medal of Technology (1989), Albany Medical Center Prize (2004), Shaw Prize in Life Science and Medicine (2004), and Double Helix Medal (2009).

Council for Biotechnology Information

United States
1201 Maryland Ave., SW, Suite 900
Washington, DC 20024
Phone: (202) 962-9200
Email: cbi@whybiotech.com
URL: http://www.whybiotech.com/

Canada
105L 111 Research Dr.
Saskatoon, SK, S7N 3R3
Phone: (416) 922-1944
Toll-Free: (1) (866) 922-1944
Email: info@canadacbi.com
URL: http://www.whybiotech.ca/

Mexico
AgroBIO Mexico A.C.
Dakota No. 2004, Oficina 302, Col. Nápoles
C.P. 03810, Mexico DF
Phone: +52 55 55438489
Email: agrobio@agrobiomexico.org.mx
URL: http://www.agrobiomexico.org.mx/

The Council for Biotechnology Information (CBI) is a non-profit 501(c)6 organization created for the purpose of providing information about the benefits and safety of agricultural bio-technology and its role in sustainable development. The organization was created in April 2000 and has major offices in three countries: Canada, Mexico, and the United States. Member organizations of the CBI as of early 2014 were BASF, Bayer CropScience, Dow AgroSciences LLC, DuPont, Monsanto, and Syngenta.

The basic premise behind the CBI program is that bioengineered organisms can improve human life around the world by increasing the size and quality of harvests, find new ways of meeting the world's energy needs, and develop new crops that can survive in otherwise inhospitable areas, such as deserts, saline environments, or unusually cold lands. Some of the specific messages that the council makes available are that

• New crops can be developed that have higher nutritional content than comparably occurring nature crops.

- GM crops can improve the quality and quantity of crops in developing nations, thus helping to solve one of the most important problems faced by those nations.

- Respected authorities around the world have come to the conclusion that bioengineered crops are safe and healthy for humans and domestic animals.

- Bioengineered crops can help farmers save water, thus helping to solve another environmental problem faced by many places in the world.

- The use of GM crops can greatly reduce the amount of pesticides used in agriculture, thus reducing both costs to farmers and potential health risks for consumers.

- Crops can be engineered so as to make them useful as biofuels, helping to deal with yet another important social issue.

The main focus of CBI's work is on the dissemination of information about the benefits and safety of GM crops and foods. It accomplishes this objective with a variety of print, electronic, and visual materials. For example, its web page provides pages on topics such as third-party (neutral) studies on the safety and efficacy of genetically engineered crops, a list of experts who are available to answer questions and provide information about GM foods, a timeline of the development of agricultural biotechnology, and a frequently asked questions (FAQ) section that provides answers to common questions about engineered crops and foods. The council also provides fact sheets in print and electronic form that deal with fundamental issues related to GM foods, including "Helping Increase Crop Yields for America's Farmers," "Biotechnology and Biofuels: Providing Renewable Energy while Reducing Carbon Emissions," "Biotechnology and Drought: Producing More Crop per Drop," "Biotechnology and Food: Helping Increase Global Food Security," and "Biotechnology and Sustainability: Supporting Sustainable Solutions in Agriculture."

The organization's visual presentations include online slideshows on topics such as "Agricultural Biotechnology and Sustainaiblity," "How Biotechnology Is Helping Increase Global Food Production," "Biotechnology and Biofuels: Fueling Growth for Today and Tomorrow," and "Biotechnology and Drought: Helping Produce 'More Crop per Drop'." CBI also offers a number of video programs on similar topics (e.g., "World without Food Science" and "Connecting Farmers"), as well as its own YouTube channel (http://www.youtube.com/user/CBIWashingtonDC) and Green State TV, which provides interviews with people interested in the use of GM foods to help solve a variety of worldwide problems.

Groups opposed to the development and use of GM foods have pointed out the association of CBI with biotechnology firms and have raised questions as to how unbiased the information is that is provided by the council. Without question, however, the council does provide a host of useful and generally accurate information about one side of the controversy about GM agricultural products.

CropGen

PO Box 38589
London SW1A 1WE
United Kingdom
Phone (in UK) 020-7025-2333
(from overseas) +44-20-8451-0784
Email: cropgen@f2s.com
URL: http://www.cropgen.org/

CropGen is an organization targeted at the media and the general public with the goal of promoting research on and the use of GM crops and foods. The organization is based in the United Kingdom, but it has members from many other parts of the world, including Egypt, Germany, the Philippines, Poland, South Africa, Switzerland, and the

United States. It provides expert advice on topics relating to the genetic modification of plants and animals in specialized fields such as bioethics, biotechnology law, economics of GM agriculture, farming and agricultural chemicals, GM foods and human health, GM issues and the public media, plant ecology and weed control, plant genetics and agriculture, plant breeding and biodiversity, and regulation and coexistence.

A core section of the association's website is the question and answer page that provides information on topics such as the history of the genetic modification of foods, the extent to which GM foods are present in the marketplace, who produces GM foods, what the justification for GM foods is, how GM foods can benefit human life, what medical benefits there may be for GM foods and other products, what contributions the genetic modification of plants may have for other fields such as energy production, and what dangers and risks GM crops and foods may pose. The web page also provides links to about four dozen organizations that can provide additional information about and support for the invention and use of GM products.

CropGen was established in 2000 with a grant of nearly £500,000 from a consortium of biotechnology firms including BASF, the Crop Protection Association, Dow AgroSciences, DuPont, Monsanto, and Syngenta. For the first three years of its existence, it was operated by the public relations firm Countrywide Porter Novelli, after which management was transferred to another public relations firm, Lexington Communications. CropGen says that its objective is to make available unbiased scientific information in support of the greater use of GM foods and that no one associated with the organization is funded by any biotechnology company or by any organization that works on behalf of GM products.

In addition to its very useful website, the organization takes part in radio and television interviews, offers speakers for debates and other types of meetings, and briefs journalists on issues related to GM foods. An item of special interest on its website is a list of articles under the section "Highlights," which have dealt most recently with topics such as the safety of GM foods for humans and domestic animals, the discovery of the presence of modified gene fragments in human blood, changes in Russian attitudes toward GM foods, the discovery of GM wheat in Oregon, and current UK policy on GM foods and crops.

Food & Water Watch

1616 P St., NW, Suite 300
Washington, DC 20036
Phone: (202) 683-2500
Fax: (202) 683-2501
Email: http://www.foodandwaterwatch.org/about/contact-us/
URL: http://www.foodandwaterwatch.org

Food & Water Watch was formed in 2005 by 12 members of the Energy and Environment Program of the nonprofit organization Public Citizen. The organization's mission is to work to ensure that the food and water available to people is safe and accessible and that it is produced by sustainable methods. Over time, the organization has expanded its array of programs that currently include specific issues such as bottled water, climate change, consumer labels desalination, factory farms and factory fish farming, the federal budget, food and water justice, food safety, fracking, genetically engineered foods, groundwater protection, irradiation, nanotechnology, water conservation, water privatization, and worldwide water resources.

The organization provides on its web page an overview of some of its most important accomplishments over the past decade. These achievements include the following:

• Playing a role in Maryland state legislation to ban the presence of arsenic in chicken feed

- Running a campaign to encourage Starbucks to stop using milk produced by rBGH cows
- Working with inspectors from the U.S. Department of Agriculture (USDA) to maintain the highest possible standards of food inspection
- Protecting small farms from new federal legislation designed more specifically for large corporate farms
- Advocating for rigorous labeling regulations on foods imported from outside the United States
- Organizing to protect water supplies by eliminating the use of the hazardous chemical triclosan in consumer products
- Cooperating with other organizations to promote adoption of a bill in New Jersey to ban fracking in the state
- Preventing the conversion of publicly owned water purification systems to private companies in a number of localities across the United States

Food & Water Watch has adopted a four-pronged approach in pursuit of its programs that includes a program of education about such issues for the general public and policy makers; lobbying of those policy makers for the adoption of programs consistent with the organization's mission; promotion of information about food and water issues through a variety of media; and encouragement of activism among members and other interested parties primarily through its Internet site.

A vital aspect of Food & Water Watch work is providing materials that educate the general public and policy makers on critical issues. These materials are often available in the form of fact sheets on topics such as "The World Food Prize," "Save Antibiotics for Medicine, Not Factory Farms," "United Water: A Corporate Profile," "Monsanto's Seed Company Subsidiaries," and "How Much Do Labels Really Tell You?" In addition to fact sheets, the organization offers other types of research information in the form of reports, issue briefs, case studies, and corporate profiles. Examples of each are "The Social Costs of Fracking," "The EPA's Failure to Track Factory Farms," "Citrus County, Florida," and "Aqua America," respectively.

Food & Water Watch also provides a variety of tools to help the average citizen better understand some important issues in the field and to learn how to deal with these issues. The "Take Back the Tap Guide to Safe Tap Water," for example, provides guidance as to how citizens can understand water quality reports that are commonly issued by local water companies and how they can use this information to purchase water filters for their home and take such other actions that will improve the likelihood of getting clean water in their homes. The "Smart Seafood Guide" helps consumers learn more about the fish products that are available for sale in their markets, including knowing whether or not the fish is caught or farmed locally, how the fish is caught or farmed, and what contaminants may be associated with fish products.

The news section of the organization's website provides access to a blog dealing with its major topics, a collection of recent news reports, press releases about important issues, events of interest to members and to the general public, and video productions dealing with food and water issues.

Robert T. Fraley (1953–)

Fraley was honored with a share of the 2013 World Food Prize, awarded annually by the World Food Prize Foundation to individuals "who have advanced human development by improving the quality, quantity or availability of food in the world." The prize was conceived in the mid-1980s by Norman Borlaug, who had himself won a Nobel Peace Prize for his contributions to the relief of human hunger around the world. Fraley was honored for his research on methods for transforming the genome of plants important in agriculture.

Robert Thomas Fraley was born in Danville, Illinois, on January 25, 1953. He was brought up on a farm in nearby Hoopeston, Illinois; grew grain; and maintained livestock. It goes almost without saying that this early experience made a life-long impression on Fraley who was eager to have a chance to improve agricultural technology to meet the needs of hungry people worldwide. Upon completing high school, Fraley entered the University of Illinois at Champagne-Urbana, where he received his bachelor's degree in biology in 1974, his master's in 1976, and his PhD in microbiology and biochemistry in 1978. He then spent a year as a postdoctoral fellow at the University of California at San Francisco.

At the conclusion of his studies, Fraley took a position with the Monsanto company, where he has remained ever since. His first appointment at Monsanto was as senior research specialist, after which he worked his way up through the ranks to eventually become executive vice president and chief technology officer.

Fraley's first technical breakthrough in the engineering of plants came in 1983 when he and three of his colleagues reported on a method for introducing genes into plants providing those plants with immunity to certain diseases and adverse environmental conditions. In recognition of this achievement, Fraley was awarded a share of the 1986 Charles A. Thomas & Carroll A. Hochwalt Award for innovative basic science by Monsanto. A year later, Fraley worked on the team that developed and tested the first genetically engineered tomato, the Flavr Savr tomato. In 1996, Fraley was also involved in research on another important GM breakthrough, the development of plants resistant to Monsanto's Roundup Ready insecticide.

In addition to the World Food Prize, Fraley has received a number of other honors for his research on the genetic manipulation of plants, including the Edgar M. Queeny award, the highest honor that Monsanto offers for research in biotechnology (1996); the National Medal of Technology, given to

Fraley in a ceremony at the White House by President Bill
Clinton (1999); and the National Academy of Sciences Award
for the Industrial Application of Science (2008). In 2004,
Fraley was also awarded an Alumni Achievement Award by
the University of Illinois. Since 1981, Fraley has also served as
adjunct professor at Washington University in St. Louis.

John E. Franz (1929–)

In the field of GM crops, few discoveries have been as important as that of the chemical known as *glyphosate*, whose
technical name is N-(phosphonomethyl)glycine. Glyphosate is
classified as a broad-spectrum systemic herbicide, a substance
that is taken up by a wide range of plants and is toxic to those
plants because it interferes with their growth. Glyphosate was
discovered in 1970 by Monsanto chemist John E. Franz, and
it is now the primary ingredient in the company's widely popular herbicide, Roundup. Roundup became a critical tool in the
arsenal of modern agriculture when Monsanto developed GM
plants carrying a gene making them resistant to glyphosate.
Thus, farmers could plant a crop of GM corn, soybeans, cotton, or some other crop resistant to glyphosate and then spray
the field with Roundup. The pesticide kills most weeds present
in the field but has no effect on the so-called Roundup Ready
GM crop.

John Edward Franz was born in Springfield, Illinois, on
December 21, 1929. He became fascinated with the study of
chemistry at the age of 10 and decided that he would make
his career in that field. His interest in chemistry was so intense
that he decided to ignore any other subject and had to be convinced by one of his high school teachers that he really needed
to focus on physics, mathematics, and other subjects to do well
in college.

Franz matriculated at the University of Illinois, from which
he earned his bachelor of science degree (in chemistry, of
course) in 1951. He then continued his studies at the

University of Minnesota, which granted him his PhD in organic chemistry in 1955. After graduation, he was offered positions with both Monsanto and Dow Chemical, eventually choosing to accept Monsanto's offer. He began work as a research chemist at the company's Organic Chemicals Division in St. Louis in 1955. He remained with the company for his entire career, become group leader of the Organic Chemicals Division in 1959, science fellow in the same division in 1962, and then science fellow in the Agricultural Products Division in 1967. It was in this position that he carried out his research on herbicides for use in agricultural settings and discovered glyphosate in the process. This research was based on an incorrect interpretation of studies conducted on herbicidal action conducted over a nine-year period by his colleagues that produced an effective compound nonetheless. Among glyphosate's many advantages is that it has no toxic effects on a broad range of animal life, ranging from most bacteria to insects, fish, birds, and mammals.

In 1975, Franz was appointed senior science fellow in the Agricultural Products Division. Five years later, he was named distinguished science fellow in the division, a title he held until his retirement from Monsanto in 1994.

Franz has more than 840 patents to his credit, most of them dealing with some aspect of glyphosate. He has also received many honors based on that one discovery, including the IR-100 award of Industrial Magazine in 1977, the first J. F. Queeny Award from Monsanto in 1981, the National Medal of Technology in 1987, the Carothers Award of the American Chemical Society in 1989, the Perkins Medal of the American Section of the Society of Chemical Industry in 1990, the Outstanding Achievement Award of the University of Minnesota in 1988, the Missouri Award of the Missouri Department of Economic Development in 1988, and the Inventor of the Year Award of the St. Louis Metropolitan Bar Association in 1986. He was inducted into the United States Inventor's Hall of Fame in 2007.

Dennis Gonsalves (1943–)

American plant pathologist Dilworth D. Jensen wrote a paper in 1949 describing a disease affecting the papaya plant in Hawaii that he attributed to the papaya ringspot virus (PRSV). The disease causes chlorosis (yellow splotches) to develop on leaves and oily liquids to escape from the plant's petioles (the region at which a leaf is attached to a stem). In more severe cases, the plant fails to produce healthy fruit and is of no economic value. Given the critical role of the papaya in the Hawaiian economy, agricultural researchers began an aggressive campaign to find ways of combating PRSV disease. Conventional methods for the control of such diseases were largely unsuccessful. For example, quarantining of plants failed to control the disease because the disease vector, an aphid, was able to reach quarantined areas rather easily. Cross-protection (the introduction of a weaker strain of PRSV with the intention of improving plant immunity) also proved unsuccessful. In 1985, Cornell plant pathologist Dennis Gonsalves began research on a genetically engineered form of the papaya plant (*Carica papaya*). That research was based on the principle that a plant that contains a gene or a DNA fragment similar to that of a pest will have immunity to that pest. So Gonsalves and his colleagues began to look for a way to insert into the papaya genome a portion of the PRSV genome, hoping that the product would have immunity to the viral disease.

Gonsalves's team achieved success in 1991 with a product known as *papaya 55-1*. Field tests confirmed that the varietal was indeed resistant to the virus, and it soon became commercially available under the trade names of SunUp and Rainbow. Researchers were so excited by their discovery that they began to distribute 55-1 seeds at no cost to Hawaiian farmers after the U.S. Department of Agriculture approved the new products. Today more than three-quarters of the papaya grown in Hawaii is some form of the genetically engineered product. It is no exaggeration to say that Gonsalves's research saved the papaya industry in Hawaii.

Dennis Gonsalves was born in Kohala, Hawaii, on April 2, 1943. His father was a Portuguese immigrant whose father's parents had come from the Azores and Madeira Islands and whose mother was Hawaiian-Chinese. Gonsalves remembers that he was not especially interested in an academic career from childhood through his high school years. However, his attitudes changed when he was accepted at the prestigious Kamehameha School in Honolulu, which had been founded for the specific purpose of educating native Hawaiian children. Gonsalves decided to continue his education as an agricultural engineer at the University of Hawaii, but when that field no longer seemed to hold employment opportunities, he switched to horticulture. He eventually earned both his BS and MS degrees from Hawaii in 1965 and 1968, respectively. He then continued his education at the University of California at Davis, from which he received his PhD in plant pathology in 1972.

The event that Gonsalves said changed his life occurred while he was still at the University of Hawaii, working as a plant technician in the laboratory of Eduardo Trujillo, a plant pathologist for the University of Hawaii on the island of Kauai. Trujillo suggested to Gonsalves that the newly discovered PRSV disease might be an interesting topic for research. As soon as he began a study of the disease, Gonsalves later said, he knew that he wanted to become a plant pathologist, with special emphasis on the study of viral diseases in plants. Gonsalves also picked up on Trujillo's suggestion that he should focus on research that has practical applications and not to get carried away with abstract studies. It was under the guidance of Trujillo, therefore, that Gonsalves set off on a career of practical research in the study of viral diseases of the papaya.

After completing his studies at Davis, Gonsalves took a job as assistant professor at the University of Florida, where he remained until 1977. While at Florida, he worked at the Agricultural Research and Education Center at the Institute of Food and Agricultural Sciences at Lake Alfred, where he carried out research on the diseases of citrus trees. He then moved to Cornell University, where he spent the rest of his academic career. He served as associate professor of plant pathology at Cornell from 1977 to 1986 and full professor from 1987 to his retirement in 2002, at which time he was named professor emeritus at Cornell. In 2002, Gonsalves also decided to return to his native Hawaii, where he took the position of University of Hawaii graduate and center director of the USDA Pacific Basin Agricultural Research Center in Hilo. Gonsalves has received the Alexander von Humboldt award of the Alexander von Humboldt Foundation (2002) and the Leadership in Science Public Service Award of the American Society of Plant Biologists (2003).

Greenpeace International

Ottho Heldringstraat 5
1066 AZ Amsterdam
The Netherlands
Phone: +31 (0) 20 718 2000
Fax: +31 (0) 20 718 2002
Email: supporter.services.int@greenpeace.org
URL: http://www.greenpeace.org/international/en/

Greenpeace United States

702 H St., NW, Suite 300
Washington, DC 20001
Phone: (202) 462-1177
Fax: (202) 462-4507
Email: info@wdc.greenpeace.org
URL: http://www.greenpeace.org/usa/en/

Greenpeace was founded in 1971 when a group of environmentalists leased a small fishing vessel to protest nuclear tests
being conducted off the coast of Alaska. The region in which
the testing was to take place was the last refuge of a number
of endangered and threatened species, so the mission was a
campaign against both the use of nuclear weapons and the
potential destruction of endangered wildlife. The fishing boat
was intercepted and prevented from reaching its destination,
and the weapons test was carried out as planned. However,
the impetus for the campaign was by no means lost, and the
organization grew over the next 40 years to become one of the
largest and most influential environmental groups in the world.
Today, Greenpeace has a worldwide membership of about
2.8 million individuals and a membership of 250,000 in the
United States. The organization has 32 national and regional
offices, as well as international headquarters in Amsterdam.

The controlling legal structure of Greenpeace is a Dutch nonprofit organization whose legal name is Stichting Greenpeace
Council that provides general oversight and direction for the
organization. A seven-member board of directors approves the
annual budget and appoints the executive director, who is responsible for the day-to-day operations of the organization. Each
regional office is organized in a similar fashion and elects a
representative to the organization's annual general meeting,
which elects the board of directors, approves new Greenpeace
organizations, authorizes the annual budget, and sets policy priorities for the coming year.

As of early 2014, Greenpeace has focused its efforts on six
major topics: climate change, forests, oceans, agriculture, toxic
pollution, and nuclear issues, for each of which it has developed
a comprehensive and detailed plan of action. The Greenpeace
campaign against GM foods is part of its agriculture mission.
The organization describes GM foods as possible threat to
human health and the environment and suggests that adequate
information on the safety of such products has not yet been
established. Their campaign is focused on three themes:

1. GM organisms should not be released into the environment until adequate scientific evidence has been obtained about their safety to human health and to the environment.
2. Food products containing GM elements should be labeled, and GM foods should be physically separated from conventional foods.
3. Patents should not be issued to organisms that have been created by genetic engineering.

An important feature of the Greenpeace experience has always been the active involvement of volunteers in achieving the organization's objectives. Some of the ways in which volunteers can participate are the following:

• Making financial donations to the organization
• Volunteering to participate in Greenpeace campaign, ranging from "licking envelopes to climbing smokestacks"
• Applying for employment with Greenpeace and putting to use some specific practical skill needed by the organization
• Taking a job on one of the three large and many smaller ships and boats used by the organization to carry out its campaigns
• Making personal lifestyle changes that will contribute to achieving the organization's overall goals, such as changing any number of factors in one's home, yard, office, and community
• Developing and carrying out a campaign of one's own choosing on a local environmental problem of interest and concern to the community (see http://www.greenpeace .org/international/en/getinvolved/ for more details on ways of becoming involved)

Greenpeace relies to a considerable extent on the use of multimedia resources to get its message out to the general public. Its website has a number of photographs, photos essays, videos, slideshows, webcams, games, e-cards, and computer supplements to describe the problems in which it is interested and the programs it has developed to deal with those issues.

Institute for Responsible Technology

PO Box 469
Fairfield, IA 52556
Phone: (641) 209-1765
Fax: (888) 386-6075
Email: info@responsibletechnology.org
URL: http://www.responsibletechnology.org/

The Institute for Responsible Technology (IRT) was founded in 2003 by Jeffrey Smith, who calls himself "the leading consumer advocate promoting healthier non-GMO choices." Smith is the author of two books on the subject, *Seeds of Deception: Exposing Industry and Government Lies about the Safety of the Genetically Engineered Foods You're Eating* and *Genetic Roulette: The Documented Health Risks of Genetically Engineered Foods.* Smith created IRT as a mechanism for providing information about GM foods to the general public and to policy makers around the world. The organization studies risks posed by GM foods on human health, agriculture, the environment, and the economy. The organization relies for its research and analysis primarily on volunteers from a wide variety of fields including media experts, social network campaigners, writers, graphic designers, communications specialists, fundraisers, outreach professionals, and support staff. Some of these individuals work out of the organization's main office in Fairfield, Iowa, whereas others work out of virtual offices throughout the United States.

A major focus of IRT's work is education about GM foods, providing publications and essays on topics such as the genetic engineering process, GMOs in foods, health risks posed by GM foods, risks to agriculture and the environment, issues related to the use of genetically engineered hormones in dairy products, special risks of GM foods posed to children, and 10 reasons to avoid using GM foods. An important section of the organization's website is devoted to the topic of alleged fraud by supporters of GM foods. The section purports to present the techniques used by pro-GM individuals and companies to make their case before the general public and decision makers, such as the use of rigged studies, the manipulation of data by pro-GM forces, the inadequacy of regulations dealing with GM crops and foods, and efforts that have been made to silence critics of the GM foods industry.

The institute also provides information for consumers about places and ways at and by which they can avoid encountering GM foods, with recommendations for places to buy non-GMO products, ways to determine whether restaurants are serving GMO products or not, and grocery stores and other purveyors of foods that are particularly sensitive to GM food issues. The organization also provides an iPhone app that can be used as a guide to the purchase of non-GMO products.

IRT sponsors a number of programs, campaigns, and other efforts to carry out its primary objectives. For example, the Tipping Point Network is a network of local activists who are committed to providing information about GMO products to their neighbors, local officials, and community organizations. The organization also provides tool kits specifically designed for parents, schools, and retailers, with information about GM foods and activities that can help people choose to purchase and eat non-GM products. IRT also has available a very wide selection of print and electronic resources on GM topics, including brochures and reports; a summary report called the *State of the Science Report*; a newsletter, *Spilling the Beans*; an archive of news reports about GM food topics; a list of speakers who are available to address GM food–related issues; and a number of audio and video programs on the topic.

Another especially helpful feature of the IRT website is a sub-banner that displays sections of interest to specialized groups, such as consumers, health care providers, retailers, manufacturers, schools, parents, and individuals who are especially interested in the subject of autism. In 2012, the organization released a new film on GMO issues titled *Genetic Roulette: The Gamble of Our Lives*, which won the 2012 Movie of the Year award given by the Solari Report and the top Transformational Film of the Year award given by AwareGuide.

International Service for the Acquisition of Agri-Biotech Applications

ISAAA SEAsiaCenter
Dr. Randy A. Hautea, Center Director and ISAAA
Global Coordinator
c/o IRRI
DAPO Box 7777, Metro Manila
The Philippines
Phone: +63 2 845-0563/0569/0573
Fax: +63 49 536-7216; +63 2 845-0606
Email: seasiacenter@isaaa.org

ISAAA AfriCenter
Dr. Margaret Karembu, Director
PO Box 70
ILRI Campus, Old Naivasha Rd.
Uthiru, Nairobi 00605
Kenya
Phone: +254 20 4223618
Fax: +254 20 4223600
Email: africenter@isaaa.org

ISAAA AmeriCenter
Ms. Patricia Meenen, Business Administrator
105 Leland Laboratory

Cornell University
Ithaca, NY 14853
Phone: (607) 255-1724
Fax: (607) 255-1215
(notify office of incoming fax)
Email: americenter@isaaa.org
URL for ISAAA: http://www.isaaa.org

The International Service for the Acquisition of Agri-Biotech Applications (ISAAA) is an international nonprofit organization established in 1992 for the purpose of providing technical information and tools related to agricultural biotechnology to poor and underserved farmers around the world. The organization's objective is to make possible the transfer of this technology to farmers who would otherwise not have access to it as a way of achieving agricultural sustainability and development. ISAAA has three centers of operation: SEAsiaCenter, hosted by the International Rice Research Institute (IRRI) in Los Baños, Laguna, Philippines; ISAAA AfriCenter, hosted by the International Livestock Research Institute (ILRI) located in Nairobi, Kenya; and ISAAA AmeriCenter, hosted by Cornell University, Ithaca, New York. Each center has additional specialized responsibilities. SEAsiaCenter also serves as the Global Coordination Office and the home of the Global Knowledge Center on Crop Biotechnology. AfriCenter is involved primarily with research on the tissue culture of bananas and rapid propagation of multipurpose trees. AmeriCenter also serves as the administrative and financial headquarters for ISAAA overall.

ISAAA is governed by a board of directors consisting of experts from around the world who are especially interested in developing agriculture systems that will help solve world hunger problems while protecting the natural environment. Current board members come from Brazil, Canada, China, India, the Philippines, Singapore, South Africa, the United Kingdom, and the United States. The organization's work receives financial support from a number of private and governmental organizations and agencies such as the African Agricultural Technology Foundation; Association for Strengthening Agricultural Research in Eastern and Central Africa; Bayer CropScience Ag; Cornell University; CropLife International; Fondazione Bussolera (Italy); Government of Kenya; Ibercaja (Spain); International Development Research Center of Canada; Maharashtra Hybrid Seeds Pvt. Ltd (India); Monsanto; National Council for Science and Technology (Kenya); Department of Agriculture (Philippines); Economic Commission for Africa; United Nations Educational, Scientific, and Cultural Organization; United States Department of Agriculture; U.S. Soybean Export Council; U.S. Agency for International Development (USAID); and Vibha Agrotech Pvt. Ltd (India).

ISAAA's work is divided into four major categories: Knowledge Sharing Initiative, Technology Transfer Projects, Impact Assessment of Crop Biotechnology, and Support Projects. The Knowledge Sharing Initiative was developed primarily in response to requests from policy makers and program directors in Southeast Asia for ISAAA to develop ways of providing information about agricultural biotechnology developments for farmers in their area. That function is now handled primarily by the Global Knowledge Center on Crop Biotechnology, which provides information and assistance through technical articles, reports, updates on developments, and a variety of useful publications. Among the most important of these is the Biotech Information Directory, which lists more than 500 links to research institutes, universities, companies, sources of biotech information, and other directories specific to agricultural biotechnology and related fields. Another useful publication is the weekly Crop Biotech Update, which provides a summary of world developments in the field of agricultural biotechnology. The center also provides a list of courses, meetings, workshops, and other events of potential interest to individuals and organizations interested in agricultural biotechnology.

ISAAA's Technology Transfer Projects have had a number of objectives, such as providing farmers with the tools to do diagnostic testing for specific plan diseases, learning how to develop transgenic crops with specific genetic characteristics, making use of molecular markers in crops, and designing plants with specific market applications. Impact studies are research attempts by ISAAA staff and colleagues to determine the economic, environmental, and social impact of agricultural biotechnology in specific areas. Some examples of studies of this type are research on the environmental impact of Bt eggplant in the Philippines, regulatory costs of commercializing papaya ringspot virus (PRSV) in the Philippines and Indonesia, effects on farm income and productivity of GM sweet potato in Kenya, and the economic impact of Bt corn in the Philippines.

The ISAAA Impact Assessment of Crop Biotechnology area of research involves using skills from the social sciences to measure the impact of crop biotechnology on factors such as economic surplus, agricultural productivity and income, human health and nutrition, and environmental effects of the technology. Previous research has focused on the impact of engineered papaya, banana, eggplant, corn, and sweet potato crops in areas such as Kenya, the Philippines, and Indonesia.

ISAAA's Support Projects are programs conducted with other agencies (e.g., Cornell University and USAID) to move GM products along the pipeline from academic research to the marketplace. One such current program, the Agricultural Biotechnology Support Project II (ABSP II), is focusing on ways in which biotechnology products can be commercialized in east and west Africa, India, Bangladesh, Indonesia, and the Philippines.

Another of the ISAAA's invaluable databases is its online GM Approval Database, which contains information on any GM crop that has been approved for use in nearly three dozen countries and the European Union. An interactive tool allows one, as just one example, to discover that three varieties of herbicide-tolerant (Roundup Ready) alfalfa are currently approved for use in eight countries around the world. The database also provides detailed information about the nature of the genetic modification that has been used in the plant and other relevant information about the product.

In addition to its regular print and electronic publications, ISAAA maintains a very useful blog on its website at http://isaaablog.blogspot.com/.

John D. Kemp (1940–)

Kemp and Timothy Hall headed a research team that, in 1983, found a way to insert a gene from one plant, the common bean (*Phaseolus vulgaris*), into a second plant, the sunflower (*Helianthus annuus*), after which the gene was expressed as an apparently normal part of the sunflower's genome. The experiment is of significance because it was the first time that the transfer of genes between two plants as the result of human intervention had been demonstrated, a procedure that provides the basis for much of the genetic engineering of plants conducted today. On August 10, 1981, *Newsweek* magazine ran a story about Kemp and Hall's "sunbeam" plant as a harbinger of the future of plant biotechnology.

John Daniel Kemp was born in Minneapolis, Minnesota, on January 20, 1940. He attended the University of California at Los Angeles (UCLA), from which he received his BS in chemistry in 1962 and his PhD in biochemistry in 1965. He then remained at UCLA for postdoctoral studies from 1965 to 1968. Upon completing his postdoctoral studies, Kemp accepted an appointment as assistant professor at the University of Wisconsin, where he eventually became professor of plant pathology in 1977. During his tenure at Wisconsin, Kemp was concurrently a research chemist for the Agricultural Research Service (ARS) of the U.S. Department of Agriculture (USDA) and vice president, head of microbiology, acting director, and associate director at the Agrigenetics Corporation in Boulder, Colorado.

In 1985, Kemp left Wisconsin to become professor of plant pathology and director of the Plant Genetic Engineering Laboratory at New Mexico State University in Las Cruces. He retired from New Mexico State in 2002 and is currently professor emeritus at the university. Hall's accomplishment is memorialized today with a plaque at the History of Genetics section of the Smithsonian Institution, in honor of the first plant-to-plant gene transfer in history.

Steve Lindow (1951–)

Lindow is a pioneer in the study of the ways in which bacteria are involved in the formation of ice crystals on plants. This process is responsible plant death caused by freezing temperatures. The ability to find ways of preventing these so-called ice-nucleating bacteria from acting on plants provides a mechanism for allowing those plants to survive low temperatures at which they would otherwise freeze. This research led to the development in the early 1980s of the first GM organism to be released into the environment, an ice-minus bacterium that was spread on a plot of strawberries. The experiment was conducted in December 1987 by the biotechnology company Advanced Genetic Sciences (AGS). Shortly thereafter, a similar experiment was conducted using ice-minus bacteria on potato seedlings. Both experiments were regarded as technical successes, suggesting a promising future for the use of GM bacteria to increase crop yields. Environmental groups took quite a different view, however, expressing concerns about possible harmful effects on other plants in the test area. Some members of these groups expressed their concerns by launching a guerilla attack on two test plots of strawberries and potatoes at Brentwood and Tule Lake, California, respectively, in 1988. They noted their objections to the experiments by simply tearing out all the plants being tested with the ice-minus bacteria.

Steven E. Lindow was born in Portland, Oregon, on May 20, 1951. He attended Oregon State University, in Corvallis, from which he earned a bachelor of science degree in botany in 1973. He then matriculated at the University of Wisconsin at Madison, where he was awarded his PhD in plant pathology in 1977. His doctoral thesis dealt with the topic on which he was eventually to spend most of his academic career, the role of bacteria in the destruction of plants by frost formation.

After completing a year's postdoctoral research at Wisconsin-Madison, he accepted an appointment as assistant professor of plant pathology at the University of California at Berkeley. He has remained at Berkeley ever since, with promotions to associate professor in 1983 and full professor in 1989, a post he continues to hold. The majority of his work has focused on ice-minus bacteria, a topic on which he has written more than 125 peer-reviewed papers and more than 70 book chapters, mini-reviews, and full books.

In addition to his academic research, Lindow has been involved in a variety of professional activities. For example, he was a member of the U.S. Department of Agriculture Biotechnology Research Advisory Committee from 1988 to 1990, the Environment Protection Agency's Subcommittee on Mitigation and Containment of Recombinant Organisms in 1989, the National Science Foundation Workgroup on Molecular Ecological Methods in 1985, the National Academy of Science Taskforce on Biological Control Research Needs and Priorities in Plant/Microbe Interactions in Agriculture in 1988, and the U.S. Department of Energy Workgroup on Molecular Methods in Ecology in 1991. He has also served on the Public and Scientific Affairs Board of the American Society for Microbiology (1988–1990); the Honors and Awards committee (1997–2000), Phyllosphere Microbiology committee (1989–1992 and 1998–2001), and Epidemiology committee (1995–1998) of the American Phytopathological Society; and the Scientific Board of the International Society for Molecular Plant-Microbe Interactions (2003 to present). He has also been organizer or co-organizer on a number of conferences on ice-nucleating bacteria, including the International Conferences on

Biological Ice Nucleation held in San Francisco (1982); Flagstaff, Arizona (1984); Newport, Oregon (1987); Saskatoon, Canada (1989); and Madison, Wisconsin (1991).

Among Lindow's many honors are the CIBA/Geigy and Ruth Allen awards of the American Phytopathological Society, election as fellow of that society in 1994, election to the National Academy of Sciences in 1999, the Procter and Gamble award of the American Society for Microbiology, and election as fellow to the American Academy of Microbiology and the American Association for the Advancement of Science. In 2004, he was given a Distinguished Teaching Award by the College of Natural Resources at Berkeley.

Mark Lynas (1973–)

Mark Lynas is a journalist, photographer, author, and environmental activist who was actively involved in the anti-GM food movement in the late 1990s. Lynas remembers that he became involved in that movement after attending a small meeting of activists in Brighton led by Jim Thomas, a campaigns director for Greenpeace. Lynas reports that his first reaction to the stories Thomas had to tell was horror at the things that modern biotechnology companies were doing to the world's food supplies. He came to the conclusion, he later said, that "[b]ig corporations were using more chemicals so that they could take over the food chain."

He soon became increasingly active in the anti-GMO movement, taking part in "actions" at fields where new GM crops were being tested. His protest activities may have reached a zenith on April 29, 1998, when he took part in a sit-in at Monsanto's offices at High Wycombe, in Buckinghamshire, England. His role in the action, he said, was that he "cased the joint, printed the leaflets and hired the buses."

Even at this early point in his career of activism against GM products, he had begun to have second feelings about his participation in such campaigns. He reports that he was increasingly aware that his colleagues in protest had a tendency to ignore the best scientific evidence about GM products and hewed to preconceived notions about their effects on human health and the natural environment. Although he remained active in the anti-GMO movement for a number of years, he finally broke with his previous allies in March 2013. That break came in an address he made to the annual Oxford Farming Conference, a meeting of the world's leading representatives of the agricultural community. It is regarded as a premier session of the members of the agriculture "establishment." At the meeting, Lynas read a 5,000-word speech in which he apologized for having worked so hard in opposition to GM products and explained that he now realized he was wrong in his understanding and interpretation of the work of agricultural biotechnology firms like Monsanto. (It perhaps goes without saying that Lynas's speech became the focus of a vigorous exchange of views between pro- and anti-GM activists.)

Mark Lynas was born in Fiji and then traveled with his family to Peru, Spain, and the United Kingdom. He attended the University of Edinburgh, from which he received his degree in history and politics. His father was a geologist who worked on mapping projects for the government, which activity was responsible for Lynas's earliest interests in climate-change issues. He describes a trip to his family's home in 2000 during which they looked at photographs taken 20 years earlier, when his father was mapping on the remote eastern side of the Cordillera Blanca, Peru's highest range. The dominant feature of these photographs was an enormous glacier in one of the region's valleys. When his father observed that the glacier was probably decreasing in size because of global warming, Lynas decided to set off on a world journey to collect evidence of the way climate change was affecting Earth features. In 2002, he completed that journey by returning to the Cordillera Blanca, where he found that the glacier in his father's photographs had completely disappeared. That discovery only confirmed Lynas's decision to devote his career to the campaign to work for the reduction of greenhouse gases and further global warming.

The result of that commitment has been a number of articles, speeches, books, films, and other productions that describe the risks posed by global climate change, the reasons for that process, and the steps that must be taken to reverse the process. The most important of those works are his books *High Tide: The Truth about Our Climate Crisis* (Picador 2004), in which he provides before-and-after pictures of the effect of climate change on geographic features, taken during his 2000–2002 trip around the world; *Gem Carbon Counter* (Collins 2007), a resource that shows how one can calculate one's own carbon footprint and how it can be changed; *Six Degrees: Our Future on a Hotter Planet* (National Geographic 2007), in which Lynas provides verbal and photographic descriptions of the effects of one-, two-, three-, four-, five-, and six-degree increases in the planet's annual average temperature; and *The God Species: Saving the Planet in the Age of Humans* (National Geographic 2011), in which he describes the threat that human life now poses to other plants and animals on Earth.

In addition to his books, Lynas has contributed to a collection of essays on environmental issues, *Fragile Earth: Views of a Changing World* (Collins 2006); been involved in the production of a film called *The Age of Stupid*, set in 2055 and showing the long-term effects of global climate change; and contributed regularly to a number of major newspapers and magazines, including *Ecologist*, *Geographical*, *Granta*, the *Guardian New Statesman*, and the *Observer*.

(Quotations in this article are taken from Will Storr, "Mark Lynas: Truth, Treachery and GM Food," *Guardian*, http://www.theguardian.com/environment/2013/mar/09/mark-lynas-truth-treachery-gm, accessed on December 9, 2013, and Mark Lynas, "Vanishing Worlds," *Guardian*, http://www.theguardian.com/society/2004/mar/31/environment.environment, accessed on December 9, 2013.)

Monsanto

800 N. Lindbergh Blvd.
St. Louis, MO 63167
Phone: (314) 694-1000
Email: http://www.monsanto.com/whoweare/Pages/contact-us.aspx
URL: http://www.monsanto.com/

Monsanto is a large, publicly traded, multinational chemical and agricultural biotechnology company. Its name is probably more closely associated with research on and the development of agricultural biotechnology products of any company in the world. It is seen by many people as having made enormous contributions to the development of new agricultural products and, therefore, contributing to the solution of some of the world's most serious problems (e.g., widespread hunger). Other people argue that it has caused more problems for the world's agricultural systems and for human nutrition than any existing corporation. The company's record is so extensive and expansive that no such generalized statement can reasonably summarize its historic and current achievements.

The Monsanto Company was founded in 1901 by John Francis Queeny, a native of Chicago who had been working in the pharmaceutical industry since the age of 12. Queeny took his wife's maiden name as the name for his new company. The first product made by the company was saccharin, a widely popular artificial sweetener, which it sold to the Coca-Cola company and to the manufacturers of canned food products. Over the years, the company diversified and expanded the variety of products it manufactured, adding the raw material salicylic acid, aspirin, and vanillin, as well as a number of chemicals used in the processing of natural rubber. It later added one of the most important of all raw chemicals for industrial processes, sulfuric acid, as well as a class of very popular industrial chemicals known as the polychlorinated biphenyls (PCBs), which were later to be associated with a variety of human health problems.

Through a series of mergers and acquisitions, and through its own research, Monsanto eventually added the personnel, technology, and facilities to extend even further the variety of products it made, which eventually include such items as light-emitting diodes (LEDs), artificial dopamine (a drug used to treat Parkinson's disease), acetic acid (an essential raw material for a variety of industrial chemical syntheses), and AstroTurf (a plastic material used on athletic fields, home lawns, and other settings in place of natural grass).

In the early 1980s, Monsanto began to focus on the development and production of GM seeds, crops, and foods. A key step in this decision was the purchase of an agricultural biotechnology company called Agracetus (founded in 1981 under the name Cetus). Agracetus had focused on the development of technology for the production of genetically transformed organisms (including the production of a "gene gun" used to fire transformed genes into host cells). Agracetus also developed the first successful genetically engineered crop, Roundup Ready soybean, which it made available commercially in 1991. Today, the Agracetus Campus of the Monsanto Company is located on a 4.5-acre site in Middleton, Wisconsin, with a staff of more than 21,000 employees.

Agracetus is only one of many Monsanto subsidiaries. Other specialized divisions are Asgrow, a seed production and marketing company specializing in research on soybeans, maize, and sorghum; Calgene, specializing in herbicide-tolerant and insect-resistant crops; DeKalb Genetics, the world's second largest seed company; First Line Seed, which sells soybean seeds primarily; EID Parry, an Indian producer of cotton seeds; Monsoy, the largest producer and seller of soybean seeds in Brazil; and Plant Breeding International Cambridge, Ltd, a British firm that specializes in research on grass seeds, potatoes, barley, wheat, and rapeseed. Monsanto's revenue for all its operations in 2013 was $14.9 billion.

The controversy over Monsanto's activities is too complex to be discussed in this short article. Two pieces of datum reflect the range of this controversy. In 2009, the business journal *Forbes* named Monsanto its Company of the Year for its enormous success during a period of economic recession in the United States and the world (see http://www.forbes.com/forbes/2010/0118/americas-best-company-10-gmos-dupont-planet-versus-monsanto.html). Only a year later, the Swiss company Covalence, which ranks companies on the basis of their business ethics, placed Monsanto last on its list of 581 international corporations (see http://web.archive.org/web/20100610062335/http://www.covalence.ch/index.php/ethical-rankings/across-sectors).

Non-GMO Project

1200 Harris Ave., Suite #305
Bellingham, WA 98225
Phone: (877) 358-9240
Fax: (866) 272-8710
Email: info@nongmoproject.org
URL: http://www.nongmoproject.org

The Non-GMO Project was born in 2005, when two grocery stores, The Natural Grocery Company in Berkeley, California, and The Big Carrot Natural Food Market in Toronto, Canada, combined to develop a standard definition for GM foods that could be used in their own buying and selling activities. This move grew out of a common experience in both stores in which customers were increasingly interested in knowing which products contained GM elements and which did not. The stores both discovered that responding to customers' concerns was especially difficult because there was no widely accepted meaning as to what it meant for a product to be a GMO food. The new organization eventually accomplished its goal through a cooperative effort with the Global ID Group, whose work is involved with the testing and certification of non-GMO foods.

Identification and promotion of foods that do not contain GM components is still a major part of the Non-GMO

Project's work. Its website, for example, provides lists of food products, restaurants, and retailers who guarantee that all their products are completely natural and contain no GM components. A visitor to the website can click on the appropriate button and find extensive lists of businesses in each category that it can trust as a supplier of non-GMO products. The organization also has a verification process in place that allows a food supplier, restaurant, or food retailer to apply for approval as a non-GMO industry.

Another aspect of the Non-GMO Project's work is community involvement. Individuals and businesses are encouraged to become involved in the effort to identify and distinguish GM foods in a variety of ways, ranging from supplying recipes that do not involve the use of GM products to participation in the Non-GMO month activities to organizing or participating in a variety of activities designed to promote the goals of the Non-GMO Project.

Retailers are a special target of the organization's activities also. The Retailer Toolkit includes activities such as a quarterly newsletter with articles relevant to the sale of non-GM foods by retailers; webinars designed specifically for retailers interested in handling non-GM foods; so-called shelf talkers, which are tags that highlight the availability on shelves of foods that contain no GM components; a FAQ trifold that contains basic facts about GM foods in a brightly illustrated and interesting format; a statement of policies about non-GMO food products; and a plan for connected retailers with the parent organization and with each other.

Non-GMO Project also has a special outreach to members of the food industry, whom it works with and encourages to promote the production and distribution of non-GM foods. Access to the food industry page on the organization's website is password protected, allowing direct access from a specific industry member directly to the organization itself.

The issue of food labeling is also a matter of major concern to the organization. It provides information on the status of current efforts throughout the United States to require the labeling of GM foods and food products, and it offers suggestions and materials for use by individuals who are interested in participating in the food labeling campaign in their own state and community.

The News and Events section of the organization's website provides a guide to forthcoming events at restaurants, food suppliers, and food producers associated with the organization. A recent listing of events, for example, mentioned the official verification recently received by a bakery, approval of certain specific non-GMO foods at another bakery, and the awarding of a seal of approval for its products to a food supplement company.

Organic Consumers Association

6771 South Silver Hill Dr.
Finland, MN 55603
Phone: (218) 226-4164
Fax: (218) 353-7652
Email: http://www.organicconsumers.org/aboutus.cfm#contact
URL: http://www.organicconsumers.org/

The Organic Consumers Association (OCA) is a nonprofit, online, grassroots, public interest 501(c)3 organization whose mission is to promote health, justice, and sustainability. The organization was founded in 1998 in response to a decision by the U.S. Department of Agriculture (USDA) to establish a set of regulations for organic food to which many food producers objected. A number of growers, distributors, and consumers of organic foods concluded that the proposed USDA regulations would dramatically degrade the quality of products sold under the rubric of "organic," and they organized a massive protest that produced more than 280,000 letters and emails complaining about the USDA decision. The organization has continued to grow since then and now claims a worldwide membership of over 850,000 individuals. Included among these members are thousands of natural food and organic grocery stores, markets, and other retail outlets, as well as producers and consumers of such products. Some of the other organizations affiliated with OCA are the National Coalition against the Misuse of Pesticides, Consumers Union, Native Forest Council of Oregon, Ashland Community Food Store (Ashland, Oregon), Network for Safe & Secure Food and Environment (Japan), Family Farm Defenders of Wisconsin, and Research Foundation for Science, Technology, & Natural Resource Policy (India).

A major feature of OCA's program is a six-point Organic Agenda 2005–2015 that calls for

1. The conversion of American agriculture to at least 30 percent organic products by 2015
2. A free trade approach to the distribution of food, in contrast to the existing system controlled by large multinational corporations
3. A global moratorium on genetically engineered crops and foods
4. A phase-out of the most dangerous industrial agriculture and factory farming practices
5. Universal health care for all Americans, with an emphasis on better nutrition, preventive health care, and wellness programs
6. Energy independence with vastly increased emphasis on the use of alternative and renewable energy sources

A major feature of OCA's work is its Take Action program, in which the organization encourages members and friends to become involved in specific activities related to its overall mission. Some recent Take Action alerts involved opposition to a federal bill that would prohibit state anti-GMO laws and regulations; letter writing to two U.S. senators expressing opposition to voluntary (but not mandatory) labeling of GM foods; action to have the use of the antibiotic streptomycin banned from use with organic apples and pears; speaking out against membership of certain organizations and individuals in the Grocery Manufacturers Association (GMA), which has been involved in actions against state laws for the labeling of GM products; letter writing to the U.S. Food and Drug Administration (FDA) in opposition to the approval of GM foods; lobbying of national representatives and senators in opposition to the proposed Farmers Assurance Provision, also known by its opponents as the Monsanto Protection Act; and expressions of opposition to new trade bills that are in conflict with OCA's stand on free trade.

The OCA website is also a gold mine of information on current events worldwide related to organic farming and related issues. In a recent posting, that website contained feature stories on the French government's initiative to double land devoted to organic farming by 2017, the signing of a bill prohibiting the farming of GM crops on the Big Island of Hawaii, the advantages of grass-fed food animals over "factory-farmed" animals, the latest news on a controversial study on the health effects of GM food by Belgian researchers Gilles Eric Séralini, and recommendations for a variety of foods with supposedly significant nutritional advantages, such as cinnamon, nutmeg, and kale.

The OCA website also has a very extensive listing of "green" businesses, ranging from buying clubs and organic snacks to holistic dentists and chiropractors to outdoor furniture and appliances. For individuals with an interest in organic crops and foods, the association also provides a variety of electronic newsletter with current news about events in the field, *Organic Bytes* (http://www .organicconsumers.org/organicbytes.cfm).

A section of the website is also a useful resource for a variety of topics relating to genetic engineering, such as pages on rBGH (recombinant bovine growth hormone), the Millions against Monsanto campaign, issues related to cloning and patenting of life forms, the nature and applications of nanotechnology, progress in the development of GM wheat, and research on GM fish.

Ingo Potrykus (1933–)

Nutrition experts recommend a varied diet consisting of vegetables and fruits, as well as animal and dairy products for the maintenance of good health. For millions of people around the world, however, such a diet is next to impossible. Many of those people rely almost entirely on a restricted diet of grains, such as corn or rice, with a limited supply of other nutritional foods. Lacking the complete diet needed to maintain good health, many people are susceptible to nutritional disorders, as well as being at increased risk for infectious diseases. These health problems can lead to a number of disabling and even fatal disorders that account for high morbidity and mortality rates in developing countries around the world.

Researchers have been working for decades on ways of resolving this basic problem of world nutrition. One of the most promising solutions devised thus far has been the invention of GM foods that contain nutrients not found in the normal basic diet of individuals who cannot afford or do not have access to a diet of healthy natural foods. A leader in this researcher has long been Ingo Potrykus, a coinventor, with German biologist Peter Beyer, of the GM food known as Golden Rice. Golden Rice is a form of the crop that has been engineered to contain the provitamin known as β-carotene, or provitamin A. A provitamin is a substance that is converted within the human body into the vitamin of the same name. Thus, provitamin A is converted in the body to vitamin A, a substance known to strengthen the human immune system in general and, more specifically, to protect against diseases of the eye that can result in blindness. According to some estimates, as many as a half-million children worldwide die each year as a result of vitamin A deficiency disorders. By genetically modifying the food that many of those children eat as a cornerstone of their daily diets—rice—Potrykus and Beyer created a mechanism for saving hundreds of thousands of lives each year. The presence of the orange-colored β-carotene in the engineered rice accounts for the golden color of the product, and hence its name.

Ingo Potrykus was born in Hirschberg im Riesengebirge, Germany, on December 5, 1933. He attended the universities of Erlangen and Cologne, where he studied biochemistry, botany, genetics, philosophy, physical education, and zoology. He received his PhD in plant genetics from the Max Planck Institute for Plant Breeding Research in Cologne in 1968. He then accepted an appointment as assistant professor at the Institute of Plant Physiology at Stuttgart–Hohenheim, where he served from 1970 to 1974 before becoming group leader at the Max Planck Institute for Genetic at Ladenburg–Heidelberg from 1974 to 1976. He then assumed a similar post at the Friedrich Miescher Institute in Basel, Switzerland, from 1976 to 1986. During his stay in Basel, Potrykus received his habilitation in botany from the University of Basel (1982). The habilitation degree is the highest honor given to an academic in Europe and some other parts of the world. It is awarded to a person with a PhD degree who has extended his or her research to a higher level that leads to life-long tenured positions in his or her field. In 1986, Potrykus received such an appointment when he was named full professor of plant sciences at the Eidgenössische Technische Hochschule Zürich (ETH, Swiss Federal Institute of Technology), a post he held until his retirement in 1999.

Potrykus and Beyer began their research on Golden Rice in the late 1980s and received a grant from the Rockefeller Foundation in 1993 to carry out a seven-year project on the development of the product. Since his retirement in 1999, Potrykus has continued to work on the engineered crop through the International Humanitarian Golden Rice Board, where he has served as president. His objective, and that of the board, is to make available the fruits of their research on Golden Rice to people living in impoverished nations where rice is the primary component of a person's diet, such as China, India, Vietnam, Bangladesh, Indonesia, and the Philippines.

Potrykus has authored more than 340 scientific papers on Golden Rice and been awarded 30 patents for the product. He has received numerous awards for his work, including the Kumho Science International Award in Plant Molecular Biology and Biotechnology (2000), the American Society of Plant Biologists Leadership in Science Public Service Award (2001), the Crop Science of America President's Award and European Culture Award in Science (2002), and the Bertebos Prize of the Royal Swedish Academy of Agriculture and Forestry (2007). He was also given an honorary doctorate by the Swedish University of Agricultural Sciences in 2002 and by the University of Freiburg in 2007. He was also named the most influential scientist in the area of agricultural, industrial, and environmental biotechnology for the decade 1995–2005 by the readers of the journal *Nature Biotechnology* in 2006 and was featured on the cover of *Time* magazine on July 31, 2000, as someone whose work could "save a million kids a year." Potrykus has also been honored by election to a number of prestigious societies, including Academia Europaea, the Swiss Academy of Technical Sciences, the Hungarian Academy of Sciences, Academia Bibliotheca Alexandria, the Pontifical Academy of Sciences, and the World Technology Network.

Maxine Singer (1931–)

In a biographical sketch of Singer, the National Library of Medicine has noted that "[d]uring the early 1970s, as debate over the environmental and health risks of the new technology of gene recombination grew ever more heated, Maxine Singer was a leading voice of prudence, patience, and dedication to balancing scientific principles and public welfare." The period called for just such an outlook on new research on genetic engineering. Only a few years earlier, the work of Arthur Kornberg, Gobind Khorana, Paul Berg, Herbert Boyer, Stanley N. Cohen, and others had shown that it was possible to modify the DNA of an organism, opening a new line of research that scientists could hardly have imagined only a few decades earlier. And it was clear to those scientists that the modifications they were now able to make could potentially produce revolutionary changes in human society. They were confronted with the challenge of finding ways of going forward with this research, gaining the greatest amount of new information from it, without placing human health or the natural environment at risk. It was a difficult and challenging balancing act on which Singer was to make as important contributions as anyone else in the field.

Maxine Frank Singer was born in New York City on February 15, 1931, to Henrietta (née Perlowitz) Frank, a hospital admissions officer, children's camp director, and model, and Hyman Frank, an attorney. She attended public schools in Brooklyn, where she developed an interest in science early in life. She has credited her high school chemistry teacher with encouraging her to continue her studies in the field when she matriculated at Swarthmore College, from which she received her bachelor's degree in 1952. Singer then continued her studies at Yale University, which granted her a PhD in biochemistry in 1957. Although her doctoral studies at Yale focused on protein chemistry, she soon became fascinated by the newly important subject of nucleic acids. (Watson and Crick had announced the chemical structure of the DNA molecule in 1953.)

Upon graduation, Singer looked for a laboratory where she could pursue her own research on nucleic acids. One of the few options then available in the United States was the laboratory run by Leon Heppel at the National Institutes of Health

(NIH) at Bethesda, Maryland. Heppel hired Singer to join his team at the laboratory of biochemistry in the National Institute of Arthritis and Metabolic Diseases (later renamed the National Institute of Arthritis, Metabolism, and Digestive Diseases [NIAMDD]). Singer was hired as a postdoctoral fellow in spite of the fact that she had not officially received her doctorate from Yale. Two years later, she was appointed to a regular full-time position at NIAMDD, where she remained until 1974.

The mid-1970s were a period of discussion and debate about the potential impacts of recombinant DNA research on human health and the natural environment. That debate reached a critical point at a 1973 session of the annual Gordon Conference, a highly regarded series of meetings on current scientific topics that always attracts leaders in the field of physical, biological, mathematical, and social sciences. Singer cochaired a session on current research on DNA, and attendees at the session discussed possible social consequences of this line of research. They recommended writing a letter that would be published in the journal *Science* calling for a meeting of researchers in the field to get closer attention to this problem. Singer was one of the authors and signers of that letter, and she went on to become one of the organizers of that meeting, the Asilomar Conference on Recombinant DNA, held at Asilomar State Park, California, in February 1975.

In 1974, Singer left NIAMDD to accept a new position at NIH as chief of the Section on Nucleic Acid Enzymology at the Division of Cancer Biology and Diagnosis (DCBD) at the National Cancer Institute (NCI). Six years later, she was promoted to chief of the DCBD Laboratory of Biochemistry, a post she held until 1988. She then accepted appointment as president of the Carnegie Institution, one of the nation's most prestigious research institutions, in Washington, DC. She retired from Carnegie in 2002. During her tenure at Carnegie, she retained her affiliation with NCI, where she continued her research on human genetics.

Singer's work has been recognized with a number of awards and honors. She has been given honorary degrees by Brandeis University, Dartmouth College, Harvard University, New York University, Swarthmore College, the Weizmann Institute of Science, Williams College, and Yale University. She was elected to the American Academy of Arts and Sciences in 1978, the National Academy of Sciences in 1979, and the Pontifical Academy of Sciences in 1986. She was given the Distinguished Presidential Rank Award in 1988 by President Ronald Reagan and the National Medal of Science in 1992 by President Bill Clinton. The citation accompanying the National Medal noted that it was given for Singer's "outstanding scientific accomplishments and her deep concern for the societal responsibility of the scientist."

Singer married fellow research Daniel Morris Singer in 1952. They have four grown children.

Marc van Montagu (1933–)

GM organisms are synthesized by inserting the DNA from some organism, or artificially produced DNA, into the cells of a host organism. Under the proper conditions, DNA in the host cell takes up the introduced DNA to form a hybrid product that consists of the host DNA and introduced DNA. A key challenge faced by genetic researchers, then, is to find a way of producing this hybrid DNA by cutting the host DNA and pasting in the foreign DNA.

During the 1970s, a number of research teams around the world were attempting to solve this problem. In the early 1980s, a breakthrough occurred almost simultaneously in two laboratories, one led by Mary-Dell Chilton, originally at the University of Washington, and Marc van Montagu, then at the University of Ghent, in Belgium. These discoveries eventually became the basis for the technology by which the vast majority of genetically engineered organisms are produced today.

Marc van Montagu was born in Ghent, Belgium, on November 10, 1933. He attended Ghent University, from which he received his MSc in chemistry and organic chemistry in 1955 and his PhD in organic chemistry and biochemistry in 1965. During the period from 1956 to 1960, van Montagu worked as director of the Bureau of Studies at the Technical School for the Nuclear Industry. Over his academic career, van Montagu divided his time among three academic appointments, as part-time professor at the Free University of Brussels (until 1989), full professor of molecular genetics at the University of Ghent (until 1999), and director of the Department of Genetics at the Flanders Institute of Biochemistry (until 1999).

In 1982, van Montagu drew on his experience with and discoveries in genetic engineering to create a new company, Plant Genetics Systems, Inc. (PGS), to bring those discoveries into commercial realization. The company was a joint venture between European investors and Advanced Genetic Systems, of Oakland, California. Van Montagu served as scientific director and a member of the board of directors of PGS until 1996. PGS was acquired by the German company AgroEvo in 1995 and was later absorbed by the pharmaceutical giant Novartis. In 1998, van Montagu founded a second biotechnology company, CropDesign, which was acquired in 1996 by BASF Plant Science.

Throughout his career, van Montagu has held a number of additional scientific research and consulting posts that include chair of the Scientific Advisory Committee of the Danforth Center, St. Louis; member of the Science Board of the Alellyx corporation, São Paulo; biotechnology advisor to the International Center for Agriculture Research in Dry and Arid Areas (ICARDA), Aleppo, Syria; member of the Board of Governors and of the Scientific Advisory Board of the Weizmann Institute of Science, Rehovot, Israel; member of the Science Advisory Committee of the Institute of Molecular Biology and Biotechnology, Heraklion, Crete; member of the International Advisory Board at King Abdulaziz University, Jeddah, Saudi Arabia; member of the Board of Directors of the Avesthagen biotechnology company, Bangalore, India; and scientific advisor to the biotechnology firms Tibotech (Belgium) and Extracta (Brazil).

Van Montagu has been honored with a number of awards and prizes, including the Theodor Bücher Medal of the Federation of European Biochemical Societies; Genome Valley Excellence Award, presented by BioAsia, India; the Rank Prize for Nutrition; the IBM-Europe Prize; the Charles Leopold Mayer Prize of the Academy of Sciences, France; the Dr. A. de Leeuw–Damry–Bourlart Prize of the Belgian National Fund for Scientific Research; the Japan Prize; and the World Food Prize, in 2013. The last of these awards is widely considered to be one of the highest honors awarded to food scientists in the world, accompanied by a $250,000 cash award (shared among three winners in 2013). He has been elected to a number of honorary societies, including the U.S. National Academy of Sciences, Belgian Royal Academy of Sciences, Academia Europea, Agricultural Academy of Russia, Academy of Engineering of Sweden, Agricultural Academy of France, Royal Academy of Overseas Sciences, Italian Academy of Sciences dei XL, American Academy of Microbiology, and Third World Academy of Sciences. He has been awarded honorary doctorates by the universities of Helsinki, Compiegne, Rio de Janeiro, Liege, Brussels, Habana, and Sofia.

Although officially retired from his academic appointments in 1999, van Montagu has remained active in GM food-related work. In 2000, for example, he founded the Institute of Plant Biotechnology Outreach to assist developing countries with the implementation of latest research in the genetic engineering of organisms and to encourage research in the field in their own countries.

World Health Organization

Avenue Appia 20
1211 Geneva 27

Switzerland
Phone: +41 22 791 21 11
Fax: +41 22 791 31 11
Email: http://www.who.int/about/contact_form/en/index.html
URL: http://www.who.int

The World Health Organization (WHO) is a division of the United Nations, the first specialized agency of the United Nations created during its founding in San Francisco in July 1946. All 61 nations present at that conference signed not only the founding documents of the United Nations but also the new constitution of the WHO. The organization formally became operational on April 7, 1948, also designated as the first World Health Day, after the 26th member state signed the ratification documents for the organization.

WHO currently consists of 194 member states, each of whom sends delegates to the World Health Assembly, which meets yearly to set overall policy for the group. That policy is carried out on a day-to-day basis by a director-general and 34-member executive board, chosen by the assembly. Much of the ongoing work of the organization is carried out through WHO's regional offices in the Brazzaville, Congo (Africa), Washington, DC (Americas), Cairo (Eastern Mediterranean), Copenhagen (Europe), New Delhi (Southeast Asia), and Manila (Western Pacific). The agency's home office is in Geneva.

Every six years, WHO establishes a global health plan that focuses on some large-scale health issue to which the organization will give major attention over the ensuing period. For the period 2008–2013, that health plan was directed at the prevention and control of four noncommunicable diseases—cardiovascular diseases, diabetes, cancers, and chronic respiratory diseases—and four shared risk factors—tobacco use, physical inactivity, unhealthy diets, and the harmful use of alcohol (see http://whqlibdoc.who.int/publications/2009/9789241597418 _eng.pdf). For the period 2014–2019, the health plan focused on the prevention of avoidable blindness and visual impairment (see http://www.who.int/blindness/Zerodraftactionplan 2014-19.pdf).

In addition to this single large-scale effort, WHO has a myriad number of specific health problems to which it devotes its energy and with which it works in partnership with member states. Some of those topics are accountability for women's and children's health, African Programme for Onchocerciasis Control, aging and life course, blood products and related biologicals, blood transfusion safety, child growth standards, children's environmental health, climate change and human health, diagnostic imaging, dracunculiasis, essential medicines for children, food safety, gender, women and health, health and human rights, HIV/AIDS, household water treatment and safe storage, immunization financing, leprosy elimination, malaria, occupational health, prevention of deafness and hearing impairment, social determinants of health, transplantation, vaccine safety, and water sanitation and health. The organization devotes a section of its website to information about biotechnology, which includes information on GM foods and the controversy that surrounds their use and labeling.

One of WHO's most important functions is the production of a large range of publications on virtually every possible health topic. These publications are led by a group of peer-reviewed and specialized journals in health science that include the monthly journal, *Bulletin of the World Health Organization*; the *Weekly Epidemiological Record*; the *Eastern Mediterranean Health Journal*; the *WHO South-East Asia Journal of Public Health*; *Western Pacific Surveillance and Response*; and *WHO Drug Information*. Publications also include reports and reference books on a wide range of health topics, such as the annual *World Health Report*, a document that summarizes the status of health status in member nations; *World Health Statistics*, an annual compilation of data from the organization's member states; *International Travel and Health*, a publication on health risks for international travelers, vaccination requirements, and precautions to take; *International Health Regulations*, a listing of public health regulations that are legally binding on WHO member states; *The International Classification of Diseases*, the international standard diagnostic classification for epidemiological and health management purposes; and *International Pharmacopoeia*, a collection of quality specifications for pharmaceutical substances and dosage forms. WHO also publishes an extensive collection of reports, reviews, statistical information, guidelines, and other documents for each of its six regions. A complete list of all WHO publications is available on the organization's website at http://apps.who.int/bookorders/anglais/home1.jsp?sesslan=1.

WHO also collects, collates, archives, and distributes statistical information on virtually every health issue of concern today. These data cover topics such as mortality and morbidity estimates, health systems, the health workforce, health financing, noncommunicable diseases, infectious diseases, road safety, substance abuse, and women's health issues.

Introduction

One can learn a great deal about the history, background, and current issues related to genetically modified (GM) foods by examining the documentary history of that subject. This chapter provides brief excerpts from a number of laws, regulations, court cases, reports, and other documents dealing with GM foods. The last part of the chapter also provides some interesting statistical data about GM foods.

Data

Table 5.1 Genetically Engineered Crops in the United States, 2000–2013 (percent of all planted crop; all genetically engineered varieties)

As of 2013, three of the most important crops in the United States, cotton, corn, and soybeans, have been planted primarily in the form of genetically engineered seeds. This table shows the increase in the use of GM seeds in the United States between 2000 and 2013.

Year	Corn	Cotton	Soybeans
2000	25	61	54
2001	26	69	68
2002	34	71	75

(continued)

Vernon Hugh Bowman, a 75-year-old Indiana soybean farmer, speaks with reporters outside the Supreme Court in Washington. On May 13, 2013, the Supreme Court said that the Indiana farmer violated Monsanto Co.'s patents on soybean seeds resistant to its weed-killer. Bowman had been growing the beans without buying new seeds from the corporation. (AP Photo/ J. Scott Applewhite)

Table 5.1   (*continued*)

Year	Corn	Cotton	Soybeans
2003	40	73	81
2004	47	76	85
2005	52	79	87
2006	61	83	89
2007	73	87	91
2008	80	86	92
2009	85	88	91
2010	86	93	93
2011	88	90	94
2012	88	94	93
2013	90	90	93

Source: "Genetically Engineered Varieties of Corn, Upland Cotton, and Soybeans, by State and for the Unites States, 2000–13." USDA Economic Research Service. http://www.ers.usda.gov/data-products/adoption-of-genetically-engineered-crops -in-the-us.aspx#.Ug0OJZLCZ8F. Accessed on August 15, 2013.

Table 5.2   Laws and Regulations on Genetically Modified Crops and Foods

No federal laws exist to prohibit the production, culturing, planting, growth, processing, sale, or other use of GM products in the United States. However, a number of state and local jurisdictions have adopted various forms of regulation to limit or promote the use of such products. This table summarizes most of those laws and regulations as of late 2013.

State	Laws and/or Regulations
Arkansas	Restrictions on production, sale, transport, use, storing, harvesting, and so on of certain types of GM rice
California	Marin county: GM crops prohibited within county Mendocino county: GM crops prohibited within county Santa Cruz county: Moratorium on propagation and growing of GM crops within county Trinity county: GM crops prohibited within county City of Arcata: GM crops prohibited within city City of Point Arena: GM crops prohibited within city
Colorado	City of Boulder: GM crops prohibited on city land
Florida	Restrictions on transport and use of Bt cotton within the state Permit required for culturing of transgenic fish
Hawaii	Bt cotton banned in the state
Idaho	GM plants and plant pests prohibited within state

(*continued*)

Table 5.2 *(continued)*

State	Laws and/or Regulations
Indiana	Seed suppliers prohibited from entering private farm land to test for GM products
Maine	Town of Montville: GMO-free zone (no GM seeds permitted)
Maryland	Permit required for the raising of GM fish in the state
Michigan	Raising of GM fish prohibited in state
Minnesota	Permit required for the release of GM organisms in the state Permit required for field experiments with GM pesticides
Mississippi	Permit required for cultivation of GM fish in the state
Missouri	Control on the planting, culturing, sale, and so on of GM rice in the state
Nebraska	Seed suppliers prohibited from entering private farm land to test for GM products
Oregon	GM fish may not be released in areas where they will compete with native fish Bentgrass Control Area established with separation between native and GM varieties of the crop
South Dakota	Seed suppliers prohibited from entering private farm land to test for GM products
Washington	San Juan county: GM crops prohibited within county Creation of Canola Control Areas to ensure separation of native and GM forms of the crop Transgenic fish banned from state
Wisconsin	Permit required for the release of GM organisms into the environment

Note: The following states have passed laws prohibiting local jurisdictions from adopting laws controlling one or another aspect of the planting, growth, cultivation, transport, sale, and other use of GM organisms: Arizona, Florida, Georgia, Idaho, Indiana, Iowa, Kansas, North Dakota, Ohio, Oklahoma, Pennsylvania, South Dakota, Texas, and West Virginia.

Source: Adapted from "State/Local Efforts to Control GMOs." Organic Consumers Association. http://www.organicconsumers.org/articles/article_27247.cfm. Accessed on August 20, 2013.

Table 5.3   Characteristics of Permits on Genetically Modified Crops Issued
by Animal and Plant Health Inspection Service

One component of the U.S. system for regulating GM crops involves approval
by the U.S. Department of Agriculture Animal and Plant Health Inspection
Service (APHIS) for the release of GMOs into the environment. Data on the
types of permits approved provide a good overview of the types of GM
products that are being tested or developed in the United States.

Number of Releases Approved by APHIS, 1985–2013

Year	Number of Approved Releases
1985	4
1986	11
1987	11
1988	16
1989	30
1990	51
1991	90
1992	160
1993	301
1994	579
1995	711
1996	612
1997	763
1998	1,071
1999	983
2000	925
2001	1,083
2002	1,194
2003	813
2004	893
2005	955
2006	865
2007	932
2008	871
2009	751
2010	660
2011	792
2012	665
2013 (as of November 1, 2013)	537

(continued)

Table 5.3   (continued)

Release Counts for 10 Most Regulated Products

Product	Number of Approved Releases
Corn	7,779
Soybean	2,225
Cotton	1,104
Potato	904
Tomato	688
Wheat	485
Alfalfa	452
Tobacco	427
Rapeseed	310
Rice	294

Number of Approved Releases by Modified Trait

Trait	Number of Approved Releases
Herbicide tolerance	6,772
Agronomic property[1]	5,293
Product quality	4,898
Insect resistance	4,809
Other	1,986
Marker gene	1,892
Virus resistance	1,425
Fungal resistance	1,191
Bacterial resistance	224
Nematode resistance	149

[1]Such as tolerance to cold, soil salinity, stress, drought, or pests.

Top 10 Permit Holders

Permit Holder	Number of Permits
Monsanto	6,782
Pioneer Hi-Bred International	1,085
Syngenta	566
Dow Agrosciences	400
U.S. Department of Agriculture	370
AgrEvo	326
Du Pont	320
ArborGen	311
Bayer CropScience	260
Seminis Vegetable Seeds	210

(continued)

Table 5.3   (*continued*)

Ten Most Frequent Locations for Release of GMO

State	Number of Permits
Hawaii	3,057
Illinois	2,937
Puerto Rico	2,931
Iowa	2,639
California	1,869
Indiana	1,504
Nebraska	1,832
Minnesota	1,183
Wisconsin	1,027
Florida	1,022

Source: All data from Release Summary Data and Charts (1987 to Present). Information Systems for Biotechnology. Virginia Tech University. http://www.isb .vt.edu/release-summary-data.aspx. Accessed on October 23, 2013. All data used by permission.

Table 5.4 Trends in Approved Phenotype Releases in the United States, 1987–2012, by Percent of All Permits Issued by APHIS (rounded to nearest whole number)

Over the past three decades, crops have been genetically altered for a variety of reasons. This table shows the proportion of GM crops approved by the U.S. Department of Agriculture Animal and Plant Health Inspection Service (APHIS) from 1987 to 2012.

Year	BR	VR	FR	OO	NR	IR	MG	HT	AP	PQ	N
1987								100			5
1988		19	6			31	6	31		5	16
1989		21		3		27	6	33		9	33
1990		37		7		24	4	19	1	7	68
1991	8	20	5	3		22	7	19	4	14	107
1992	2	25	2	2		16	1	33	3	15	201
1993	1	15	4	2	1	21	1	32	2	22	362
1994	1	16	3	2	1	19	2	26	3	29	674
1995	1	14	4	4	1	26	2	22	4	24	829
1996	1	15	7	5		25	3	24	3	17	746
1997	1	13	6	4	1	21	3	31	7	15	986
1998	1	13	8	2		23	3	28	7	15	1,465
1999	1	15	5	6		21	5	21	10	15	1,255
2000	1	8	6	6	1	25	5	29	8	13	1,109
2001	1	5	5	6	1	32	6	23	8	15	1,269
2002	1	2	3	4		33	4	29	9	16	1,426
2003	1	3	4	5	1	18	6	31	11	21	1,022

(continued)

Table 5.4 (continued)

Over the past three decades, crops have been genetically altered for a variety of reasons. This table shows the proportion of GM crops approved by the U.S. Department of Agriculture Animal and Plant Health Inspection Service (APHIS) from 1987 to 2012.

Year	BR	VR	FR	OO	NR	IR	MG	HT	AP	PQ	N
2004	1	2	4	7	1	16	6	29	16	20	1,155
2005	1	1	4	6	1	15	6	24	17	27	1,358
2006	1	2	5	8	1	13	8	29	19	24	1,386
2007	1	2	3	6	1	22	7	24	22	14	1,774
2008	1	1	4	15	1	9	8	20	26	17	1,854
2009	1	1	3	5	1	11	7	22	30	29	1,279
2010	1	1	3	9	1	8	9	22	28	18	1,688
2011	1	1	4	9	1	9	10	20	31	14	2,143
2012	1	1	4	11	1	10	10	21	29	13	2,109

BR, bacterial resistance; VR, virus resistance; FR, fungal resistance; OO, other; NR, nematode resistance; IR, insect resistance; MG, marker gene; HT, herbicide tolerance; AP, agronomic properties; PQ, product quality; N, number of all permits issued.

Source: Adapted from "Releases and Permits by Phenotype per Year." Information Systems for Biotechnology. Virginia Tech University. http:// www.isb.vt.edu/phenotype-by-years.aspx. Accessed on October 24, 2013.

Table 5.5   Global Farm Income Benefits from Growing Genetically Modified
Crops, 1996–2011 (million US$)

The British research firm of PG Economics, Ltd, has been following the economic costs and benefits to farmers worldwide as a result of the use of GM
crops for more than a decade. Tables 5.5, 5.6, and 5.7 reprint some of the most
basic data they have found in their most recent (2013) study.

Trait	Increase in farm income 2011	Increase in farm income 1996–2001	Percent of total value[1]	Percent of total value[2]
GM herbicide-tolerant soybeans	3,879.2	32,211.9	3.8	3.2
GM herbicide-tolerant maize	1,540.2	4,212.2	1.5	0.7
GM herbicide-tolerant cotton	166.9	1,224.1	0.4	0.3
GM herbicide-tolerant canola	433.2	3,131.4	1.4	1.2
GM insect-resistant maize	7,104.9	25,762.0	6.8	3.3
GM insect-resistant cotton	6,559.6	31,263.2	14.7	11.6
Others	83.3	412.0	n/a	n/a
Total	19,767.3	98,216.8	6.3	5.9

n/a, not applicable.
[1]Farm income benefit in 2011 as percent of total value of production of those crops
in GM adopting countries.
[2]Farm income benefit in 2011 as percent of total value of global production of crop.
Source: Brookes, Graham, and Peter Barfoot. 2013. GM Crops: Global Socio-
economic and Environmental Impacts 1996–2011, Table 1, 10–11. Dorchester,
UK: PG Economics, Ltd.

Table 5.6 Genetically Modified Crop Farm Income Benefits of 1996–2011: Selected Countries (million US$)

More data from the 2013 PG Economics, Ltd, survey.

Country	GM HT soybeans	GM HT maize	GM HT cotton	GM HT canola	GM IR maize	GM IR cotton	Total
United States	13,835.9	3,110.5	924.8	241.5	21,497.3	3,769.4	43,379.4
Argentina	12,624.6	510.5	89.0	n/a	380.7	362.3	13,967.1
Brazil	4,314.5	431.5	82.6	n/a	1,796.9	19.9	6,645.4
Paraguay	732.4	n/a	n/a	n/a	n/a	n/a	732.4
Canada	231.6	66.7	n/a	2,862.5	820.5	n/a	3,981.3
South Africa	7.0	3.8	3.0	n/a	887.3	31.6	932.7
China	n/a	n/a	n/a	n/a	n/a	13,067.8	13,067.8
India	n/a	n/a	n/a	n/a	n/a	12,579.5	12,579.5
Australia	n/a	n/a	58.4	27.5	n/a	525.4	611.3
Mexico	4.9	n/a	51.4	n/a	n/a	123.9	180.2
Philippines	n/a	88.2	n/a	n/a	176.1	n/a	264.3
Romania	44.6	n/a	n/a	n/a	n/a	n/a	44.6
Uruguay	83.4	n/a	n/a	n/a	11.7	n/a	95.1
Spain	n/a	n/a	n/a	n/a	139.1	n/a	139.1
Other EU	n/a	n/a	n/a	n/a	16.2	n/a	16.2
Colombia	n/a	0.9	14.9	n/1	29.2	13.7	58.7
Bolivia	327.0	n/a	n/a	n/a	n/a	n/a	327.0
Burma	n/a	n/a	n/a	n/a	n/a	338.7	338.7
Pakistan	n/a	n/a	n/a	n/a	n/a	334.2	334.2

HT, herbicide tolerant; IR, insect resistant; n/a, not applicable.

Source: Brookes, Graham, and Peter Barfoot. 2013. *GM Crops: Global Socio-economic and Environmental Impacts 1996–2011*, Table 2, 11. Dorchester, UK: PG Economics, Ltd.

Table 5.7   Genetically Modified Crop Farm Income Benefits of 2011: Developing versus Developed Countries (million US$)

Additional data from the 2013 PG Economics, Ltd, survey.

Crop	Developed Countries	Developing Countries[1]
GM HT soybeans	1,794.2	2,085.0
GM IR maize	5,710.4	1,394.5
GM HT maize	897.1	643.1
GM IR cotton	650.7	5,908.9
GM HT cotton	80.7	86.2
GM HT canola	433.2	0
GM virus-resistant papaya and squash and GM HT sugar beets	83.3	0
Total	9,649.6	10,117.7

HT, herbicide tolerant; IR, insect resistant.
[1]Developing countries: all countries in South America, Mexico, Honduras, Burkina Faso, India, China, the Philippines, and South Africa.

Source: Brookes, Graham, and Peter Barfoot. 2013. *GM Crops: Global Socio-economic and Environmental Impacts 1996–2011*, Table 3, 12. Dorchester, UK: PG Economics, Ltd.

Documents

Plant Patent Act of 1930

During the first three decades of the twentieth century, American botanist Luther Burbank developed a number of new plant species through the process of hybridization. As a result of his work, a number of political figures recommend that the U.S. Congress adopt a law permitting Burbank and inventors like him to patent their discoveries. And thus was born the Plant Patent Act of 1930, which, in 1980, the U.S. Supreme Court extended to cover genetically engineered plants, as well as naturally occurring plants.

§161. Patents for plants

Whoever invents or discovers and asexually reproduces any distinct and new variety of plant, including cultivated sports, mutants, hybrids, and newly found seedlings, other than a tuber propagated plant or a plant found in an uncultivated state, may obtain a patent therefor, subject to the conditions and requirements of this title.

The provisions of this title relating to patents for inventions shall apply to patents for plants, except as otherwise provided.

§162. Description, claim

No plant patent shall be declared invalid for noncompliance with section 112 if the description is as complete as is reasonably possible.

The claim in the specification shall be in formal terms to the plant shown and described.

§163. Grant

In the case of a plant patent, the grant shall include the right to exclude others from asexually reproducing the plant, and from using, offering for sale, or selling the plant so reproduced, or any of its parts, throughout the United States, or from importing the plant so reproduced, or any parts thereof, into the United States.

Source: U.S. Code. Chapter 15, Sections 161–163. http://uscode.regstoday.com/35USC_CHAPTER15.aspx. Accessed on May 17, 2014.

Diamond v. Chakrabarty, 447 U.S. 303 (1980)

In 1971, microbiologist Ananda Mohan Chakrabarty, while employed by the General Electric (GE) corporation, invented a bacterium capable of digesting crude oil, a potentially useful invention for the removable of oil spills on water or land. GE applied for a patent for Chakrabarty's discovery, which was denied by the U.S. Patent Office on the grounds that patents could not be issued for living objects. That decision was appealed through the courts until it reached the U.S. Supreme Court, which decided on a five-to-four vote that the patent could be issued. Portions of the majority and dissenting opinions are quoted here. Omitted sections are indicated by ellipses (. . .).

Chief Justice Burger, for the majority:

We have also cautioned that courts "should not read into the patent laws limitations and conditions which the legislature has not expressed." . . . Guided by these canons of construction, this Court has read the term "manufacture" in § 101 [*the relevant patent law, Title 35 U.S.C. § 101*] in accordance with its dictionary definition to mean "the production of articles for use from raw or prepared materials by giving to these materials new forms, qualities, properties, or combinations, whether by hand labor or by machinery." . . . Similarly, "composition of matter" has been construed consistent with its common usage to include "all compositions of two or more substances and . . . all composite articles, whether they be the results of chemical union, or of mechanical mixture, or whether they be gases, fluids, powders or solids." . . . In choosing such expansive terms as "manufacture" and "composition of matter," modified by the comprehensive "any," Congress plainly contemplated that the patent laws would be given wide scope.

. . .

Judged in this light, respondent's micro-organism plainly qualifies as patentable subject matter. His claim is not to a hitherto unknown natural phenomenon, but to a nonnaturally occurring manufacture or composition of matter—a product of human ingenuity "having a distinctive name, character [and] use."

. . .

Our task, rather, is the narrow one of determining what Congress meant by the words it used in the statute; once that is done, our powers are exhausted. Congress is free to amend § 101 so as to exclude from patent protection organisms produced by genetic engineering. . . . Or it may choose to craft a statute specifically designed for such living things. But, until Congress takes such action, this Court must construe the language of § 101 as it is. The language of that section fairly embraces respondent's invention.

Writing for the four dissenting judge, Justice Brennan pointed out that:

In this case, however, we do not confront a complete legislative vacuum. The sweeping language of the Patent Act of 1793, as reenacted in 1952, is not the last pronouncement Congress has made in this area. In 1930, Congress enacted the Plant Patent Act affording patent protection to developers of certain asexually reproduced plants. In 1970, Congress enacted the Plant Variety Protection Act to extend protection to certain new plant varieties capable of sexual reproduction. Thus, we are not dealing—as the Court would have it—with the routine problem of "unanticipated inventions." . . . In these two Acts, Congress has addressed the general problem of patenting animate inventions and has chosen carefully limited language granting protection to some kinds of discoveries, but specifically excluding others. These Acts strongly evidence a congressional limitation that excludes bacteria from patentability.

. . .

. . . the 1970 Act clearly indicates that Congress has included bacteria within the focus of its legislative concern, but not within the scope of patent protection. Congress specifically excluded bacteria from the coverage of the 1970 Act. . . . The Court's attempts to supply explanations for this explicit exclusion ring hollow. It is true that there is no mention in the legislative history of the exclusion, but that does not give us license to invent reasons. The fact is that Congress, assuming that animate objects as to which it had not specifically legislated could not be patented, excluded bacteria from the set of patentable organisms.

Source: "Diamond v. Chakrabarty—447 U.S. 303 (1980)." Justia.com. http://supreme.justia.com/cases/federal/us/447/303/case.html. Accessed on August 15, 2013.

Coordinated Framework for the Regulation of Biotechnology (1986)

Authority for the control over the approval of research on and commercialization of bioengineered products in the United States is a complex system first announced in a 1986 document issued by the Office of Science and Technology Policy (OSTP). The key sections of that document that divide up this responsibility are reprinted here. For acronyms, see footnotes; FDA = Food and Drug Administration, EPA = Environmental Protection Agency, and S&E = Science and Education Administration of the U.S. Department of Agriculture.

CHART I.—COORDINATED FRAMEWORK—APPROVAL OF COMMERCIAL BIOTECHNOLOGY PRODUCTS

Subject	Responsible Agency(ies)
Foods/Food Additives	FDA* FSIS[1]
Human Drugs, Medical Devices, and Biologics	FDA
Animal Drugs	FDA
Animal Biologics	APHIS
Other Contained Uses	EPA
Plants and Animals	APHIS* FSIS[1] FDA[2]
Pesticide Microorganisms Released in the Environment	EPA* APHIS[3]

(continued)

CHART I.   (*continued*)

Subject	Responsible Agency(ies)
All	
Other Uses (Microorganisms)	EPA*
Intergeneric Combination	APHIS[3]
Intrageneric Combination	APHIS
Pathogenic Source Organism	EPA*,[4]
1. Agricultural Use	APHIS[3]
2. Nonagricultural Use	EPA Report
No Pathogenic Source Organisms	
Nonengineered Pathogens	APHIS
1. Agricultural Use	EPA[4]
2. Nonagricultural Use	APHIS[3]
Nonengineered Nonpathogens	EPA Report

*Lead agency.
[1]FSIS, Food Safety and Inspection Service, under the assistant secretary of agriculture for marketing and inspection services, is responsible for food use.
[2]FDA is involved when in relation to a food use.
[3]APHIS, Animal and Plant Health Inspection Service, is involved when the microorganism is plant pest, animal pathogen, or regulated article requiring a permit.
[4]EPA requirements will only apply to environmental release under a "significant new use rule" that EPA intends to propose.

CHART II.—COORDINATED FRAMEWORK—BIOTECHNOLOGY RESEARCH JURISDICTION

Subject	Responsible Agency(ies)
Contained Research, No Release in the Environment	Funding agency[1]
	NIH or S&E
1. Federally Funded	Voluntary review
2. Nonfederally Funded	APHIS[2]
Foods/Food Additives, Human Drugs, Medical Devices, Biologics, Animal Drugs	FDA*, NIH
	Guidelines and review
1. Federally Funded	FDA*, NIH
2. Nonfederally Funded	Voluntary review
Plants, Animals, and Animal Biologics	Funding agency*,[1]
1. Federally Funded	APHIS[2]
2. Nonfederally Funded	APHIS*
	S&E
	Voluntary review

(*continued*)

CHART II. *(continued)*

Subject	Responsible Agency(ies)
Pesticide Microorganisms	EPA*
Genetically Engineered	APHIS[2]
Intergeneric	S&E
Pathogenic Intergeneric	Voluntary review
Intrageneric Nonpathogen	EPA*
Nonengineered	APHIS[2]
Nonindigenous Pathogens	S&E
Indigenous Pathogens	Voluntary review
Nonindigenous Nonpathogen	EPA,* S&E
	Voluntary review
	EPA*
	APHIS
	EPA*,3
	APHIS
	EPA*
Other Uses (Microorganisms) Released in the	Funding agency*,[1]
Environment:	APHIS[2]
Genetically Engineered	EPA[4]
Intergeneric Organisms	EPA, APHIS
1. Federally Funded	S&E
2. Commercially Funded	Voluntary review
Intrageneric Organisms	Funding agency*,[1]
Pathogenic Source Organism	APHIS,[2]
1. Federally Funded	EPA[4]
2. Commercially Funding	APHIS[2]
Intrageneric Combination	EPA (*if nonagricultural use)
No Pathogenic Source Organisms	EPA Report
Nonengineered	EPA Report*
	APHIS[2]

*Lead Agency.
[1]Review and approval of research protocols conducted by NIH, S&E, or NSF.
[2]APHIS issues permits for the importation and domestic shipment of certain plants and animals, plant pests and animal pathogens, and for the shipment or release in the environment of regulated articles.
[3]EPA jurisdiction for research on a plot greater than 10 acres.
[4]EPA reviews federally funded environmental research only when it is for commercial purposes.

Source: Office of Science and Technology Policy. 1986. *Coordinated Framework for Regulation of Biotechnology*. http://www.aphis.usda.gov/brs/fedregister/coordinated _framework.pdf. Accessed on August 19, 2013.

Cartagena Protocol on Biosafety (2000)

The Cartagena Protocol on Biosafety was adopted in 2000 and signed by 77 nations. It entered into force on September 11, 2003, when a sufficient number of nations had ratified the treaty. The treaty outlines provisions for the movement of living modified organisms (LMOs) resulting from modern biotechnology from one country to another. The treaty has a number of provisions, perhaps the most important of which is Article 11, which is reproduced in its entirety here.

Article 11

Procedure for Living Modified Organisms Intended for Direct Use as Food or Feed, Or For Processing

1. A Party that makes a final decision regarding domestic use, including placing on the market, of a living modified organism that may be subject to transboundary movement for direct use as food or feed, or for processing shall, within fifteen days of making that decision, inform the Parties through the Biosafety Clearing-House. This information shall contain, at a minimum, the information specified in Annex II. The Party shall provide a copy of the information, in writing, to the national focal point of each Party that informs the Secretariat in advance that it does not have access to the Biosafety Clearing-House. This provision shall not apply to decisions regarding field trials.

2. The Party making a decision under paragraph 1 above, shall ensure that there is a legal requirement for the accuracy of information provided by the applicant.

3. Any Party may request additional information from the authority identified in paragraph (b) of Annex II.

4. A Party may take a decision on the import of living modified organisms intended for direct use as food or feed, or for processing, under its domestic regulatory framework that is consistent with the objective of this Protocol.

5. Each Party shall make available to the Biosafety Clearing-House copies of any national laws, regulations and guidelines applicable to the import of living modified organisms intended for direct use as food or feed, or for processing, if available.

6. A developing country Party or a Party with an economy in transition may, in the absence of the domestic regulatory framework referred to in paragraph 4 above, and in exercise of its domestic jurisdiction, declare through the Biosafety Clearing-House that its decision prior to the first import of a living modified organism intended for direct use as food or feed, or for processing, on which information has been provided under paragraph 1 above, will be taken according to the following:

(a) A risk assessment undertaken in accordance with Annex III; and

(b) A decision made within a predictable timeframe, not exceeding two hundred and seventy days.

7. Failure by a Party to communicate its decision according to paragraph 6 above, shall not imply its consent or refusal to the import of a living modified organism intended for direct use as food or feed, or for processing, unless otherwise specified by the Party.

8. Lack of scientific certainty due to insufficient relevant scientific information and knowledge regarding the extent of the potential adverse effects of a living modified organism on the conservation and sustainable use of biological diversity in the Party of import, taking also into account risks to human health, shall not prevent that Party from taking a decision, as appropriate, with regard to the import of that living modified organism intended for direct use as food or feed, or for processing, in order to avoid or minimize such potential adverse effects.

9. A Party may indicate its needs for financial and technical assistance and capacity-building with respect to living

modified organisms intended for direct use as food or feed, or for processing. Parties shall cooperate to meet these needs in accordance with Articles 22 and 28.

Source: "Text of the Cartagena Protocol on Biosafety." Convention on Biological Diversity. http://bch.cbd.int/ protocol/text/. Accessed on September 6, 2013.

Guidance for Industry: Voluntary Labeling Indicating Whether Foods Have or Have Not Been Developed Using Bioengineering (2001)

As of late 2013, there were no federal, state, or local laws that require foods containing genetically modified ingredients to carry that information on their labels. However, in 2001, the U.S. Food and Drug Administration (FDA) did release a statement suggesting the types of information that food producers might include on labels, indicating the presence of GM products. A portion of that statement is as follows (omitted footnotes are indicated by ellipses [. . .]):

STATEMENTS ABOUT FOODS DEVELOPED USING BIOENGINEERING

FDA recognizes that some manufacturers may want to use informative statements on labels and in labeling of bioengineered foods or foods that contain ingredients produced from bioengineered foods. The following are examples of some statements that might be used. The discussion accompanying each example is intended to provide guidance as to how similar statements can be made without being misleading.

"Genetically engineered" or "This product contains cornmeal that was produced using biotechnology."

The information that the food was bioengineered is optional and this kind of simple statement is not likely to be misleading. However, focus group data indicate that consumers would prefer label statements that disclose and explain the goal of the technology (why it was used or what it does for/to the food). . . . Consumers also expressed some preference for the term "biotechnology" over such terms as "genetic modification" and "genetic engineering". . . .

"This product contains high oleic acid soybean oil from soybeans developed using biotechnology to decrease the amount of saturated fat."

This example includes both required and optional information. As discussed above in the background section, when a food differs from its traditional counterpart such that the common or usual name no longer adequately describes the new food, the name must be changed to describe the difference. Because this soybean oil contains more oleic acid than traditional soybean oil, the term "soybean oil" no longer adequately describes the nature of the food. Under section 403(i) of the act, a phrase like "high oleic acid" would be required to appear as part of the name of the food to describe its basic nature. The statement that the soybeans were developed using biotechnology is optional. So is the statement that the reason for the change in the soybeans was to reduce saturated fat.

"These tomatoes were genetically engineered to improve texture."

In this example, the change in texture is a difference that may have to be described on the label. If the texture improvement makes a significant difference in the finished product, sections 201(n) and 403(a)(1) of the act would require disclosure of the difference for the consumer. However, the statement must not be misleading. The phrase "to improve texture" could be misleading if the texture difference is not noticeable to the consumer. For example, if a manufacturer wanted to describe a difference in a food that the consumer would not notice when purchasing or consuming the product, the manufacturer should phrase the statements so that the consumer can understand the significance of the difference. If the change in the tomatoes was intended to facilitate processing but did not make a noticeable difference in the processed consumer product, a phrase like "to improve texture for processing" rather than "to improve texture" should be used to ensure that the consumer is not misled. The statement that the tomatoes were genetically engineered is optional.

"Some of our growers plant tomato seeds that were developed through biotechnology to increase crop yield."

The entire statement in this example is optional information. The fact that there was increased yield does not affect the characteristics of the food and is therefore not necessary on the label to adequately describe the food for the consumer. A phrase like "to increase yield" should only be included where there is substantiation that there is in fact the stated difference.

Where a benefit from a bioengineered ingredient in a multi-ingredient food is described, the statement should be worded so that it addresses the ingredient and not the food as a whole; for example, "This product contains high oleic acid soybean oil from soybeans produced through biotechnology to decrease the level of saturated fat." In addition, the amount of the bioengineered ingredient in the food may be relevant to whether the statement is misleading. This would apply especially where the bioengineered difference is a nutritional improvement. For example, it would likely be misleading to make a statement about a nutritionally improved ingredient on a food that contains only a small amount of the ingredient, such that the food's overall nutritional quality would not be significantly improved.

Source: "Guidance for Industry: Voluntary Labeling Indicating Whether Foods Have or Have Not Been Developed Using Bioengineering; Draft Guidance." http://www.fda.gov/Food/ GuidanceRegulation/GuidanceDocumentsRegulatoryInformation/ LabelingNutrition/ucm059098.htm. Accessed on August 17, 2013.

Regulation of Genetically Modified Foods by the European Union (2003)

Genetically modified (GM) foods are regulated in the European Union by an extensive body of legislation adopted by a variety of organizations. Probably the most important single document is Regulation (EC) No 1829/2003 of the European Parliament, adopted in 2003. The document is a very long one that explains the basis for the regulations provided and that includes every conceivable aspect of the production, distribution, and consumption of GM foods. The core of that document is reprinted here.

Article 4

Requirements

1. Food referred to in Article 3(1) must not:

(a) have adverse effects on human health, animal health or the environment;

(b) mislead the consumer;

(c) differ from the food which it is intended to replace to such an extent that its normal consumption would be nutritionally disadvantageous for the consumer.

2. No person shall place on the market a GMO for food use or food referred to in Article 3(1) unless it is covered by an authorisation granted in accordance with this Section and the relevant conditions of the authorisation are satisfied.

3. No GMO for food use or food referred to in Article 3(1) shall be authorised unless the applicant for such authorisation has adequately and sufficiently demonstrated that it satisfies the requirements of paragraph 1 of this Article.

4. The authorisation referred to in paragraph 2 may cover:

(a) a GMO and foods containing or consisting of that GMO as well as foods produced from or containing ingredients produced from that GMO; or

(b) food produced from a GMO as well as foods produced from or containing that food;

(c) an ingredient produced from a GMO as well as food containing that ingredient.

5. An authorisation as referred to in paragraph 2 shall not be granted, refused, renewed, modified, suspended or revoked except on the grounds and under the procedures set out in this Regulation.

6. The applicant for an authorisation as referred to in paragraph 2 and, after the authorisation is granted, the authorisation-holder or his representative, shall be established in the Community.

7. Authorisation under this Regulation shall be without prejudice to Directive 2002/53/EC, Directive 2002/55/EC and Directive 68/193/EEC.

Source: "Regulation (EC) No 1829/2003 of the European Parliament and of the Council of 22 September 2003 on Genetically Modified Food and Feed." EUR-Lex. http://eur-lex .europa.eu/LexUriServ/LexUriServ.do?uri=CELEX:32003R1829 :EN:HTML. Accessed on August 15, 2013.

Mendocino County (California) Ban on Genetically Modified Crops (2004)

In 2004, the voters of Mendocino County, California, voted by a margin of 57 percent to 43 percent to ban the planting of GM crops in the county. The text of that law, in part, is as follows (omitted text is indicated by ellipses [. . .]):

CHAPTER 10A.15 PROHIBITION ON
THE PROPAGATION, CULTIVATION, RAISING
AND GROWING OF GENETICALLY MODIFIED
ORGANISMS IN MENDOCINO COUNTY

Sec. 10A.15.010 Finding.

The people of Mendocino County wish to protect the County's agriculture, environment, economy, and private property from genetic pollution by genetically modified organisms. (Measure H-2004, passed March 2, 2004.)

Sec. 10A.15.020 Prohibition.

It shall be unlawful for any person, firm, or corporation to propagate, cultivate, raise, or grow genetically modified organisms in Mendocino County. (Measure H-2004, passed March 2, 2004.)

Sec. 10A.15.030 Definitions.

... [This section defines terms used in the law.]

Sec. 10A.15.040 Penalties.

(A) The Agricultural Commissioner shall notify any person, firm, or corporation that may be in violation of Section 10A.15.020 of this Chapter, that any organisms in violation of this Chapter are subject to confiscation and destruction.

(B) Any person, firm, or corporation that receives notification under subsection (A) shall have five (5) days to respond to such notification with evidence that such organisms are not in violation of this Chapter.

(C) Upon receipt of any evidence under subsection (B), the Agricultural Commissioner shall consider such evidence and any other evidence that is presented or which is relevant to a determination of such violation. The Agricultural Commissioner shall make such determination as soon as possible, but at least before any genetic pollution may occur.

(D) Upon making a determination that a violation of this Chapter exists, the Agricultural Commissioner shall cause to be confiscated and destroyed any such organisms that are in violation of this Chapter before any genetic pollution may occur.

(E) If the Agricultural Commissioner determines there has been a violation of this Chapter, in addition to confiscation and destruction of any organisms that are found to be in violation, the Agricultural Commissioner shall impose a monetary penalty on the person, firm, or corporation responsible for the violation, taking into account the amount of damage, any potential damage, and the willfulness of the person, firm, or corporation. (Measure H-2004, passed March 2, 2004.)

Source: "Chapter 10A.15 Prohibition on the Propagation, Cultivation, Raising and Growing of Genetically Modified Organisms in Mendocino County." Municode. http://library .municode.com/index.aspx?clientId=16484. Accessed on August 20, 2013.

The Safety of Genetically Modified Foods, GAO Report (2002)

In 2002, U.S. Representatives John E. Baldacci and John F. Tierney asked the U.S. General Accounting Office (GAO) to conduct a study on the safety of GM crops and foods. The GAO summarized its findings on that topic as follows:

GM foods pose the same types of inherent risks to human health as conventional foods: they can contain allergens, toxins, and compounds known as antinutrients, which inhibit the absorption of nutrients. Before marketing a GM food, company scientists evaluate these risks—even though they are not routinely evaluated in conventional foods—to determine if the foods pose any heightened risks. While some GM foods have contained allergens, toxins, and antinutrients, the levels have been comparable to those foods' conventional counterparts. In evaluating GM foods, scientists perform a regimen of tests. Biotechnology experts whom we contacted agree that this regimen of tests is adequate in assessing the safety of GM foods. While some consumer groups, as well as some scientists from the European Union, have questioned the ethical or cultural appropriateness of genetically modifying foods, experts whom we contacted from these organizations also believe the tests are adequate for assessing the safety of these foods.

While FDA reports that its evaluation process includes the necessary controls for ensuring it obtains the safety data needed to evaluate GM foods, some biotechnology experts state that aspects of its evaluation process could be enhanced. FDA's controls include (1) communicating clearly—through the agency's 1992 policy statement and subsequent guidance—what safety data are necessary for its evaluations of GM food safety; (2) having teams of FDA experts in diverse disciplines evaluate company submissions for GM foods and request additional safety data, if necessary; and (3) tailoring the level of evaluation to match the degree of each submission's novelty, thereby assuring that staff have time to obtain necessary safety data. Nonetheless, FDA's overall evaluation process could be enhanced, according to some experts, by randomly verifying the test data that companies provide and by increasing the transparency of the evaluation process—including communicating more clearly the scientific rationale for the agency's final decision on a GM food safety assessment.

In the future, scientists generally expect that genetic modifications will increasingly change the composition of GM foods to enhance their nutritional value. For example, one company has modified a type of rice to contain beta-carotene. In countries where rice is a dietary staple, this rice may reduce the incidence of blindness caused by vitamin-A deficiency. Current tests have been adequate for evaluating the few GM foods with relatively simple compositional changes that FDA has reviewed so far. New testing technologies are being developed to evaluate the increasingly complex compositional changes expected. Some scientists view these new technologies as a potentially useful supplement for existing tests, while others believe that the technologies will offer a more comprehensive way of assessing the safety of all changes in GM foods.

Monitoring the long-term health risks of GM foods is generally neither necessary nor feasible, according to scientists and regulatory officials we contacted. In their view, such monitoring is unnecessary because there is no scientific evidence, or even a hypothesis, suggesting that long-term harm (such as increased cancer rates) results from these foods. Furthermore, there is consensus among these scientists and regulatory officials that technical challenges make long-term monitoring infeasible.

Experts cite, for example, the technical inability to track the health effects of GM foods separately from those of their conventional counterparts. A recent report by food and health organizations affiliated with the United Nations also expresses skepticism about the feasibility of identifying long-term health effects from GM foods.

Source: *Genetically Modified Foods: Experts View Regimen of Safety Tests as Adequate, but FDA's Evaluation Process Could Be Enhanced.* 2002. United States General Accounting Office. GAO-02-566. http://www.gao.gov/assets/240/234718.pdf. Accessed on August 21, 2013.

Invoking of Preemption (North Dakota, SB2277; 2005)

A number of states have become concerned about the actions of individual towns, cities, counties, and other jurisdictions in passing legislation outlawing the use of genetically modified crops within their boundary. (See "Mendocino County," presented earlier, as an example.) In reaction to these actions, some states have adopted preemptive legislation that bans individual jurisdictions within the state from taking such actions. An example is a bill passed in the state of North Dakota in 2005, where such action is prohibited by the clause reproduced here. Brief comments by legislators at a meeting of the House Agriculture Committee at the time on both sides of the bill are also reproduced here. The comments are taken from notes taken at the committee session and are reproduced here verbatim.

4-35-06.1 LIMITATION ON AUTHORITY OF POLITICAL SUBDIVISIONS REGARDING PESTICIDES

No political subdivision, including a home rule city or county, may adopt or continue in effect any ordinance, resolution, or home rule charter regarding the registration, labeling, distribution, sale, handling, use, application, transportation, or disposal of pesticides. This section does not apply to city zoning ordinances.

CHAIRMAN NICHOLAS: Committee Members, I would like to roll out one more bill. It is the preemption bill SB 2277. This bill committee members we heard last week and this bill is dealing with regulation and distribution of seed. It will allow preemption [by the state] and somewhat over rule local ordinances. County ordinances that such in California where the map of California looks like a checkerboard as to regulations on seeding, etc. Environmentally groups Coming in and basically over ruling farmers abilities to use the type of seed and grow The kind of crops they want. This, hopefully, is a farmer friendly bill.

. . .

REPRESENTATIVE MUELLER: . . . I guess given what this bill is doing is a pretty far reaching bill. We are actually saying to the townships in the counties that you can't put any laws in place. Like that. I think that is kind of what the problem is. We are tying the hands of our people back home in our townships and counties to say which ever direction you can't do anything about it and for that reason I am in opposition to the bill.

Source: 2005 State Agriculture. OMB/Records Management Division. SFN 2053. http://www.legis.nd.gov/files/resource/59-2005/library/sb2277.pdf?20131023162344. Accessed on October 23, 2013. Also see "State/Local Efforts to Control GMOs." Organic Consumers Association. http://www.organic consumers.org/articles/article_27247.cfm. Accessed on October 23, 2013.

Monsanto Co. v. Geertson Seed Farms, 561 U.S. ___ (2010)

The first case reaching the U.S. Supreme Court regarding genetically engineered crops came on appeal by the Monsanto Company of a pair of adverse rulings from a District Court and from the U.S. Court of Appeals for the Ninth Circuit. Both these courts ruled that U. S. Department of Agriculture's Animal and Plant Health Inspection Service (APHIS) had improperly deregulated a

Monsanto product, Roundup Ready alfalfa (RRA), for use by farmers. The courts said that further studies were needed to ensure that genes from the engineered plant would not enter those of natural alfalfa. The Supreme Court ruled 7 to 1 that the lower courts were in error in making those decisions for a number of complex reasons. The core of their decision was as follows (ellipses [. . .] indicated the omission of notes and unrelated text):

We agree that the District Court's injunction against planting went too far, but we come to that conclusion for two independent reasons. First, the impropriety of the District Court's broad injunction against planting flows from the impropriety of its injunction against partial deregulation. If APHIS may partially deregulate RRA before preparing a full-blown EIS *[environmental impact statement]*—a question that we need not and do not decide here—farmers should be able to grow and sell RRA in accordance with that agency determination. Because it was inappropriate for the District Court to foreclose even the possibility of a partial and temporary deregulation, it necessarily follows that it was likewise inappropriate to enjoin any and all parties from acting in accordance with the terms of such a deregulation decision.

Second, respondents have represented to this Court that the District Court's injunction against planting does not have any meaningful practical effect independent of its vacatur *[a court order setting aside an administrative decision].* . . . An injunction is a drastic and extraordinary remedy, which should not be granted as a matter of course. . . . If a less drastic remedy (such as partial or complete vacatur of APHIS's deregulation decision) was sufficient to redress respondents' injury, no recourse to the additional and extraordinary relief of an injunction was warranted. . . .

In sum, the District Court abused its discretion in enjoining APHIS from effecting a partial deregulation and in prohibiting the possibility of planting in accordance with the terms of such a deregulation. Given those errors, this Court need not express any view on whether injunctive relief of some kind was available to respondents on the record before us. Nor does the Court address the question whether the District Court was required to conduct an evidentiary hearing before entering the relief at issue here. The judgment of the Ninth Circuit is reversed, and the case is remanded for further proceedings consistent with this opinion.

In his dissent, Justice Breyer succinctly summed up the issues involved in the case and explained why he could not agree with the majority in its decision:

The Court does not dispute the District Court's critical findings of fact: First, Roundup Ready Alfalfa (RRA) can contaminate other plants. . . . Second, even planting in a controlled setting had led to contamination in some instances. . . . Third, the Animal and Plant Health Inspection Service (APHIS) has limited ability to monitor or enforce limitations on planting. . . . And fourth, genetic contamination from RRA could decimate farmers' livelihoods and the American alfalfa market for years to come. . . . Instead, the majority faults the District Court for "enjoining APHIS from partially deregulating RRA." . . .

. . .

In my view, the District Court may not have actually ordered such relief, and we should not so readily assume that it did. Regardless, the District Court did not abuse its discretion when, after considering the voluminous record and making the aforementioned findings, it issued the order now before us.

* * *

The District Court in this case was put in an "unenviable position." . . . In front of it was strong evidence that RRA poses a serious threat to the environment and to American business, and that limits on RRA deregulation might not be followed or enforced—and that even if they were, the newly engineered gene might nevertheless spread to other crops. Confronted with those disconcerting submissions, with APHIS's unlawful deregulation decision, with a group of farmers who had staked their livelihoods on APHIS's decision, and with a federal statute that prizes informed decisionmaking on matters that seriously affect the environment, the court did the best it could. In my view, the District Court was well within its discretion to order the remedy that the Court now reverses. Accordingly, I respectfully dissent.

Source: "Monsanto Co. vs. Geertson Seed Farms, 561 U.S. ___." http://www.supremecourt.gov/opinions/09pdf/09-475 .pdf. Accessed on August 28, 2013.

Proposition 37. Genetically Engineered Foods. Labeling. Initiative Statute (2012)

In November 2012, a citizen-initiative placed on the California ballot a proposition requiring the labeling of genetically modified food sold in the state. The proposition was defeated by a vote of 6,442,371 (51.4%) to 6,088,714 (48.6%). A summary of the provisions of the proposition was provided by the state's legislative analyst, which read, in part:

This measure makes several changes to state law to explicitly require the regulation of GE foods. Specifically, it (1) requires that most GE foods sold be properly labeled, (2) requires DPH *[Department of Public Health]* to regulate the labeling of such foods, and (3) allows individuals to sue food manufacturers who violate the measure's labeling provisions.

Labeling of Foods. This measure requires that GE foods sold at retail in the state be clearly labeled as genetically engineered. Specifically, the measure requires that raw foods (such as fruits and vegetables) produced entirely or in part through genetic engineering be labeled with the words "Genetically Engineered" on the front package or label. If the item is not separately packaged or does not have a label, these words must appear on the shelf or bin where the item is displayed for sale. The measure also requires that processed foods produced entirely or in part through genetic engineering be labeled with the words "Partially Produced with Genetic Engineering" or "May be Partially Produced with Genetic Engineering."

Retailers (such as grocery stores) would be primarily responsible for complying with the measure by ensuring that their food products are correctly labeled. Products that are labeled as GE would be in compliance. For each product that is not labeled as GE, a retailer generally must be able to document why that product is exempt from labeling. There are two main ways in which a retailer could document that a product is exempt: (1) by obtaining a sworn statement from the provider of the product (such as a wholesaler) indicating that the product has not been intentionally or knowingly genetically engineered or (2) by receiving independent certification that the product does not contain GE ingredients. Other entities throughout the food supply chain (such as farmers and food manufacturers) may also be responsible for maintaining these records. The measure also excludes certain food products from the above labeling requirements. For example, alcoholic beverages, organic foods, and restaurant food and other prepared foods intended to be eaten immediately would not have to be labeled. Animal products—such as beef or chicken—that were not directly produced through genetic engineering would also be exempted, regardless of whether the animal had been fed GE crops.

In addition, the measure prohibits the use of terms such as "natural," "naturally made," "naturally grown," and "all natural" in the labeling and advertising of GE foods. Given the way the measure is written, there is a possibility that these restrictions would be interpreted by the courts to apply to some processed foods regardless of whether they are genetically engineered.

Source: "Prop 37. Genetically Engineered Foods. Labeling. Initiative Statute." Official Voter Information Guide. http://vig.cdn.sos.ca.gov/2012/general/pdf/complete-vig-v2.pdf. Accessed on August 17, 2013.

Bowman v. Monsanto, et al. 569 U.S. 11-796 (2013)

This case arose when an Indiana farmer, Vernon Bowman, decided to harvest some of the seeds from the first generation of a soybean crop, originally grown with seeds purchased from the Monsanto Company, holder of a patent on those seeds. The seeds are genetically engineered to survive treatment with a popular Monsanto pesticide, Roundup. Bowman argued that Monsanto's patent was exhausted when it sold the seeds to him (a doctrine known as patent exhaustion*) and did not apply to future generations of seeds grown from the original seeds. The case ruled against Bowman in a unanimous verdict. Commentators on the case noted that the decision was likely to have "significant consequences" for growers who choose to use GM seeds. The core of the Court's decision is as follows (omitted text is indicated by ellipses [. . .]):*

The doctrine of patent exhaustion limits a patentee's right to control what others can do with an article embodying or containing an invention. Under the doctrine, "the initial authorized sale of a patented item terminates all patent rights to that item." . . . And by "exhaust[ing] the [patentee's] monopoly" in that item, the sale confers on the purchaser, or any subsequent owner, "the right to use [or] sell" the thing as he sees fit.

. . .

Unfortunately for Bowman, that principle decides this case against him. Under the patent exhaustion doctrine, Bowman could resell the patented soybeans he purchased from the grain elevator; so too he could consume the beans himself or feed them to his animals. Monsanto, although the patent holder, would have no business interfering in those uses of Roundup Ready beans. But the exhaustion doctrine does not enable Bowman to make additional patented soybeans without Monsanto's permission (either express or implied). And that is precisely what Bowman did. He took the soybeans he purchased home; planted them in his fields at the time he thought best; applied glyphosate to kill weeds (as well as any soy plants lacking the Roundup Ready trait); and finally harvested more (many more) beans than he started with. That is how "to 'make' a new product," to use Bowman's words, when the original product is a seed. . . . Because Bowman thus reproduced Monsanto's patented invention, the exhaustion doctrine does not protect him.

Source: *Vernon Hugh Bowman, Petitioner v. Monsanto Company et al.*, 569 U.S. 11-796 (2013). http://www.supreme court.gov/opinions/12pdf/11-796_c07d.pdf. Accessed on August 17, 2013.

H. R. 1699 (2013)

Bills that require the labeling of genetically modified foods have been introduced into the U.S. Congress on a number of occasions, but as of the end of 2013, none had proceeded any further than assignment to committee. The most recent example of such a bill is one offered by Rep. Peter De Fazio (D-OR) and Sen. Barbara Boxer (D-CA). It read as follows (ellipses [. . .] indicate the omission of text):

A BILL

To amend the Federal Food, Drug, and Cosmetic Act to require that genetically engineered food and foods that contains genetically engineered ingredients be labeled accordingly.

. . .

SEC. 2. PURPOSE AND FINDINGS

(a) PURPOSE.—The purpose of this Act is to establish a consistent and enforceable standard for labeling of foods produced using genetic engineering, including fish, thereby providing consumers with knowledge of how their food is produced.

(b) FINDINGS.—Congress finds that—

(1) the process of genetically engineering food organisms results in material changes to food derived from those organisms;

(2) the Food and Drug Administration requires the labeling of more than 3,000 ingredients, additives, and processes;

(3) individuals in the United States have a right to know if their food was produced with genetic engineering for a variety of reasons, including health, economic, environmental, religious, and ethical;

(4) more than 60 countries, including the United Kingdom and all other countries of the European Union, South Korea, Japan, Brazil, Australia, India, China, and other key United States trading partners have laws or regulations mandating disclosure of genetically engineered food on food labels;

(5) in 2011, Codex Alimentarius, the food standards organization of the United Nations, adopted a text that indicates that governments can decide on whether and how to label foods produced with genetic engineering; and

(6) mandatory identification of food produced with genetic engineering can be a critical method of preserving the economic value of exports or domestically sensitive markets with labeling requirements for genetically engineered foods.

SEC. 3. AMENDMENTS TO THE FEDERAL FOOD, DRUG, AND COSMETIC ACT

(a) IN GENERAL.—Section 403 of the Federal Food, Drug, and Cosmetic Act (21 U.S.C. 343) is amended by adding at the end the following:

"(z)(1) If it is a food that has been genetically engineered or contains 1 or more genetically engineered ingredients, unless such information is clearly disclosed, as determined by the Secretary.

"(2) This paragraph does not apply to food that—

"(A) is served in restaurants or other similar eating establishments, such as cafeterias and carryouts;

"(B) is a medical food (as defined in section 5(b) of the Orphan Drug Act);

"(C) is a food that would be subject to this paragraph solely because it was produced using a genetically engineered vaccine; or

"(D) is a food or processed food that would be subject to this paragraph solely because it includes the use of a genetically engineered processing aid (including yeast) or enzyme.

[Remaining sections of the bill deal with technical issues associated with its implementation.]

Source: H.R. 1699, 113th Congress (2013–2014). http://beta. congress.gov/bill/113th-congress/house-bill/1699. Accessed on March 31, 2014.

Raised Bill No. 6519, State of Connecticut (2013)

Connecticut became the first state to pass a law requiring the labeling of foods that contain genetically modified components. The following are the relevant portions of that act.

Sec. 3. (NEW) (Effective October 1, 2013) (a) On October first following the date the Commissioner of Consumer Protection recognizes the occurrence of both of the following: (1) Four states, not including this state, enact a mandatory labeling law for genetically-engineered foods that is consistent with the provisions of this subsection, provided one such state borders Connecticut; and (2) the aggregate population of such states located in the northeast region of the United States that have enacted a mandatory labeling law for genetically-engineered foods that is consistent with this subsection exceed twenty million based on 2010 census figures, (A) food intended for human consumption, and (B) seed or seed stock that is intended to produce food for human consumption, that is entirely or partially genetically-engineered, except a processed food subject to the provisions of this section solely because one or more processing aids or enzymes were produced or derived from genetic engineering, shall be labeled as follows: (i) In the case of such food that is sold wholesale and is not intended for retail sale, on the bill of sale accompanying such food during shipping, with the clear and conspicuous words: "Produced with Genetic Engineering"; (ii) in the case of such food for retail sale contained in a package, with the clear and conspicuous words: "Produced with Genetic Engineering"; (iii) in the case of such food that is a raw agricultural commodity, on the package offered for retail sale or, in the case of any such commodity that is not separately packaged or labeled, on the bill of sale or invoice for such commodity and on the retail store shelf or bin that holds such commodity displayed for sale with the clear and conspicuous words: "Produced with Genetic Engineering"; and (iv) in the case of any such seed or seed stock, on the container holding the seed or seed stock displayed for sale or on any label identifying ownership or possession of the commodity with the clear and conspicuous words: "Produced with Genetic Engineering". Such food labeling shall be displayed in the same size and font as the ingredients in the nutritional facts panel on the food label. Not later than thirty days after the Commissioner of Consumer Protection recognizes the occurrence of the events described in subdivisions (1) and (2) of this subsection, the commissioner shall cause to be published in the five newspapers in the state having the largest circulation, notice of the date the requirements of this section become effective. For purposes of this section, "states located in the northeast region of the United States" means Maine, Vermont, New Hampshire, Massachusetts, Rhode Island, New York, New Jersey and Pennsylvania.

The act continues with a revised section on the misbranding of foods:

(a) A food shall be deemed to be misbranded: . . . (12) if it is intended for human consumption and genetically-engineered, as defined in section 2 of this act, and does not bear labeling as required in accordance with section 3 of this act, unless (A) it is a food intended for human consumption produced without the producer's knowledge that a seed or other component of such food was genetically-engineered, or (B) on or before July 1, 2019, it is a processed food, as defined in section 2 of this act, that is subject to the provisions of section 3 of this act, solely because it contains one or more materials that have been produced with genetic engineering, as defined in section 2 of this act, provided such genetically-engineered materials do not, in the aggregate, account for more than nine-tenths of one per cent of the total weight of the processed food.

(b) Seed or seed stock that is intended to produce food for human consumption shall be deemed misbranded if it is genetically-engineered, as defined in section 2 of this act, and does not bear labeling as required in accordance with section 3 of this act.

Protection for food retailers is provided in subsection (f) of section 2 of the act:

(f) Notwithstanding the provisions of subsection (c) of this section, a retailer shall not be penalized or otherwise held liable for the failure to label pursuant to this section unless (1) the retailer is the producer or the manufacturer of the genetically-engineered food, seed or seed stock and sells the genetically-engineered food under a brand it owns, or (2) the retailer's failure to label was knowing and wilful. In any action in which it is alleged that a retailer has violated the provisions of this section, it shall be a defense that such retailer reasonably relied on (A) any disclosure concerning genetically-engineered foods contained in the bill of sale or invoice provided by the wholesaler or distributor pursuant to subsection (a) of this section, or (B) the lack of any such disclosure.

Source: Amendment: *HB0652708508SDO*. General Assembly. State of Connecticut. http://www.cga.ct.gov/2013/lcoamd/2013LCO08508-R00-AMD.htm. Accessed on December 5, 2013.

The topic of genetically modified (GM) food is one that has aroused a great deal of debate and controversy in the past, a situation that continues to the present day. This chapter provides an annotated bibliography of a selection of the books, articles, reports, and Internet sources that provide background for this debate and that present some of the arguments on all sides of the controversy.

Books

Andersson, Meike S., and M. Carmen de Vicente. 2010. *Gene Flow between Crops and Their Wild Relatives*. Baltimore: Johns Hopkins University Press.

This book provides an extensive review of all that is known about the transfer of genes in the wild between domesticated GM crops and their wild relatives.

Bennett, David J., and Richard C. Jennings, eds. 2013. *Successful Agricultural Innovation in Emerging Economies: New*

Products labeled with Non Genetically Modified Organism (GMO) are sold at the Lassens Natural Foods & Vitamins store in Los Feliz district of Los Angeles. A number of states and local communities have now voted to require the labeling of genetically modified foods in their jurisdictions. (AP Photo/Damian Dovarganes)

Genetic Technologies for Global Food Production. Cambridge, UK: Cambridge University Press.

The authors point out that a growing world population requires the development of new types of agriculture to feed that population. They suggest that genetic engineering may be one method for doing so. The essays in this book are organized into four major sections: issues relating to plant science and food security; new genetic crops in developing nations; policy lessons learned in the development of genetically modified foods; and social, legal, and ethical issues related to GM foods.

Bertheau, Yves, ed. 2013. *Genetically Modified and Non-genetically Modified Food Supply Chains: Co-existence and Traceability.* Chichester, West Sussex, UK: Co-Extra; Wiley-Blackwell.

The essays in this book are divided into eight major sections: introduction; managing gene flow; co-existence in food and feed supply chains; traceability and controls in food and feed supply chains; legal regimes, liability, and redress issues; data integration and DSS (decision support systems); related issues; and conclusion.

Bodiguel, Luc, and Michael Cardwell, eds. 2010. *The Regulation of Genetically Modified Organisms: Comparative Approaches.* New York: Oxford University Press.

The question as to how genetically modified organisms should be regulated has been answered in a variety of ways by different governmental jurisdictions around the world. This collection of essays reviews some of the regulatory mechanisms that have been developed in the European Union, which has perhaps devoted the greatest amount of time and energy to the issue, and in other parts of the world.

Carter, Colin Andre, GianCarlo Moschini, and Ian M. Sheldon, eds. 2011. *Genetically Modified Food and Global Welfare.* Bingley, UK: Emerald Group Publishing.

The essays in this book deal with the belief that genetically modified crops and foods can be a significant factor in dealing with the world's hunger issues, but that unnecessarily harsh regulatory systems (e.g., those in place in the European Union) have hampered the development of the full potential of the new technology.

Epstein, Samuel, and Beth Leibson. 2013. *Good Clean Food: Shopping Smart to Avoid GMOs, rBGH, and Products That May Cause Cancer and Other Diseases.* New York: Skyhorse Publishing, Inc.
   Operating on the assumption that GM foods are *not* "good clean foods," the authors recommend a number of practices that will allow consumers to find, purchase, and prepare such foods.

Falck-Zepeda, José, Guillaume Gruère, and Idah Sithole-Niang, eds. 2013. *Genetically Modified Crops in Africa: Economic and Policy Lessons from Countries South of the Sahara.* Washington, DC: International Food Policy Research Institute.
   This book deals with the unique opportunities and problems faced by nations in southern Africa in the use of genetically modified products for the improvement of crop and food systems as a crucial way of meeting the nutritional needs of their citizens.

Ferry, Natalie, and A. M. R. Gatehouse, eds. 2009. *Environmental Impact of Genetically Modified Crops.* Wallingford, UK; Cambridge, MA: CABI.
   The essays in this anthology discuss the results of research on the environmental impact of GM plants and seeds and the significance of this research on the development of policy on GM products. Some attention is also paid to the effects of GM products on human health.

Flachowsky, Gerhard, ed. 2014. *Animal Nutrition with Transgenic Plants.* Wallingford, UK: CAB International.

This valuable book provides a comprehensive review of the types of transgenic plants that have been developed for use as animal feeds and detailed information about specific aspects of that topic, such as studies on both first- and second-generation GM crops, applications in different parts of the world, public attitudes about the use of GM crops for animals, and ethical issues raised by the development of GM food crops.

Forman, Lillian E. 2009. *Genetically Modified Foods.* Minneapolis, MN: Abdo Group.
This book is a part of the publisher's Essential Viewpoints series in which a variety of positions on the use of genetically modified products is provided by specialists and stakeholders in the field.

Halford, Nigel G. 2012. *Genetically Modified Crops*, 2nd ed. London: Imperial College Press.
This book provides a general introduction to the subject of GM crops, with a review of the history of the technology, steps in its practical development for today's agriculture, and problems and issues that have arisen as a result of its introduction to the field.

Hauter, Wenonah. 2012. *Foodopoly: The Battle over the Future of Food and Farming in America.* New York: New Press.
The author is an organic farmer who is also a member of the national Community Supported Agriculture (CSA) movement. She explains in this book why efforts by local organic food farmers and the organizations they have created are not going to be enough to stem the growing control of the nation's food supply by international industries such as Monsanto and Dow Chemical.

Heller, Chaia. 2013. *Food, Farms & Solidarity: French Farmers Challenge Industrial Agriculture and Genetically Modified Crops.* Durham, NC: Duke University Press.

The author reviews the events that led up to an uprising of French farmers in opposition to the use of genetic seeds and genetic crops in French agriculture, and the significance this movement has had and is likely to have for the expanded use of GM products in agriculture in France and elsewhere.

Herring, Ronald J., ed. 2013. *Transgenics and the Poor: Biotechnology in Development Studies.* Hoboken, NJ: Taylor and Francis.

Genetically modified crops and foods have been touted as a potentially critical element in helping to solve the world's hunger problems. Yet that success has been somewhat limited. The essays in this book review some of the hoped-for achievements of modern agricultural biotechnology, some problems that have prevented more widespread adoption of the technology, and some specific case studies where the technology has and has not succeeded.

Hillstrom, Kevin. 2012. *Genetically Modified Foods.* Detroit: Gale Cengage Learning.

This book provides a general introduction for young adults to the topic of genetically modified foods and the debates surrounding their use.

Ho, Mae-Wan, and Eva Sirinathsinghji. 2013. *Ban GMOs Now: Health & Environmental Hazards: Especially in the Light of the New Genetics.* London: ISIS.

This book summarizes the risks to human health and the natural environment posed by the released of genetically engineered product into the environment. The authors encourage local communities to begin to take action against the continuing and expanded use of such products in countries throughout the world.

Jain, S. Mohan, and S. Dutta Gupta. 2013. *Biotechnology of Neglected and Underutilized Crops.* Dordrecht; London: Springer.

The 16 essays in this book are divided into four sections that deal with (1) three relatively unknown plants as possible food sources, (2) the development of techniques for dealing with certain so-called *orphan crops*, (3) a discussion of some neglected but potential oil crops, and (4) the potential for the genetic engineering of some better-known crops, such as Safflower, Jatropha, Bael, Taro, and Mangrove.

Kaufman, Frederick. 2012. *Bet the Farm: How Food Stopped Being Food.* Hoboken, NJ: John Wiley & Sons.
Kaufman discusses the scientific basis for the development of GM foods, reviews the history of their development and spread throughout the world, and points out the connection between GM foods and crops and worldwide economics and politics.

Kempken, Frank, and Christian Jung, eds. 2010. *Genetic Modification of Plants.* New York: Springer.
This collection of essays provides a comprehensive and complete overview of the technologies involved in the production of genetically modified plants.

Kimbrell, Andrew. 2007. *Your Right to Know: Genetic Engineering and the Secret Changes in Your Food.* San Rafael, CA: Earth Aware Editions.
This well-illustrated book is organized into five sections, dealing with human health issues, effects on the natural environment, the use of genetically altered seeds, GM foods found in the supermarket, and the future of food. Appendices provide useful guides for consumers who wish to know more about GM foods and their alternatives.

Komen, John, and David Wafula. 2013. *Trade and Tribulations: An Evaluation of Trade Barriers to the Adoption of Genetically Modified Crops in the East African Community.* Washington, DC: Center for Strategic & International Studies.

East Africa would appear to be one of the places in the world where the adoption of genetically modified crops would provide a key factor in dealing with the region's food security issues. Yet, that process has been slow in happening. The authors explore trade, political, social, and other reasons for this situation.

Marchant, Gary Elvin, Guy A. Cardineau, and Thomas P. Redick. 2010. *Thwarting Consumer Choice: The Case against Mandatory Labeling for Genetically Modified Foods.* Washington, DC: AEI Press.
The authors argue that mandatory labeling of GM food products will not provide consumers with more choices about which they have greater information but fewer choices overall. They say that such laws and regulations only tend to reduce the number and quantity of GM foods that are available in the marketplace when, overall, the presence of such food products poses no threats to consumers and may actually improve their food choices and overall nutritional opportunities.

Miller, Debra A., ed. 2012. *Genetically Engineered Food.* Detroit: Greenhaven Press.
This book is part of Greenhaven's At Issue series that focuses on important and controversial social issues. A number of writers express a variety of views on the topic of GM foods.

Oliver, Melvin J., and Yi Li, eds. 2013. *Plant Gene Containment.* Ames, IA: Wiley-Blackwell.
One of the most contentious issues surrounding the use of genetically modified seed and crops is the risk of escape of modified genes into other crops and/or wild plants. This book provides a number of articles dealing with technical aspects of this problem and its potential solutions.

Panesar, Parmjit S., and Satwinder S. Marwaha, eds. 2013. *Biotechnology in Agriculture and Food Processing: Opportunities and Challenges.* Boca Raton, FL: CRC Press.

The 16 essays in this book deal with topics such as plant cell and tissue culture techniques in crop improvement, genetic transformation and crop improvement, production of biofertilizers, production of biopesticides, biotechnology in food processing, production of fermented foods, functional foods, and enzymes in food processing.

Pechlaner, Gabriela. 2012. *Corporate Crops: Biotechnology, Agriculture, and the Struggle for Control.* Austin: University of Texas Press.

This book deals with the issues that have been raised involved large multinational corporations and individual farming units over the purchase and use of genetically modified seeds and crops. The author presents four case studies dealing with specific examples of the types of issues that arise, using regulatory provisions, court cases, and other types of source documents.

Pollack, Mark A., and Gregory C. Shaffer. 2009. *When Cooperation Fails: The International Law and Politics of Genetically Modified Foods.* Oxford; New York: Oxford University Press.

The authors review the systems that have been developed for the regulation of genetically modified products, primarily in the European Union and the United States, how those policies differ, and what effects they have had on the development of GM food technology.

Popp, Jennie, Marty D. Matlock, Nathan Kemper, and Molly Jahn. 2012. *The Role of Biotechnology in a Sustainable Food Supply.* Cambridge, UK: Cambridge University Press.

The 15 essays in this book consider a number of facets of the question as to whether genetically modified crops and foods can play a significant role in dealing with the world's hunger problems, and what challenges and issues are raised by that question.

Robin, Marie-Monique. 2010. *The World According to Monsanto: Pollution, Corruption, and the Control of the World's Food Supply*, trans. from French by George Holoch. New York: New Press.

One of the best of the many books written about the history and activities of the world's largest biotechnology firm, which was the innovator of a host of genetically engineered foods, seeds, crops, and other products.

Segger, Marie-Claire Cordonier, Frederic Perron-Welch, and Christine Frison, eds. 2013. *Legal Aspects of Implementing the Cartagena Protocol on Biosafety*. Cambridge, UK: Cambridge University Press.

The Cartagena Protocol on Biosafety was a complex document that laid out provisions for the shipment of GM crops and foods in the European Union and its trade partners. This book deals with the variety of legal issues that have arisen—and that may be expected to arise—as a consequence of that agreement. Various chapters deal with topic such as the involvement of the general public in the process, the compliance mechanism laid out by the treaty, the development of systems permitted by the treaty in various countries and regions, and global policy trends with regard to biosafety.

Smith, Jeffrey M. 2007. *Genetic Roulette: The Documented Health Risks of Genetically Engineered Foods*. Fairfield, IA: Yes! Books.

This book is a classic in the field because of its wide-ranging attack on the use of genetically modified organisms in agriculture and the food supply system. The author is the founding executive director of the Institute for Responsible Technology, an organization created to provide information about the risks and dangers of genetically modified crops and foods. His earlier book on the topic, *Seeds of Deception: Exposing Industry and Government Lies about the Safety of the Genetically Engineered Foods You're Eating*, was published by Yes! Books in 2003.

Thompson, R. Paul. 2011. *Agro-technology: A Philosophical Introduction*. Cambridge; New York: Cambridge University Press.

This textbook reviews the development of agricultural biotechnology over the centuries and considers the moral and ethical issues that have arisen as the technology of the field has expanded to include a host of processes from the field of genetic engineering.

Thomson, Jennifer A. 2013. *Food for Africa: The Life and Work of a Scientist in GM Crops*. Claremont, South Africa: UCT Press.

The author has been involved in research and development of GM crops since the 1970s. She describes her experiences in all aspects of that program, from development of GM plants to policy making to implementation of technology throughout Africa over a period of four decades.

Tutelyan, Victor, ed. 2013. *Genetically Modified Food Sources*. Amsterdam: Academic Press.

The essays in this book provide a comprehensive and technically detailed description of the safety issues involved in the production, distribution, and use of GM food products, along with the many actions that have been taken to regulate specific GM products.

Weasel, Lisa H. 2009. *Food Fray: Inside the Controversy over Genetically Modified Food*. New York: Amacom.

The author notes that the spread of GM foods and crops has, largely without concern in the United States, grown rapidly over the past few decades. She reviews that process and highlights some of the most important issues relating to the use of GM crops and foods.

Weirich, Paul, ed. 2007. *Labeling Genetically Modified Food: The Philosophical and Legal Debate.* Oxford; New York: Oxford University Press.

The dozen essays in this book deal with a variety of issues associated with the labeling of GM foods, such as the current art and state of the procedure, European Union regulations, ethical issues in labeling GM foods, consumer responses to labeling procedures and regulations, and differing conceptions by consumer of GM food labeling.

Wozniak, Chris A., and Alan McHughen, eds. 2012. *Regulation of Agricultural Biotechnology: The United States and Canada.* Dordrecht; New York: Springer.

The 17 essays in this book focus on a general overview of the regulations dealing with genetically engineered products in the United States and Canada, as well as discussions of individual more specific issues related to this topic.

Zhang, Baohong, ed. 2013. *Transgenic Cotton: Methods and Protocols.* New York: Humana Press.

This book provides a technical review of the procedures for developing strains of transgenic cotton, places and types of adoptions, and effects on agriculture and the natural environment.

Articles

Acharjee, Sumita, and Bidyut Kumar Sarmah. 2013. "Biotechnologically Generating 'Super Chickpea' for Food and Nutritional Security." *Plant Science: An International Journal of Experimental Plant Biology* 207: 108–116.

The authors present a fascinating case study of an agricultural product, chickpeas, with a number of nutritional deficits that, in theory, could be improved by genetic engineering. They point out the technical problems involved with this challenge and describe some technical fixes for them.

Agarwal, Pradeep K., et al. 2013. "Bioengineering for Salinity Tolerance in Plants: State of the Art." *Molecular Biotechnology* 54(1): 102–123.

This article provides an excellent introduction to the technology whereby plans can be genetically engineered for the development of specific desirable characteristics, in this case, an ability to grow and thrive in soil that would otherwise not be acceptable for their cultivation.

Aris, Aziz, and Samuel Leblanc. 2011. "Maternal and Fetal Exposure to Pesticides Associated to Genetically Modified Foods in Eastern Townships of Quebec, Canada." *Reproductive Toxicology* 31(4): 528–533.

The authors report finding Bt toxins from GM crops in the blood of pregnant women and their fetuses at a hospital in Eastern Canada. The findings may contradict general expectations that the use of GM foods would have any significant effects on human health.

Arjó, G., et al. 2013. "Plurality of Opinion, Scientific Discourse and Pseudoscience: An In Depth Analysis of the Séralini et al. Study Claiming That Roundup™ Ready Corn or the Herbicide Roundup™ Cause Cancer in Rats." *Transgenic Research* 22(2): 255–267.

The authors mount a vigorous attack on an article (mentioned in the title; also see later), claiming possible health effects from two popular Monsanto GM products. Also see "Robinson" under Internet resources and "Séralini et al." in this section.

Armenakas, Sophia, and Macrene Alexiades-Armenakas. 2013. "Genetically-Modified Organisms in United States Agriculture:

Mandate for Food Labeling." *Food and Nutrition Sciences* 4(8): 807–811.

The authors review the role of GM organisms in the American agricultural system and suggest reasons for the labeling of food products with GM components.

Bennett, Alan B., et al. 2013. "Agricultural Biotechnology: Economics, Environment, Ethics, and the Future." *Annual Review of Environment and Resources* 38: 249–279.

The authors provide an overview of the development of agricultural biotechnology over the past 15 years and suggest some possible future directions for genetic engineering of crops and foods.

Bouët, Antoine, Guillaume Gruère, and Laëtitia Leroy. 2013. "Market Effects of Information Requirements under the Biosafety Protocol." *International Economics* 134: 15–28.

The authors attempt to predict the effect on world markets of the document requirements imposed by the Cartagena Protocol on Biosafety. They find that signatories to the treaty and producers of GM crops and food are likely to suffer significant market losses, whereas producers of non-GM foods in signatory nations are likely to benefit from the treaty. Developing nations are likely to experience a negative impact also under terms of the treaty.

Brookes, Graham, and Peter Barfoot. 2013. "The Global Income and Production Effects of Genetically Modified (GM) Crops 1996–2011." *GM Crops & Food* 4(1): 74–83.

The authors estimate that the planting of the four major GM crops—corn, soybeans, cotton, and canola—have resulted in a total benefit of $98.2 billion over the period covered by the report, with the majority of that profit going to developing nations.

Burening, G., and J. M. Lyons. 2000. "The Case of the FLAVR SAVR Tomato." *California Agriculture* 54(4): 6–7.

The authors provide a concise history of the development, testing, and attempted commercialization of the world's first GM tomato, a product that ultimately failed in the marketplace.

Dibden, Jacqui, David Gibbs, and Chris Cocklin. 2013. "Framing GM Crops as a Food Security Solution." *Journal of Rural Studies* 29(2): 59–70.

The adoption of GM foods is often recommended as a contribution to the improvement of food safety.

Du, Bin, and Feng-Mei Zhu. 2013. "Safety Assessment and Countermeasures of Genetically Modified Food Advance." *Journal of Food Science and Technology* 5(3): 318–322.

The authors review the general question of the safety of GM foods and discuss methods by which safety can be improved.

Entine, Jon. 2013. "Notorious Séralini GMO Cancer Rat Study Retracted, Ugly Legal Battle Looms." *Forbes*. http://www.forbes.com/sites/jonentine/2013/11/29/notorious-seralini-gmo-cancer-rat-study-retracted-ugly-legal-battle-looms/. Accessed on November 30, 2013.

This article was written in response to a decision by the editor of the journal *Food and Chemical Toxicology* to retract an article about the health effects of GM foods on rats. See Séralini et al. (2012) in this section.

Espley, Richard V., et al. 2013. "Analysis of Genetically Modified Red-Fleshed Apples Reveals Effects on Growth and Consumer Attributes." *Plant Biotechnology Journal* 11(4): 408–419.

The authors discuss tests they have conducted on a genetically engineered apple with consumers and find that those consumers have no negative response to changes that have been made in the apple (improved color and flavor).

Flipse, Steven M., and Patricia Osseweijer. 2013. "Media Attention to GM Food Cases: An Innovation Perspective." *Public Understanding of Science* 22(2): 185–202.

The authors discuss in detail three specific cases in which media attention to a specific GM food–related case caused food manufacturers to alter their business practices. They make some generalizations about the relationship of media attention to GM food cases and innovation by the food industry.

Forabosco, F., et al. 2013. "Genetically Modified Farm Animals and Fish in Agriculture: A Review." *Livestock Science* 153(1–3): 1–9.

The authors provide a very complete and helpful review of the status of the development of GM animals. They note that a number of modified species are being studied in research laboratories, but that only a small number of GM animals are close to being ready for marketing.

Frewer, L. J., et al. 2013. "Genetically Modified Animals from Life-Science, Socio-economic and Ethical Perspectives: Examining Issues in an EU Policy Context." *New Biotechnology* 30(5): 447–460.

The Pegasus project is a program designed to study issues raised by the development, implementation, and commercialization of genetically modified animals and products produced from them. This paper describes a wide variety of activities designed by member of the project to determine public attitudes about these animals and products, with a view toward developing base concepts in the design of EU regulations of such products.

Galli, Gad, and Rachel Amir. 2013. "Fortifying Plants with the Essential Amino Acids Lysine and Methionine to Improve

Nutritional Quality." *Plant Biotechnology Journal* 11(2): 211–222.

Lysine and methionine are two essential amino acids that humans are unable to synthesize and that must, therefore, be obtained from plants in the diet. The authors discuss efforts to engineer plants to introduce or improve their ability to produce these two amino acids. They also discuss some of the technical problems involved in this line of research.

Gayen, Dipak, et al. 2013. "Comparative Analysis of Nutritional Compositions of Transgenic High Iron Rice with Its Non-transgenic Counterpart." *Food Chemistry* 138(2–3): 835–840.

The nutritional value of GM and non-GM rice are compared, with the results being that the two are essentially identical except for the one trait (higher iron content) introduced by the GM process.

Heap, Brian. 2013. "Europe Should Rethink Its Stance on GM Crops." *Nature* 498(7455): 409.

Heap, president of the European Academies Science Advisory Council, suggests that changes in second-generation GM crop production have made it possible for the European Union to reconsider its tradition of relatively severe restrictions on the use of such crops.

Hollingworth, Robert M., et al. 2003. "The Safety of Genetically Modified Foods Produced through Biotechnology." *Toxicological Sciences* 71(1): 2–8.

The Society of Toxicologists presents its official view on the use of GM foods in this editorial, pointing out that the issue is not so much GM foods as it is the principle of "substantial equivalence," in which the safety of foods is based on a comparison with comparable natural, traditional, or conventional foods. On the basis of that standard, the writers say, most GM foods appear to be safe for human use.

Kamle, Suchitra, and Sher Ali. 2013. "Genetically Modified Crops: Detection Strategies and Biosafety Issues." *Gene* 522 (2): 123–132.

This paper provides "an overview on the production of GM crops, their acceptabilities, detection strategies, biosafety issues and potential impact on society" and "overall future prospects."

Kouser, Shahzad, and Matin Qaim. 2013. "Valuing Financial, Health, and Environmental Benefits of Bt Cotton in Pakistan." *Agricultural Economics* 44(3): 323–335.

This article attempts to place a dollar value of the conversion of cotton farming in Pakistan from traditional to GM crops. The authors report that the conversion has resulted in an increase in value of $79 per acre, half of which is attributable to health benefits and half to environmental benefits.

Lang, John T. 2013. "Elements of Public Trust in the American Food System: Experts, Organizations, and Genetically Modified Food." *Food Policy* 41(2): 145–154.

When confronted with complex socioscientific issues, such as the use of GM foods, the public may turn to trusted organizations for reliable information on which to base their opinions and decisions. How does the public decide which organizations to trust? That question provides the motivation of the research that led to this paper.

Lemaux, Peggy G. 2008. "Genetically Engineered Plants and Foods: A Scientist's Analysis of the Issues (Part I)." *Annual Review of Plant Biology* 59: 771–812.

The author provides a very complete and even-handed review of the process of plant biotechnology and a discussion of the pros and cons associated with that technology.

Marcous, Jean-Michel, and Lyne Létourneau. 2013. "A Distorted Regulatory Landscape: Genetically Modified Wheat and the Influence of Non-safety Issues in Canada." *Science and Public Policy* 40(4): 514–528.

> The authors discuss the ways in which social and political factors were involved in the normal process of regulatory decision making on the release of GM crops in Canada, showing that this process was treated quite differently from comparable issues in the same general category because of these factors.

Martin, Cyrus. 2013. "The Psychology of GMO." *Current Biology* 23(9): R356–R359.

> The author notes that GM foods have received the "seal of approval" from most scientists, yet large numbers of the general population remain opposed to the production and use of these foods. He explores some political and cultural reasons for this phenomenon.

Martinelli, Lucia, Malgorzata Karbarz, and Helena Siipi. 2013. "Science, Safety, and Trust: The Case of Transgenic Food." *Croatian Medical Journal* 54(1): 91–96.

> The authors consider the reality that scientists and the lay public view safety issues associated with GM products in quite different ways, largely determined by the attitudes required of researchers about controversial topics.

Masip, Gemma, et al. 2013. "Paradoxical EU Agricultural Policies on Genetically Engineered Crops." *Trends in Plant Science* 18(6): 312–324.

> The authors review current regulatory policies in the European Union with regard to genetically modified crops and foods and raise a number of issues about those policies. They call those policies "contradictory and irrational" and suggest that they are damaging EU and world economies.

McColl, K. A., B. Clarke, and T. J. Doran. 2013. "Role of Genetically Engineered Animals in Future Food Production." *Australian Veterinary Journal* 91(3): 113–117.

> The authors note that the commercialization of genetically engineered animals has proceeded at a pace much slower than that for GM plants. They review progress in the field for the purpose of providing information "so that veterinarians and animal health scientists are better able to participate in the debate on GE animals."

McHughen, Alan, and Stuart Smyth. 2008. "US Regulatory System for Genetically Modified [Genetically Modified Organism (GMO), rDNA or Transgenic] Crop Cultivars." *Plant Biotechnology Journal* 6(1): 2–12.

> This paper provides a superb review of the history of regulatory actions in both the United States and the European Union beginning in the mid-1980s until almost the present day.

Mehrotra, Shweta, and Vinod Goyal. 2013. "Evaluation of Designer Crops for Biosafety—a Scientist's Perspective." *Gene* 515(2): 241–248.

> Noting the essential role that safety determination plays in the development and commercialization of GM crops, the authors explore the methods that are available to scientists for determining how safe these crops are likely to be.

Mutuc, Maria, Roderick M. Rejesus, and Jose M. Yorobe, Jr. 2013. "Which Farmers Benefit the Most from Bt Corn Adoption? Estimating Heterogeneity Effects in the Philippines." *Agricultural Economics* 44(2): 231–239.

> The authors point out that a number of studies have been done on the extent to which farmers adopt the technology of GM crops, but few studies have been done on factors that affect differences in acceptance within a country or region. In this study, they find that the new technology

is least likely to be adopted by farmers who do not irrigate their farms, who are located far from seed distribution centers, and who have little background in disease identification.

Nap, Jan-Peter, et al. 2003. "The Release of Genetically Modified Crops into the Environment." *The Plant Journal* 33: 1–18.
This early article discusses the environmental effects of releasing GM crops into the natural environment and regulations dealing with the procedure.

Nep, Shauna, and Kieran O'Doherty. 2013. "Understanding Public Calls for Labeling of Genetically Modified Foods: Analysis of a Public Deliberation on Genetically Modified Salmon." *Society & Natural Resources* 26(5): 506–521.
The authors describe their analysis of public discussion in British Columbia about the possible approval of genetically engineered salmon in Canada and classify the types of arguments they heard in the discussion.

Nielsena, Thea. 2013. "Consumer Buying Behavior of Genetically Modified Fries in Germany." *Journal of Food Products Marketing* 19(1): 41–53.
The author describes an experiment in which consumers in Germany are given the option of purchasing French fries from street carts that are either GM or non-GM products. She analyzes the reasons that purchasers gave for choosing one product over another.

Oczek, Jeremy P. 2000. "In the Aftermath of the 'Terminator' Technology Controversy: Intellectual Property Protections for Genetically Engineered Seeds and the Right to Save and Replant Seed." *Boston College Law Review* 41(3): 627–658.
The author discusses legal issues related to the development and use of genetic use restriction technology (GURT; so-called terminator technology) for the production and sale of seed for crops.

Okeno, James A., et al. 2013. "Africa's Inevitable Walk to Genetically Modified (GM) Crops: Opportunities and Challenges for Commercialization." *New Biotechnology* 30(2): 124–130.

The authors argue that the lack of sufficient arable land in most parts of Africa means that African nations will inevitably take greater advantage of the opportunities of improved food production provided to them by GM goods. They review some of the policy decisions that have already been take for the encouragement of research and expanded planting of GM crops on the continent.

Panda, Rakhi, et al. 2013. "Challenges in Testing Genetically Modified Crops for Potential Increases in Endogenous Allergen Expression for Safety." *Allergy* 68(2): 142–151.

This article reviews the regulatory procedures involved in testing for the possible allergenicity of genetically modified food products and raises the question as to the efficacy of such procedures and the conditions under which such testing may or may not be necessary.

Phillips, Diane M., and William K. Hallman. 2013. "Consumer Risk Perceptions and Marketing Strategy: The Case of Genetically Modified Food." *Psychology & Marketing* 30(9): 739–748.

The authors note that the way new products are received by consumers is determined to a considerable extent on the way they are marketed. They examine this idea by presenting a series of consumer panels with GM foods labeled in a variety of ways to see how the labeling process affects acceptance of the products.

Price, William D., and Lynne Underhill. 2013. "Application of Laws, Policies, and Guidance from the United States and Canada to the Regulation of Food and Feed Derived from Genetically Modified Crops: Interpretation of Composition Data." *Journal of Agricultural and Food Chemistry* 61(354): 8349–8355.

The authors provide a review of the ways in which Canadian and U.S. governmental agencies have dealt with the problem of regulating and labeling genetically modified foods and feeds.

Schwartz, Stephan A. 2013. "The Great Experiment: Genetically Modified Organisms, Scientific Integrity, and National Wellness." *Explore* 9(1): 12–16.

The author comments in detail on the controversial report that ingestion of GM foods reduces the life span of rats and increases the risk of tumors. (See Arjó et al. and Seralini et al. in this section and Robinson in the Internet section.

Séralini, Gilles-Eric, et al. 2012. "Long Term Toxicity of a Roundup Herbicide and a Roundup-Tolerant Genetically Modified Maize." *Food and Chemical Toxicology* 50(11): 4221–4231.

This is a very important paper that reports on a study in which rats fed food containing GM products died at a greater rate and developed more tumors than did control animals who did not receive those foods. This article was late attacked vigorously by a number of scientists who objected to a variety of features of the report. See Arjó et al. in this section and Robinson in the Internet section. In November 2013, Elsevier, publisher of *Food and Chemical Toxicology*, announced that it was retracting the paper, not because the data were fraudulent or incorrect, but because the results were "inconclusive" and therefore "do not reach the threshold of publication." The publisher's decision was met with a firestorm of protest by opponents of GM crops and foods who claimed that the retraction was motivated by political, economic, or other nonscientific factors. For more on the case, also see the Elsevier announcement at http://www.elsevier.com/about/press-releases/research-and-journals/elsevier-announces-article

-retraction-from-journal-food-and-chemical-toxicology and articles by "Entine" in this section.

Silva Dias, João, and Rodomiro Ortiz. 2012. "Transgenic Vegetable Breeding for Nutritional Quality and Health Benefits." *Food and Nutrition Sciences* 3: 1209–1219.
This article provides an excellent review of research done on the genetic modification of plants for the purpose of increasing their nutritional value. It deals both with products that are well along in the development stage and with those that are still in the early stages of research.

Van Zwanenberg, Patrick, and Valeria Arza. 2013. "Biotechnology, Controversy, and Policy: Challenges of the Bioeconomy in Latin America." *Technology in Society* 35(2): 105–117.
The authors consider the various ways in which new forms of agricultural biotechnology can impact farming communities by comparing the process by which GM cotton crops were introduced into two very different farms in Argentina.

Vàzquez-Salat, Núria, and Louis-Marie Houdebine. 2013. "Will GM Animals Follow the GM Plant Fate?" *Transgenic Research* 22(1): 5–13.
The authors of this paper trace the history of the development and commercialization of genetically engineered plants and animals and point out common issues and differences between the two experiences retrospectively and prospectively.

Verma, Charu, et al. 2011. "A Review on Impacts of Genetically Modified Food on Human Health." *The Open Nutraceuticals Journal* 4: 3–11.
The authors of this article cite a large number of studies that support their views that the health risks posed by

genetically modified foods and crops are too extensive and too well studied to ignore.

Zhao, J., et al. 2013. "Nutritional Composition Analysis of Meat from Human Lactoferrin Transgenic Bulls." *Animal Biotechnology* 24(1): 44–52.

The researchers compared the nutritional value of traditional (non-GM) and GM beef and found no differences on a number of measures.

Reports

Barker, Debbie, Bill Freese, and George Kimbrell. 2013. *Seed Giants vs. U.S. Farmers: A Report by the Center for Food Safety & Save Our Seeds*. Washington, DC: Center for Food Safety.

This report discussed the ways in which seed production and sales have changed over the past few decades in the United States and how farmers have essentially become "serfs" to large biotechnology companies that invent, produce, and sell those seeds.

Bull, Alan T., Geoffrey Holt, and Malcolm D. Lilly. 1982. *Biotechnology: International Trends and Perspectives*.

This report discusses in detail virtually all that was known at the time about the risks and benefits involved in the genetic engineering of plants and animals for a variety of purposes.

Cartagena Protocol on Biosafety to the Convention on Biological Diversity. 2000. Montreal: Secretariat of the Convention on Biological Diversity. http://bch.cbd.int/protocol/text/. Accessed on August 18, 2013.

This treaty provides an outline for the transport of engineered organisms across international borders. It is an addendum to the 1993 Convention on Biological Diversity.

Committee on Identifying and Assessing Unintended Effects of Genetically Engineered Foods on Human Health, Board on

Life Sciences, Food and Nutrition Board, Board on Agriculture and Natural Resources, Institute of Medicine, and National Research Council of the National Academies. *Safety of Genetically Engineered Foods: Approaches to Assessing Unintended Health Effects.* Washington, DC: The National Academies Press, 2004.

Although now somewhat dated, this book is important because it provides the views of a group of the most highly qualified scientists and other stakeholders in the debate over GM foods with regard to the safety of GM products and steps that should be taken to continue testing for and validity that safety.

Genetically Engineered Crops: Agencies Are Proposing Changes to Improve Oversight, but Could Take Additional Steps to Enhance Coordination and Monitoring. 2008. Washington, DC: U.S. Government Accountability Office. GAO-09-60. http://www .gao.gov/assets/290/283060.pdf. Accessed on August 21, 2013.

The Government Accountability Office (GAO) reports on its investigation of six instances in which GM seeds or crops were released into the environment and the ways in which federal agencies responsible for oversight of GM crop use responded to these events. The agency makes a number of recommendations for improving the response to such events.

Genetically Modified Foods: Experts View Regimen of Safety Tests as Adequate, but FDA's Evaluation Process Could Be Enhanced. 2002. Washington, DC: U.S. General Accounting Office. GAO-02-566.   http://www.gao.gov/assets/240/234718.pdf. Accessed on August 21, 2013.

In the single most important report on GM foods by a U.S. governmental agency, the General Accounting Office (now the Government Accountability Office) assesses the risks posed by such products and concludes that they "pose the same types of inherent risks to human health as conventional foods."

Gurian-Sherman, Doug. 2009. *Failure to Yield: Evaluating the Performance of Genetically Engineered Crops.* Cambridge, MA: Union of Concerned Scientists.

The author begins by noting the promises made by proponents of GM crops and foods with regard to an expected increase in crop yields. He then surveys the available literature and comes to the conclusion that these promises have not been kept, and crop yield improvements were seen over the preceding decade where the result of factors other than the use of GM products.

National Research Council, et al. 2010. *The Impact of Genetically Engineered Crops on Farm Sustainability in the United States.* Washington, DC: National Academies Press.

The authors of this extensive and intensive report call it "the first comprehensive assessment of the effects of GE-crop adoption on farm sustainability in the United States." The study examined the ways in which genetically engineered crops have affected the incomes, agronomic practices, production decisions, environmental resources, and personal well-being of American farmers.

Safety Evaluation of Foods Derived by Modern Biotechnology: Concepts and Principles. 1993. Paris: Organisation of Economic Co-operation and Development.

This report provides a general overview of the principles involved in the genetic modification of organisms, some of the many applications that may result from such research, potential risks associated with genetic engineering, and some principles on which the monitoring and regulation of GM genetically modified organisms can be based.

"State/Local Efforts to Control GMOs." Organic Consumers Association. http://www.organicconsumers.org/articles/article_27247.cfm. Accessed on August 20, 2013.

This website provides an invaluable resource on the types of laws and regulations adopted by state and local jurisdictions on the use or prohibition of GM organisms within their districts.

Strategies for Assessing the Safety of Foods Produced by Biotechnology. 1991. Geneva: Food and Agriculture Organisation and World Health Organisation.

This joint report reviews some applications to which genetic engineering has been put and is likely to be put in the future, along with potential risks associated with those applications and methods for assessing those risks in the future.

Internet Sources

"8.1 Genetically Modified Organisms (GMOs)." World Trade Organization. http://www.wto.org/english/tratop_e/sps_e/sps _agreement_cbt_e/c8s1p1_e.htm. Accessed on August 30, 2013.

This publication by the World Trade Organization deals with the special issues involved in the transboundary trade of such products among different countries and steps that have been taken to deal with those issues.

"20 Questions on Genetically Modified Foods." World Health Organization. http://www.who.int/foodsafety/publications/biotech/ 20questions/en/. Accessed on August 29, 2013.

This fact sheet provides a very complete and detailed introduction to the subject of GM foods, dealing with issues such as why GM foods are produced, how they differ from traditional foods, what potential risks they pose to human health and to the environment, and how they are regulated nationally.

"AgBioWorld." http://www.agbioworld.org. Accessed on December 12, 2013.

AgBioWorld is the website of the AgBioWorld Foundation, a 501(c)(3) nonprofit organization located in Auburn, Alabama, designed to provide science-based information on all aspects of agricultural biotechnology. The website provides not only current news and information on agricultural biotechnology but also current and past issues of the organization's newsletter, *AgBioView Newsletter*.

Antoniou, Michael, Claire Robinson, and John Fagan. 2012. "GMO Myths and Truths." Earth Open Source.org. http://earthopensource.org/files/pdfs/GMO_Myths_and_Truths/GMO_Myths_and_Truths_1.3.pdf. Accessed on December 13, 2013.
A very well-documented and written report on many essential aspects of GM foods, such as the techniques used in genetic engineering, regulations on GM products, health hazards of GM foods, specific health issues related to Roundup products and glyphosate, effect of GM crops on farms and the natural environment, the effects of climate change on the debate over GM crops and foods, and problems involved in feeding the world now and in the future.

"Are Biotech Foods Safe to Eat?" WebMD. http://www.webmd.com/food-recipes/features/are-biotech-foods-safe-to-eat. Accessed on August 29, 2013.
WebMD is a highly regarded and trustworthy website dealing with a host of health and medical issues. On this web page, it reviews the nature of GM foods, their risks and benefits, and the best current information available on their safety.

Beans, Laura. 2013. "New Generation of Genetically Engineered Crops Found to Drastically Increase Use of Toxic Pesticides." EcoNews. http://ecowatch.com/2013/08/30/new-generation-genetically-engineered-crops-increase-toxic-pesticides/. Accessed on December 13, 2013.

The author reports on and discusses new research that suggests that farmers in the United States are drastically increasing their use of pesticide because of the genetically modified crops they are now planting.

Benbrook, Charles M. 2012. "Impacts of Genetically Engineered Crops on Pesticide Use in the U.S.—the First Sixteen Years." *Environmental Sciences Europe.* http://www.enveurope.com/content/24/1/24/abstract. Accessed on August 21, 2013.
The author finds that the amount of herbicide used on engineered corn, cotton, and soybean crops has actually increased over the period of time for his study, a seeming contradiction to what one might expect. The change has occurred because of the evolution of herbicide-resistant weeds that require ever-increasing amounts of herbicide for their control.

Biello, David. 2010. "Genetically Modified Crop on the Loose and Evolving in U.S. Midwest." *Scientific American.* http://www.scientificamerican.com/article.cfm?id=genetically-modified-crop. Accessed on December 13, 2013.
This very interesting article reports on the spread of GM canola among native and cultivated version of the crop in parts of the Midwest. Especially interesting is the host of comments from readers about the role that Monsanto's policies and practices have or have not had in this phenomenon.

Bocco, Diana. "Top 10 Genetically Modified Food Products." Science and Society. http://dsc.discovery.com/tv-shows/curiosity/topics/10-genetically-modified-food-products.htm. Accessed on September 2, 2013.
The author reviews the status of 10 major food products that have been genetically modified: sugar beets, corn, potatoes, tomatoes, squash, Golden Rice, soybeans, oils, animal feed, and salmon.

Boyle, Rebecca. 2011. "How to Genetically Modify a Seed, Step by Step." *Popular Science.* http://www.popsci.com/science/article/2011-01/life-cycle-genetically-modified-seed. Accessed on December 13, 2013.

This very well-written article explains the process of genetically engineering a seed in sufficient detail to understand the process but not to overwhelm the reader.

Carpenter, Janet, and Leonard Gianessi. 1999. "Herbicide Tolerant Soybeans: Why Growers Are Adopting Roundup Ready Varieties." AgBioForum. http://agbioforum.org/v2n2/v2n2a02-carpenter.htm. Accessed on August 21, 2013.

The authors provide a very detailed history and discussion of the development of genetically modified soybean crops in the United States.

"Contribution from the Network of 'GM-Free' European Regions and Local Authorities on the Subject of Co-existence between GMOs and Conventional and Organic Farming." http://www.gmo-free-regions.org/fileadmin/files/gmo-free-regions/GMO-Free-Network_Flyer_EN.pdf. Accessed on August 21, 2013.

This brochure was developed by the Network for the Vienna conference held in April 2006. Its purpose was to explain the goals and activities of the Network in regulating and controlling the use of GMO products within the region that, at the time, consisted of 43 regions in Europe.

"Daisy Q&As." AgResearch, New Zealand. http://www.agresearch.co.nz/news/Lists/news/Attachments/74/Daisy%20Q+A%201%20Oct%2012%20for%20web.pdf. Accessed on December 11, 2013.

This fact sheet provides answers to a number of basic questions about a genetically engineered cow, Daisy, produced by this New Zealand company that produces hypoallergenic milk, milk lacking in a protein that causes allergic reaction in humans who consume it.

Dugan, Sean. "The Pros and Cons of Genetically Modifying Your Foods." Article 3. http://www.article-3.com/the-pros-and-cons-of-genetically-modifying-your-food-912185. Accessed on August 29, 2013.

The author provides a good general introduction to the topic of GM foods, mentions that, for the most part, they are safe to eat, and then explains why such a controversy has arisen over them.

"Environmental Concerns." Biotechnology and Agricultural Education Program. University of Hawaii. http://www.cta hr.hawaii.edu/biotech/EnvironmentalConcerns.html. Accessed on December 4, 2013.

This web page provides a clear and concise summary of the potential risks to the natural environment posed by the presence of GM seeds and crops.

Enviropig™. University of Guelph. http://www.uoguelph.ca/enviropig/. Accessed on December 11, 2013.

This website provides a comprehensive description of the research program conducted at Guelph to produce a more environmentally friendly domestic pig, along with information about the technology involved, environmental benefits, commercialization, societal issues, and other related topics.

Fresco, Louise O. "Genetically Modified Crops Are Here to Stay." Spotlight 2001. http://www.fao.org/ag/magazine/0111 sp.htm. Accessed on August 29, 2013.

The author is assistant director-general of the Food and Agriculture Organization Agriculture Department. As the title makes clear, she does not think there is any way to stop the use of GM crops around the world. She recommends instead considering the role of GM crops in the overall scheme of agriculture, remaining aware of the many other forms of agriculture to which farmers do and should have access.

"Genetically Engineered Animals." U.S. Food and Drug Administration. http://www.fda.gov/animalveterinary/development approvalprocess/geneticengineering/geneticallyengineeredanimals/ default.htm. Accessed on December 13, 2013.

> This website provides a host of useful information about the genetic engineering of animals from the standpoint of one of the U.S. government's primary regulatory agencies. Included are sections on the process by which the genetic engineering of animals is carried out, current research in the field, general questions and answers about genetically engineered animals, and actions by the Food and Drug Administration related to supervision and regulation of genetically engineered animals in the United States.

"Genetic Engineering." Grace Communications Foundation. http://www.sustainabletable.org/264/genetic-engineering. Accessed on December 13, 2013.

> This website provides a comprehensive and easy-to-understand introduction to the topic of GM foods with links to useful articles and websites that provide more detailed information on the topic.

"Genetically Modified Crops." Case Studies in Agricultural Biosecurity. Federation of American Scientists. http://www .fas.org/biosecurity/education/dualuse-agriculture/2.-agricultural -biotechnology/genetically-engineered-crops.html. Accessed on December 12, 2013.

> This excellent video and accompanying text reviews all major aspects of the technology of and debate over the use of GM crops, including sections on methods of gene transfer in plants, Bt corn, StarLink corn, Biopharming, edible vaccines, and the potential risks involved in genetic modification of plants.

"Genetically Modified Crops." Green Facts. http://www.green facts.org/en/gmo/index.htm. Accessed on December 11, 2013.

This website is an excellent resource of information on a variety of environmental issues, such as air pollution, biodiversity, chemical substances, climate change, consumer safety, and GM crops.

"Genetically Modified Food." Social Issues Research Center. http://www.sirc.org/gate/. Accessed on August 30, 2013.
This organization claims to believe in a balanced debate on issues surrounding the use of GM food. The majority of its articles appear to argue in support of such foods, however. In any case, the articles do provide a fair presentation of reasons not to fear about the use of GM foods as well as to understand the benefits they may offer human societies.

"Genetics and Genomics Timeline." Genome News Network. http://www.genomenewsnetwork.org/resources/timeline/index .php. Accessed on August 13, 2013.
This website provides a comprehensive and understandable introduction to major events in the story of the research on genes, DNA, and DNA technology.

Gilbert, Natasha. 2013. "Case Studies: A Hard Look at GM Crops." *Nature*. http://www.nature.com/news/case-studies-a -hard-look-at-gm-crops-1.12907#/superweeds. Accessed on August 21, 2013.
This article reviews the status of three specific issues related to the development and use of GM crops: the appearance and spread of herbicide-resistant "superweeds," the spread of transgenes to nonengineered natural crops, and the psychological stress on some farmers as a result of dealing with these new products. The same article is available on the *Scientific American* website at http:// www.scientificamerican.com/article.cfm?id=a-hard-look-at -3-myths-about-genetically-modified-crops.

"GM-Free Regions Networks Declaration of Rennes." http:// www.gmo-free-regions.org/fileadmin/files/declaration_rennes_en _051130.pdf. Accessed on August 21, 2013.

> This web page contains the text of the Declaration of Rennes, adopted in 2005 by member regions of the European Network for the control of genetically modified organisms.

"GMOs: Engineering and Environmental Disaster." Earth Justice. http://earthjustice.org/gmo. Accessed on August 21, 2013.

> This website presents the argument that the distribution of GM organisms in the environment will produce a host of new problems, such as the growth of herbicide-resistant "superweeds" and the spread of new genetic material throughout the environment.

"Golden Rice Is Part of the Solution." Golden Rice. http:// www.goldenrice.org/. Accessed on August 26, 2013.

> This web page provides a good background on the history, nature, and applications of one of the world's best-known (and often controversial) engineered food crops, Golden Rice.

Gonsalves, Carol, David R. Lee, and Dennis Gonsalves. 2004. "Transgenic Virus-Resistant Papaya: The Hawaiian 'Rainbow' was Rapidly Adopted by Farmers and Is of Major Importance in Hawaii Today." APSnet. http://www.apsnet.org/publications/ apsnetfeatures/Pages/PapayaHawaiianRainbow.aspx. Accessed on December 11, 2013.

> The authors describe the problems created in Hawaii by the spread of papaya ringspot virus (PRSV) beginning in 1992, and the way in which a genetically modified form of the papaya plant, introduced in 1998, provided a rapid and highly effective solution to this problem.

Grant, Bob. "AAAS: Don't Label GM Foods." *The Scientist.* http://www.thescientist.com/?articles.view/articleNo/33057/title/ AAASDontLabelGMFoods/. Accessed on August 30, 2013.

This article reports on an action by the American Association for the Advancement of Science in opposition to the labeling of GM foods. Of special interest is the extensive list of responses and commentaries to the article.

Harmon, Amy, and Andrew Pollack. 2012. "Battle Brewing over Labeling of Genetically Modified Food." *New York Times.* http://www.nytimes.com/2012/05/25/science/dispute -over-labeling-of-genetically-modified-food.html?_r=0. Accessed on December 13, 2013.

The authors review the debates going on in state legislatures and at the ballot box over the labeling of GM foods, providing a nice review of both the pros and cons of that practice. The article drew a very large number of comments from readers that are well worth reading.

Jaffe, Greg. 2013. "What You Need to Know about Genetically Engineered Food." *The Atlantic.* http://www.theatlantic.com/ health/archive/2013/02/what-you-need-to-know-about-genetically -engineered-food/272931/#comments. Accessed on December 13, 2013.

The value of this article is not so much the clear, general introduction it provides to the topic but the vigorous exchange of views in the blog section of the website that discusses the activities of a variety of organizations that support or oppose the use of GM products.

"Journal Retraction of Séralini Study Is Illicit, Unscientific, and Unethical." GM Watch. http://www.gmwatch.org/index.php/ news/archive/2013/15184-journal-retraction-of-seralini-study -is-illicit-unscientific-and-unethical. Accessed on November 30, 2013.

This article was written about the decision by the journal *Food and Chemical Technology* to retract an important article on the health effects of GM corn on rats. See Séralini et al. in the Articles section.

Mannion, A. M., and Stephen Morse. 2013. "GM Crops 1996–2012: A Review of Agronomic, Environmental and Socio-economic Impacts." University of Surrey Centre for Environmental Strategy Working Paper 04/13. http://www.surrey.ac.uk/ces/files/pdf/04-13%20Morse_Mannion_GM%20Crops.pdf. Accessed on December 4, 2013.

This research paper examines the available research on a host of issues related to the use of GM products, including advantages and disadvantages of such products, agronomic impacts, environmental and ecological impacts, economic impacts, and social impacts, followed by a discussion of the import of this evidence and conclusions that can be drawn from the available research. A very useful list of references is also included.

Mather, Robin. 2012. "The Threats from Genetically Modified Foods." Mother Earth News. http://www.motherearthnews.com/homesteading-and-livestock/genetically-modified-foods-zm0z12amzmat.aspx#axzz2nNYmt2k7. Accessed on December 13, 2013.

The author argues that "[g]enetically modified foods and crops pose serious threats to human and animal health, but Big Ag doesn't want you to know that." Some interesting reactions and responses from readers are included in the blog for this website.

McCarthy, Erin. 2011. "Label GM Foods? Our Right2Know." Grace Communications Foundation. http://gracelinks.org/blog/661/label-gmo-foods-our-right2know. Accessed on December 13, 2013.

This essay makes the point that the debate over GM foods is not likely to end soon, but one fundamental point that remains is that consumers have the right to know what is in their foods and that, therefore, there should be no hesitation in labeling of foods containing GM products.

Mestel, Rosie. 2012. "GMO Foods Don't Need Special Label, American Medical Assn. Says." *Los Angeles Times.* http://articles.latimes.com/2012/jun/21/news/la-heb-gmo-foods-medical-association-20120620. Accessed on August 30, 2013.

This article reviews the actions of the American Medical Association in opposition to the required labeling of GM foods.

Meyer, Hartmut. 2007. "GMO-Free Regions Manual: Case Studies from around the World." http://www.gmo-freeregions.org/fileadmin/files/gmo-free-regions/GMO_free_regions_manual.pdf. Accessed on August 21, 2013.

This brochure describes the general philosophy and practice of GM-free zones in regions around the world, with detailed descriptions of such programs in the United States, Chile, New Zealand, Philippines, and the European Union.

Miller, Henry I. 2013. "Debunking 'The Big Lie' about Genetically Engineered Crops." *Forbes.* http://www.forbes.com/sites/henrymiller/2013/05/23/debunking-the-big-lie-about-genetically-engineered-crops/. Accessed on December 13, 2013.

Miller writes in response to the upcoming March Against Monsanto by pointing out what he sees as the many fallacies perpetrated by opponents of GM crops and foods.

"Outcrossing and Gene Flow." GM Compass. http://www.gmo-compass.org/eng/safety/environmental_safety/170.genetically_modified_plants_out_crossing_gene_flow.html. Accessed on December 4, 2013.

This article explains the process by which genes can be transferred from one organism to another organism of the same or different species in nature and how this information relates to safety issues posed by GM crops.

Pearce, Fred. 2012. "What Are Environmentalists Taking Anti-Science Positions?" Environment 360. http://e360.yale.edu/

feature/why_are_environmentalists_taking_anti-science_positions/2584/. Accessed on December 4, 2013.

> The writer accuses some members of the environmental movement of ignoring sound scientific evidence on some controversial topics, including GM crops and foods. The article engendered a large number of (generally) very thoughtful responses.

"Pest Resistant Crops." Gene Watch. http://www.genewatch .org/sub-568238. Accessed on August 28, 2013.

> This valuable web page provides a very complete discussion of the history and current use of pest-resistant crops, with a number of useful links to related pages.

Phillips, Theresa. 2008. "Genetically Modified Organisms (GMOs): Transgenic Crops and Recombinant DNA Technology." Scitable by Nature Education. http://www.nature.com/ scitable/topicpage/genetically-modified-organisms-gmos-transgenic -crops-and-732. Accessed on December 13, 2013.

> This article provides an excellent general overview of the current and possible future uses of GM crops and foods, with a discussion of some of the safety and other issues related to the field.

Pollack, Andrew. 2013. "In a Bean, a Boon to Biotech." *New York Times.* November 15, 2013. http://www.nytimes.com/ 2013/11/16/business/in-a-bean-a-boon-to-biotech.html?page wanted=all&_r=0. Accessed on December 11, 2013.

> The author describes the development of a genetically modified form of soybeans that have reduced (or zero) trans fat, making the product safer and healthier for the human diet. The product was first introduced in the United States in 2011, and its use was promoted indirectly by the Food and Drug Administration's 2013 decision to recommend or require the elimination of trans fat from many foods.

Robinson, Clare. 2013. "Tumorous Rats, GM Contamination, and Hidden Conflicts of Interest." Spinwatch. http://www .spinwatch.org/index.php/issues/more/item/5495-tumorous-rats -gm-contamination-and-hidden-conflicts-of-interest. Accessed on August 21, 2013.

> Robinson discusses in detail the publication of a report on possible health risks posed by GM foods, reaction to that report by a number of scientists, and possible conflicts of interest associated with those reactions. For more detail, see Séralini et al. and Arjo et al. under the **Articles** section.

Ronald, Pamela. 2013. "The Truth about GMOs." Boston Review. http://www.bostonreview.net/forum/pamela-ronald -gmo-food. Accessed on October 30, 2013.

> The author points out that the development of GM crops can provide one important way of increasing the world's food supply, thus helping to solve one of the world's most serious problems: mass hunger. She explains why she thinks GM crops are a safe and effective way for dealing with this issue.

Schauzu, Marianna. 2000. "The Concept of Substantial Equivalence in Safety Assessment of Foods Derived from Genetically Modified Organisms." AgBiotechNet. http://www .bfr.bund.de/cm/349/schauzu.pdf. Accessed on August 20, 2013.

> The author reviews the development and meaning of the term *substantial equivalence* and its continued use in the assessment of the safety of GM foods around the world.

"Should We Grow GM Crops?" Harvest of Fear. PBS. http:// www.pbs.org/wgbh/harvest/exist/yes2.html. Accessed on December 4, 2013.

> This web page reviews some of the socioeconomic objections that have been raised to the use of GM crops.

Then, Christoph. 2013. "30 Years of Genetically Engineered Plants—20 Years of Commercial Cultivation in the United

States: a Critical Assessment." Testbiotech. http://www
.testbiotech.de/sites/default/files/TESTBIOTECH%20Cultivation
_GE_%20plants_US.pdf. Accessed on September 11, 2013.

This report provides an excellent review of the development of agricultural biotechnology in the United States
and Europe since the 1980s, with emphasis on differences
in the ways in which the two regions have dealt with the
new technology.

Tyson, Peter. "Show We Grow GM Crops?" Frontline. Harvest
of Fear. http://www.pbs.org/wgbh/harvest/exist/. Accessed on
August 30, 2013.

This presentation is an extraordinary piece that allows
readers to hear arguments both for and against the use of
GM crops in such a way that they can adjust their opinions as they hear more and more points on each side of
the debate.

"Weighing the GMO Arguments: For/Against." FAO
Newsroom. http://www.fao.org/english/newsroom/focus/2003/
gmo7.htm and http://www.fao.org/english/newsroom/focus/
2003/gmo8.htm. Accessed on August 29, 2013.

These two pieces by the U.N. Food and Agriculture
Organization provided two of the most complete, lucid,
and unbiased arguments for and against the use of GM
foods available on the Internet.

Humans have been modifying plants and animals for thousands of years. For most of that time, the process of organism modification was carried out knowing little or nothing about the actual genetic mechanism by which such changes occurred. Since the last half of the twentieth century, plant and animal organism has become a much more sophisticated art and science that has resulted in the production of genetically modified (GM) seeds, crops, foods, and other organisms today. This chapter provides a brief overview of some of the most important events in that long history, including some of the important social, political, economic, and other events that have accompanied that progress.

c. 12000 BCE   The date often cited for the first domestication of a wild animal, the dog from the grey wolf. Estimated dates for the domestication of other animals are about 8000 BCE for sheep and goats, about 7000 BCE for pigs, and 4000 BCE for horses. All domestication occurred by cross-breeding on a trial-and-error basis.

Greenpeace activists hold banners reading "Contaminated by Monsanto?" after they dumped nine tons of corn in front of the headquarters of the French conservative Union for a Popular Movement party in Paris on March 31, 2008, to protest against the planting of genetically modified corn. (AP Photo/Jacques Brinon)

c. 10000 BCE Estimated date for the first domestication of a wild plant, wild emmer (*Triticum dicoccum*), to a domesticated variety.

c. 1800 BCE Possible earliest date for the hybridization of plants, carried out by farmers in Babylonia.

c. 1550 BCE First hybrid animal, the mule, reputed to have been developed during the Egyptian New Kingdom (c. 1550–1067 BCE).

1720 English gardener Thomas Fairchild is credited with having produced the first hybrid plant in Europe, *Dianthus Caryophyllus barbatus*, a cross between sweet william and pink carnation species.

1865 Austrian monk Gregor Mendel announces the results of his research on the transmission of genetic traits in pea plants in a paper titled "Versuche über Pflanzenhybriden" ("Experiments on Plant Hybridization") at two meetings of the Natural History Society of Brno. The paper is published a year later in the journal *Verhandlungen des naturforschenden Vereins Brünn* (*Proceedings of the Natural History Society of Brünn*).

1869 Swiss biologist Friedrich Miescher discovers a weakly acidic substance whose function is unknown in the nucleus of cells, the first mention of what was to become known as deoxyribonucleic acid (DNA).

1908 American plant geneticist George Harrison Shull invents the first commercially successful corn hybrid.

1909 Danish botanist Wilhelm Johannsen suggests the name *gene* for the unit in cells responsible for the transmission of hereditary characteristics.

1919 Hungarian agricultural engineer Károly Ereky invents the word *biotechnology* to describe methods for converting waste agricultural products into useful materials.

1926 Future vice president of the United States Henry A. Wallace develops the first commercial hybrid corn and founds the Pioneer Hi-Bred Corn Company to market his product.

1928   British bacteriologist Frederick Griffith provides the first experimental evidence that a bacterium is able to change in both form and function. Griffith attributes this change to the presence in the bacterium of a *transforming factor*, later shown to be DNA.

1935   Russian chemist Andrei Nikolaevitch Belozersky isolates pure DNA for the first time.

1941   American geneticists George Beadle and Edward Tatum propose the one-gene, one-protein hypothesis, namely that each gene in an organism's genome is responsible for the production of a single unique protein.

1944   The research team of Canadian-born American molecular biologist Oswald Avery, Canadian microbiologist Colin MacLeod, and American geneticist Maclyn McCarty demonstrate that DNA is the "transforming factor" identified by Frederick Griffith (1928), responsible for changing the form and function of a bacterium.

1952   American molecular biologist Joshua Ledeberg suggests the name *plasmid* for all extra-chromosomal material in a cell capable of transmitting genetic information. Plasmids have become an essential tool in the practice of genetic engineering.

1952   American bacteriologist Alfred Hershey and American geneticist Martha Chase provide convincing evidence that DNA is the genetic material through which traits are inherited in organisms.

1953   English chemist Francis H. C. Crick and American biologist James D. Watson discover the chemical structure of DNA.

1957   Crick proposes the Central Dogma of molecular biology, namely that the direction of events in a cell is always DNA —> RNA —> protein and never the reverse.

1967   Researchers at five different laboratories announce the discovery of DNA ligases, substances that joined two separate molecules or fragments to form a new molecule or fragment.

1970   American microbiologist Hamilton O. Smith isolates the first restriction enzyme, a substance that recognizes and cleaves DNA at specific points in the molecule. Almost concurrently, American molecular biologist Daniel Nathans uses that enzyme, HindII, to make the first restriction map of the simian virus SV40.

1970   Morton Mandel and Akiko Higa provide the first demonstration of induced (artificial) competence, when they use a solution of calcium chloride to induce *Escherichia coli* bacteria to incorporate a bacteriophage λ unit.

1970   Indian geneticist Chandrakant T. Patel develops the world's first commercial cotton hybrid, known as Sankar-4 (Hybrid-4).

1972   American biochemist Paul Berg produces the first recombinant DNA molecule.

1973   American biochemists Herbert Boyer and Stanley N. Cohen devise a method for cloning genetically engineered DNA molecules in foreign cells, providing the first reliable system of recombinant DNA synthesis.

1974   German biochemist and geneticist Rudolf Jaenisch produces the first transgenic mouse by splicing viral DNA into an early-stage mouse embryo.

1975   About 140 biologists, physicians, and lawyers meet at the Asilomar Conference Center, near Monterey, California, to discuss safety issues associated with research involving recombinant DNA technology.

1976   Biochemist Herbert Boyer and venture capitalist Robert Swanson found Genentech, the first company devoted entirely to genetic engineering. The company's first commercial production somatostatin is produced a year later.

1976   Belgian molecular biologist Walter Fiers sequences the genome of bacteriophage MS2, which was thought by some historians to be the first complete sequencing of an organism's genome.

1976   The U.S. National Institutes of Health (NIH) creates an advisory committee on research and development of recombinant DNA research.

1976   The Monsanto Company patents Roundup® herbicide.

1980   In the case of *Diamond v. Chakrabarty*, the U.S. Supreme Court rules that genetically altered life forms can be patented.

1982   The European Organisation for Economic Co-operation and Development (OECD) issues a report, the first of its kind, outlining issues related to the development of genetic engineering of plants and animals.

1982   The U.S. Food and Drug Administration (FDA) approves the first genetically engineered drug, Humulin, a form of insulin produced by genetically altered bacteria.

1983   Four independent groups of researchers almost simultaneously announce the synthesis of the first transgenic plant, a genetically engineered tobacco plant.

1983   The biotechnology company Advanced Genetic Sciences (AGS) requests permission from the U.S. government to field test a type of bacterium (called Frostban) capable of resisting low temperatures at which it would normally freeze. Legal challenges delay the test for four years.

1983   An advisory committee on rDNA research and applications is established in the White House Office of Science and Technology Policy (OSTP).

1983   The World Health Organization (WHO) uses the *Bacillus thuringiensis* (Bt) bacterium to combat infections by black flies in Africa.

1985   Researchers from the U.S. Department of Agriculture and the University of Pennsylvania produce the first transgenic domestic animal, a pig.

1986   In a document called the "Coordinated Framework for the Regulation of Biotechnology," the OSTP assigns various aspects of the regulation of GMOs to the Department of Agriculture (USDA), FDA, and Environmental Protection Agency (EPA).

1986   The EPA approves the release of the first commercial crop produced by biotechnology, GM tobacco plants.

1987   AGS field tests its experimental *ice-minus* bacterium, Frostban, on strawberry and potato plots in experiments that are disrupted by protestors. Frostban never reaches commercial production, although not primarily because of these protests.

1987   Researchers at the Waite Institute in Australia modify a type of soil bacterium that causes crown gall disease. The modified bacterium is tested successfully on almond seedlings.

1987   The U.S. Department of Agriculture approves commercial production of a modified type of tomato with extended shelf life by the Calgene company. The product is the forerunner of the first commercially available GM plant, the Flavr Savr tomato (1994).

1991   A joint committee of the Food and Agriculture Organisation (FAO) and the World Health Organisation (WHO) issues a report on strategies for assessing the safety of foods produced by genetic engineering.

1991   The U.S. Department of Agriculture's Animal and Plant Health Inspection Service (APHIS) publishes guidelines for the field testing of genetically engineered crops.

1992   China becomes the first nation in the world to permit the growing of a GM crop, tobacco.

1992   The FDA announces that it has concluded that GM foods are "not inherently dangerous" and, therefore, do not require governmental regulation.

1993   The FDA approves the use of Monsanto's recombinant bovine somatotrophin (rBST) for use in cows to produce milk production. The company makes available the product under the trade name Posilac in 1994.

1993   The first herbicide-resistant soybeans (resistant to the herbicide sulfonylurea) become available.

1993   The OECD publishes a report dealing with the monitoring of the safety of GM foods titled "Safety Evaluation of Foods Derived by Modern Biotechnology: Concepts and Principles," laying down many of the fundamental principles on that topic that remain in force today. The report introduces the concept and terminology of the *substantial equivalence* of GM foods.

1994   France approves the planting of the first genetically engineered crop in Europe, tobacco.

1994   The FDA approves the sale of Calgene's Flavr Savr tomato, although the product never becomes commercially successful.

1996   The first domestic mammal to be cloned from an adult somatic cell, a sheep named Dolly, is born at the Roslin Institute in Scotland.

1996   Monsanto introduces its first genetically engineered crop (cotton), resistant to the Roundup Ready® herbicide.

1996   The first glyphosate-resistant weed (*Lolium rigidum*) is detected in a canola crop in Australia.

1997   The European Union adopts Regulation 258/97/EC, the Novel Foods Regulation, which requires that products containing GM materials carry labels to that effect.

1997   Austria bans the planting of a GM form of corn, an action followed quickly by seven other European nations.

1998   Rainbow, a GM form of papaya resistant to papaya ringspot virus (PRSV) is planted for the first time in Hawaii, making possible the survival of an important cash crop that had nearly been destroyed by the pest.

1998   In Directive 90/220, the European Union adopts a policy for the use of GM crops and foods in Europe but delays the implementation of that policy for a period of six years while further research and analysis is conducted.

1998   The European Union approves the first GM crop in the region, a modified form of maize known as MON810, produced by Monsanto.

1998   Researchers at the Sanger Institute and Washington University announce the complete genome for the first animal, a nematode *Caenorhabditis elegans*.

1998   The Delta & Pine Land Company, an American cotton seed company, and the USDA receive a patent for genetic use restriction technology (GURT), also known as *terminator technology*, a procedure that produces sterile seeds, thereby preventing farmers from harvesting seeds from first-year plants to be used for replanting a year later.

2000   The invention of Golden Rice is announced. Golden Rice is a genetically engineered form of natural rice enriched with three genes for the biosynthesis of beta-carotene.

2000   The Cartagena Protocol on Biosafety (CPB) is adopted as an extension to the Convention on Biological Diversity, adopted in 1993. The CPB is designed to govern the movement of biologically engineered organisms across international borders. The treaty comes into effect in September 2003 after 50 nations had ratified it. The United States is not a signatory to the treaty.

2000   An international team of researchers sequence the complete genome of the plant *Arabidopsis thaliana*, the first such accomplishment for a plant.

2001   The European Commission publishes a report on the safety of genetically engineered crops, concluding that they pose no more of a threat to human health and the environment than do conventional crops.

2001   The European Union adopts Directive 2001/18/EC, which repeals Directive 90/220 and replaces it with significantly more stringent requirements for the planting, production, and distribution of GM crops and foods. (Also see **1998**.)

2001   Researchers at the University of California at Davis and the University of Toronto announce to production of a new type of tomato tolerant of high-salt environments.

2003   Argentina, Canada, and the United States file a complaint with the World Trade Organization (WTO), claiming that the European Union's policies on GM food constitute an unfair and illegal protectionist move against foreign trade.

2003   Ten European regions organize to form a network of GMO-free jurisdictions. They include Aquitaine (France), Basque Country (Spain), Thrace-Rodopi (Germany), Limousin (France), Marche (Italy), Upper Austria (Austria), Salzburg (Austria), Schleswig-Holstein (Germany), Tuscany (Italy), and Wales (United Kingdom).

2003   The Codex Alimentarius Commission of the FAO/ WHO publishes a document, "Principles and Guidelines on Foods Derived from Biotechnology," designed to assist European nations to coordinate and standardize their regulation of GM food as a way of ensuring public safety and facilitating international trade.

2003   The first Bt-toxin-resistant organism, the bollworm moth *Helicoverpa zea*, is found in parts of Arkansas and Mississippi.

2004   The European Union's total prohibition on the planting of GM crops ends with its authorization for the use of a GM form of corn, Bt-11 maize.

2005   In February, the European Network (see **2003**), grown to 20 members, adopts a *Charter of the Regions and Local Authorities of Europe on the Subject of Coexistence of Genetically Modified Crops with Traditional and Organic Farming*, otherwise known as the Charter of Florence, outlining the group's philosophy about GM organisms and their common intentions to prevent their use in the regions.

2005   In November, the Network meets again in Rennes, France, now grown to 40 members to revise and update the

Charter of Florence with a new document known as the Declaration of Rennes.

2006   The WTO rules in favor of Argentina, Canada, and the United States on the 2003 (*q.v.*) complaint against the European Union's ban on GM crops and food. Some individual European nations ignore this decision, at least in the short term.

2008   The FDA announces that meat and milk from cow, pig, and goat clones is of equal safety and equal nutritional value as that from nonengineered animals.

2009   Researchers from the Monsanto company announce that the pink bollworm in certain parts of India has become resistant to the company's GM Bt cotton, the first instance in which an organism has become resistant to a GM crop in the world.

2010   The Canadian Department of Environment approves the release of Enviropigs into the environment, as long as they are kept separate from traditional pigs. The pigs have been genetically engineered to digest large quantities of phosphorus, reducing dramatically the amount of wastes they produce. (Also see **2012**.)

2011   Researchers at the University of Sherbrooke Hospital Centre find Bt toxins from GM crops in the blood of pregnant women and their fetuses.

2011   A form of soybeans genetically engineered to be high in monounsaturated fats is made commercially available for the first time.

2012   New Zealand researchers announce the development of a cow, Daisy, that produces milk free of ß-lactoglobulin protein that can causes allergic skin, digestive, and respiratory reactions, predominantly in infants.

2012   The University of Guelph, in Ontario, loses its funding for the Enviropig program (see **2010**), and all remaining animals are destroyed.

2012   Voters in California defeat Proposition 37, requiring that all foods containing GM components be so labeled. The vote was 51.41 percent to 48.59 percent.

2012   A French court finds Monsanto guilty of poisoning farmer Paul Francois, who had claimed that he had suffered neurological problems, including memory loss, headaches, and stammering as a result of inhaling Monsanto's Lasso weedkiller in 2004.

2013   A farmer in eastern Oregon discovers a strain of GM wheat growing on his property. Researchers are unable to trace the origin of the strain, which the Monsanto company had developed but had ceased testing in 2005.

2013   Opponents of GM foods carry out two March against Monsanto rallies in more than 400 cities in more than 50 countries. Organizers claim 2 million marchers in the first event and 3 million in the second.

2013   Voters in Washington state defeat Initiative 522 requiring the labeling of all GM food products. The final vote was 51.09 percent "no" to 48.91 percent "yes."

2013   Connecticut becomes the first state to pass a law requiring the labeling of food that contains GM components. The state of Maine follows with a similar law a few weeks later.

2014   The FDA approves public sale and distribution of AquAdvantage Salmon, a type of salmon that has been genetically modified to grow year around instead of only in spring and summer.

The study of genetically modified (GM) organisms involves an extensive vocabulary of terms from a variety of fields. This chapter provides definition of some of the terms most commonly used in speaking and writing about GM products.

allergen   A substance capable of producing an allergic reaction in an animal.

androgenesis   A process by which an embryo is produced that contains genetic data only from the male parent; a process that is sometimes used in the production of genetically modified organisms.

antisense technique   A method used in genetic engineering that involves the production of a gene that has the opposite effect of some desired gene, such that the two forms of the genes bond to each other, producing an inactive complex.

artificial competence   *See* **competence**.

Bacillus thuringiensis **(Bt)**   A soil bacterium that produces toxins that are deadly to some pests.

bacteriophage   A virus that infects a bacterium.

baculovirus   A virus that is effective against a host organism at only certain states of that organism's life cycle; a principle that is used in the development of genetically modified organisms needed at only certain times in a growing cycle.

ballistic gun   *See* **gene gun**.

biofortification Any process by which the nutritional value of a plant or animal is improved by genetic modification or some other synthetic process.

bioremediation Any process by which the natural environment or some other system is improved by a synthetic procedure, such as the use of genetic engineering.

Bt *See Bacillus thuringiensis* **(Bt)**.

Bt crop A crop that has been genetically engineered to carry the gene for the bacterium *Bacillus thuringiensis*, thus allowing it to produce natural pesticides for a number of organisms.

competence The ability of a cell to take up free DNA in a cell and be thereby transformed into a new form. Competence can be either *natural*, when it occurs without external actions, or *induced* or *artificial*, when it occurs under such external action.

complementary herbicide The herbicide that is selected for use with a crop that has been genetically engineered to be tolerant of that herbicide.

cross-pollination Fertilization of a plant with pollen from another plant.

cultivar A form of a plant that has been produced by selective breeding and maintained by cultivation but that is not different enough from the parents to be classified as a distinct species; from *culti*vated *vari*ety.

DNA sequencing *See* **gene sequencing**.

electroporation A method for introducing a gene into a host organism by directing a pulse of electricity at the organism that briefly opens the pores of the organisms and allows the gene to enter.

field trial A test of a new type of plant or form of technology, including genetically modified organisms, which is carried out outside the laboratory. Such tests are carefully controlled with specific requirements for location, plot size, weather conditions, and other factors.

food security The extent to which adequate supplies of food are available to a country, a region, or individual consumers.

gene flow *See* **horizontal gene flow; vertical gene flow.**

gene gun A device that is used to fire a gene into a host organism; one of the methods used to produce a chimeric product. Also known as a *ballistic gun* or *particle gun.*

gene mapping The process of determining the relative physical locations of genes on a chromosome.

gene sequencing The process of determining the exact sequence of nucleotide bases in a strand of DNA. Also known as *DNA sequencing.*

genetic engineering The deliberate modification of the DNA of an organism by any one of a number of methods.

genetic use restriction technology (GURT) A procedure used for the production of sterile seeds, thus requiring farmers to purchase new seeds for their crops every year. Also known as *terminator technology.*

genetically engineered organism (GEO) *See* **genetically modified organism.**

genetically modified organism (GMO) Any organism that has been modified by the insertion or removal of one or more genes. Also called *genetically engineered organism* (GEO).

GEO *See* **genetically modified organism.**

GMO *See* **genetically modified organism.**

horizontal gene flow (HGF) The transfer of genes between two organisms in some manner other than traditional reproduction. Also known as *horizontal gene transfer.*

horizontal gene transfer (HGT) *See* **horizontal gene flow.**

identity preservation A technical and administrative procedure for segregating one crop type from another crop type at every stage from production and processing to distribution.

induced competence *See* **competence.**

intellectual property rights Creations of the mind, such as works of art, literary works, and inventions for which the creator receives exclusive rights of production and use.

molecular marker A specific section of DNA that can "flag" the position of a particular gene or a specific genetic characteristic.

mutagen Any substance or other factor that is capable of producing mutations.

natural competence *See* **competence**.

oncogenic Capable of causing cancer.

organic agriculture A method of farming that avoids the use of synthetic materials, including any type of genetically modified organism. Unlike somewhat similar terms such as *natural, healthy,* or *safe,* organic has official governmental definitions.

particle gun *See* **gene gun**.

pharming The practice of genetically engineering a plant or animal so as to have it produce a drug or pharmaceutical.

polymerase chain reaction (PCR) A type of chemical technology used for making multiple copies of sections of DNA.

recombinant DNA (rDNA) DNA that consists of DNA segments from two different organisms.

substantial equivalence The concept that, if a new food is found to be essentially equivalent to a natural or existing food, it can be regarded as safe as the natural or existing food.

sustainability The conditions under which humans can exist in harmony with nature in such a way as to ensure that adequate supplies of necessary materials will continue to be available to humans over time.

terminator technology *See* **genetic use restriction technology (GURT)**.

traceability With regard to genetically modified products, the ability to verify the origin, history, transport, use, and other characteristics of a synthetically produced seed, crop, or food.

transgenic   Referring to an organism whose genome has been altered by the insertion of DNA from a different species.

vector   A material, such as a bacteriophage or virus, that can be used to insert a gene from one organism or synthetic source into a second organism.

vertical gene flow (VGF)   The transfer of genes from one organism to another by traditional means of reproduction, from parents to offspring. Also known as *vertical gene transfer* (VGT).

vertical gene transfer (VGT)   *See* **vertical gene flow**.

wild type   The form of an organism that occurs naturally, in contrast to a form produced by breeding, genetic engineering, or some other procedure.

About the Author

David E. Newton holds an associate's degree in science from Grand Rapids (Michigan) Junior College, a BA in chemistry (with high distinction) and an MA in education from the University of Michigan, and an EdD in science education from Harvard University. He is the author of more than 400 textbooks, encyclopedias, resource books, research manuals, laboratory manuals, trade books, and other educational materials. He taught mathematics, chemistry, and physical science in Grand Rapids, Michigan, for 13 years; was professor of chemistry and physics at Salem State College in Massachusetts for 15 years; and was adjunct professor in the College of Professional Studies at the University of San Francisco for 10 years.

Previous books for ABC-CLIO include *Global Warming* (1993), *Gay and Lesbian Rights—A Resource Handbook* (1994, 2009), *The Ozone Dilemma* (1995), *Violence and the Mass Media* (1996), *Environmental Justice* (1996, 2009), *Encyclopedia of Cryptology* (1997), *Social Issues in Science and Technology: An Encyclopedia* (1999), *DNA Technology* (2009), and *Sexual Health* (2010). Other recent books include *Physics: Oryx Frontiers of Science Series* (2000), *Sick!* (4 volumes; 2000), *Science, Technology, and Society: The Impact of Science in the 19th Century* (2 volumes; 2001), *Encyclopedia of Fire* (2002), *Molecular Nanotechnology: Oryx Frontiers of Science Series* (2002), *Encyclopedia of Water* (2003), *Encyclopedia of Air* (2004), *The New Chemistry* (6 volumes; 2007), *Nuclear Power* (2005), *Stem Cell Research* (2006), *Latinos in the*

Sciences, Math, and Professions (2007), and *DNA Evidence and Forensic Science* (2008). He has also been an updating and consulting editor on a number of books and reference works, including *Chemical Compounds* (2005), *Chemical Elements* (2006), *Encyclopedia of Endangered Species* (2006), *World of Mathematics* (2006), *World of Chemistry* (2006), *World of Health* (2006), *UXL Encyclopedia of Science* (2007), *Alternative Medicine* (2008), *Grzimek's Animal Life Encyclopedia* (2009), *Community Health* (2009), *Genetic Medicine* (2009), *The Gale Encyclopedia of Medicine* (2010–2011), *The Gale Encyclopedia of Alternative Medicine* (2013), *Discoveries in Modern Science: Exploration, Invention, and Technology* (2013–2014), and Cengage *Science in Context* (2013–2014).